D1608393

PREHISTORY AT CAMBRIDGE AND BEYOND

PREHISTORY AT CAMBRIDGE AND BEYOND

GRAHAME CLARK

Emeritus Disney Professor of Archaeology
University of Cambridge

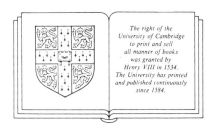

The right of the
University of Cambridge
to print and sell
all manner of books
was granted by
Henry VIII in 1534.
The University has printed
and published continuously
since 1584.

CAMBRIDGE UNIVERSITY PRESS

CAMBRIDGE

NEW YORK   PORT CHESTER

MELBOURNE   SYDNEY

Published by the Press Syndicate of the University of Cambridge
The Pitt Building, Trumpington Street, Cambridge CB2 1RP
40 West 20th Street, New York, NY 10011, USA
10 Stamford Road, Oakleigh, Melbourne 3166, Australia

First published 1989

Printed in Great Britain by the University Press, Cambridge

British Library cataloguing in publication data
Clark, Grahame.
Prehistory at Cambridge and beyond
1. University of Cambridge
2. Archaeology – Research – England – Cambridge (Cambridgeshire).
3. Man, prehistoric – Research – England – Cambridge (Cambridgeshire)
I. Title
930.1'072042659   GN761

Library of Congress cataloguing in publication data
Clark, Grahame, 1907–
Prehistory at Cambridge and beyond
Grahame Clark
         p.   cm.
Bibliography.
Includes index.
ISBN 0 521 35031 X
1. Anthropology, Prehistoric – England – History.
2. Archaeology – England – History.
3. University of Cambridge – History.
I. Title. GN722. G7C57 1988
936.2 – dc 19   87–33393

ISBN 0 521 35031 X

CONTENTS

ILLUSTRATIONS

PREFACE

This book has been written very largely in the light of the author's personal experience as undergraduate, research student, and teaching officer of Cambridge University. Even for the early period before he read for the Tripos (1928–30) the author was able to draw on personal memories of the pioneers. In the case of Sir William Ridgeway who died earlier in the year he himself matriculated (1926) and of Baron von Hügel who died in retirement in 1928 the author profited from the vivid recollections of those still working in the department and museum when he arrived on the scene himself. In the case of A. C. Haddon, who worked actively in the museum until his death in 1940 he was fortunate to enjoy close personal contact and hear much about the early days. Further, he was admitted to read the Archaeological and Anthropological Tripos by the first full-time Disney Professor of Archaeology, Sir Ellis Minns, under whom in due course he served for some years as a junior colleague. Again, he was supervised as a research student by Miles Burkitt, who gave the first lectures before the university on prehistory in 1916 and served for over thirty years as University Lecturer until his retirement in 1957. From his appointment as a Faculty Assistant Lecturer in 1935 until his retirement in 1974 the author played an active part along with colleagues in the developments chronicled in this book. For this reason it has seemed appropriate to end this account so far as the department itself is concerned with the author's retirement. The doings of Cambridge prehistorians on the other hand have been followed down to the present.

The author has drawn on two main categories of printed source. For official records of appointments and structural changes in the Cambridge department, details of changes in the teaching syllabus and the results of Tripos examinations he has been able to rely on the *Cambridge University Reporter*. For information about teaching in other British universities he has relied partly on the good-will of colleagues in answering tiresome queries by correspondence, but partly also on the comprehensive *Guide to Undergraduate Courses in Archaeology*, compiled by Fiona Roe and Jeffrey May for the Council for British Archaeology, a second edition of which was published in 1983.

His other main source has been the publications of books and papers by Cambridge prehistorians, colleagues and pupils, which embody an impressive expansion of knowledge about the unwritten past and between them justify the faith of those who laid the foundations at Cambridge. The contributions of Cambridge prehistorians have been too numerous to document fully in a work of this kind. All that has been aimed at is to point to the main areas of antiquity explored by those who taught at Cambridge and above all by their pupils, undergraduates and research students, many of whom now have departments of their own. The present writer would welcome information about particular fields he may have overlooked.

In seeing the book through the press the author has received much critical help and guidance, notably from Dr Peter Richards, editor, and Dr Caroline Murray, sub-editor. He is further indebted to his wife for correcting numerous errors and infelicities. Illustrations have been a problem. The most active prehistorians are more likely to stand behind rather than in front of the camera. Where old photographs exist it is often tedious to locate them, and the author is most grateful to all those who made the effort. Grateful acknowledgement is made to the following: Anglia Television (24); *Antiquity*, vol. 7, 1934 (16); Dr G.N. Bailey (30); Professor Peter Bellwood (45); the British Academy (7, 14, 22); the British Institute in Eastern Africa, courtesy Dr David Phillipson (40); the Trustees of the British Museum (59); Cambridge University Archives (9); Cambridge University Department of Botany (32); Cambridge University Faculty of Archaeology and Anthropology, courtesy John Alexander (34); Cambridge University Museum of Archaeology and Anthropology (1, 3, 4, 12, 15, 17, 21); Professor J. Desmond Clark (36, 37); Professor J.M. Coles (31); Professor Barry Cunliffe (60); Mrs Ruth Daniel (23); the late Bernard Fagg (39); Professor J. Golson (photo R. Ambrose) (44); Professor Norman Hammond (48); Professor Charles Higham (52); Dr Rhys Jones (46); Mr Peter Kain (courtesy Richard Leakey) (41); Mrs M. Lethbridge (13); Mrs Anne McBurney (28); Dr Paul Mellars (33); Professor J.D. Mulvaney (43); Dr Joan and Professor David Oates (49); Otago Museum, Dunedin (42); the late Dr Margaret M. Phillips (18, 19); the Press Agency (Yorkshire) Ltd (58); Professor Colin Renfrew (54); Dr Robert Rodden (29); Mr Andrew Selkirk (55, 57); Professor Thurstan Shaw (38); Dr Gale Sieveking (6, 50, 51); the Syndics of the Fitzwilliam Museum, Cambridge (5); Lord William Taylour (53); Professor Richard Wright (47); the York Archaeological Trust (56).

CHAPTER I

INTRODUCTORY

A main reason why the granting of full academic status to prehistoric archaeology at Cambridge merits more than local attention is that the example has been so widely followed. In Britain archaeology is now taught at undergraduate level in over twenty centres, many of the larger of which have been staffed from Cambridge. A feature of Cambridge teaching which it shares with that prevalent in North America is that it has from the beginning been closely associated with anthropology. Instead of being confined to Britain, Europe or the territories from which Europe has derived significant elements of its civilization, Cambridge prehistory has sought to comprehend and integrate the experience of human societies the world over. It has aimed not only to recover the antecedents of Old World civilizations, but also to explore the unwritten histories of peoples occupying large parts of the world where until modern times few or no written records were made. Cambridge teaching has sought above all to uncover the community of men. It has emphasized that prehistory serves to link human societies irrespective of the absence, presence or duration of written records. It has consistently recalled that prehistory studied over its entire span records the steps by which men have emerged from their primate stem in the course of evolution. Prehistory not only links human beings of every culture and period, but tells them how they have made themselves human in the course of evolution.

In essence every kind of archaeology, to whatever period it is applied, depends on the notion that it is possible to learn what happened in the past by reference to material artefacts or traces of human activity as well as, or even in the absence of, written documents or inscriptions. Antiquarianism stemmed from historical curiosity. It began to emerge in Europe during the sixteenth century. In large measure it reflected the anxiety of nation states newly emerged from medieval Christendom to establish and validate their distinct identities. In part also it came from a desire to learn more about the peoples from whom they derived so many of their more cherished tastes and values. These included the Greeks and Romans and the peoples of the Ancient East featured in the Bible. It was only as men became more aware of their biological status in the family of primates and conscious of their geological antiquity that interests began to focus on the remoter phases of prehistory. Increasingly prehistory has been seen as a key to anthropology as well as to history. Yet before prehistoric archaeology could earn acceptance as a subject for teaching and research in universities it had first to be turned from a pastime into a discipline calling for professional competence. This was a lengthy process but it is one which has yielded rich dividends in terms of human understanding.

Up till the First World War prehistoric archaeology in Britain was almost entirely a private pursuit. The country was still rich, and disposable income remained largely in the hands of a relatively small class. British archaeology was a leisure interest of comparatively few people. Ancient sites remained at the disposal of private persons who only comparatively rarely explored them for themselves. Most excavation was carried out by men who lived by a profession like medicine or who made their money by businesses, such as banking, milling or paper-making. For such people field archaeology made a congenial summer break and the preparation of reports an agreeable pursuit for the winter months. The collection and classification of artefacts made a special appeal to the acquisitive instincts of men concerned with money. Few public museums were equipped to undertake detailed research. As to universities it was something of a vicious circle. Until archaeology was pursued professionally[1] it could hardly qualify for academic recognition, and until universities brought themselves to teach and engage in research in archaeology, it was hard to see where the professionals were to come from. When Cambridge addressed itself to prehistoric archaeology after the First World War it had to draw its expertise from France. Similarly, when Edinburgh was looking for someone to fill its newly established Abercromby chair of Prehistoric Archaeology in 1926 it had to call upon an Australian graduate whose only formal training in the subject was obtained by taking an Oxford B.Litt.

When Henry VIII appointed John Leland as Royal Antiquary in 1533, he did so to promote the search for historical documents. Half a century later William Camden the historian thought it worthwhile to take some account of ancient monuments. He took the trouble to visit the Roman Wall and was the first to illustrate Stonehenge even if he termed it *insana substructio*. The first Englishman to practise field archaeology was the Wiltshire antiquary, John Aubrey, active during the Restoration period. Aubrey's most signal achievement was the chance discovery of Avebury, but his reputation rests most palpably on his *Monumenta Britannica*, still preserved in manuscript in the Bodleian Library at Oxford. It is a tribute to Aubrey that when O. G. S. Crawford was composing *The Long Barrows of the Cotswolds* (1925), he considered entries in the *Monumenta* sufficiently reliable to be worth citing.[2] Aubrey's successor William Stukeley gave free rein to fantasy in the books he published on Avebury and Stonehenge respectively in 1740 and 1743. Yet the elaboration and scale of his illustrations showed that the ancient Britons were capable of erecting noble if enigmatic structures before the dawn of history. In the face of Stukeley's books no one could overlook British prehistory as a palpable fact.

Systematic excavation on which the future of archaeology depended got under way in Britain during the final decades of the eighteenth century and subsequently have proceeded apace. Until the present century it remained exclusively in the hands of amateurs and was concentrated on sites readily visible from the surface, notably burial mounds, megaliths and defended sites; from the third decade of the nineteenth century a certain number of caves were also investigated. Interest was reflected in and stimulated by numerous learned societies. The Society of Antiquaries of London was founded in its present form as early as 1717 and began the publication of *Archaeologia*, a journal which continues to appear in a stately format, in 1770. The growth of interest during the nineteenth century was accompanied by the formation of numerous county societies. So long as excavation remained an amateur hobby much of the evidence was missed and therefore destroyed. It was not until General Pitt Rivers, an experienced Royal Engineer, inherited Cranborne Chase in 1880 that professional standards were first applied to the excavation of British prehistoric sites.[3] For financial reasons alone the General's standards have seldom been fully emulated. Yet the example he set of making an accurate survey before as well as after excavation and the recording, retention and identification of everything found have remained standard ever since, as well prompt publication accompanied by accurate plans and sections. When Mortimer Wheeler took over the Director-Generalship of Archaeology in India he transformed the standard of excavation prevailing in the sub-continent by introducing the methods developed some eighty years previously in southern England.[4]

Those who wrote general works about prehistory or compiled works of reference about archaeology were handicapped by having to earn their living in other ways. John Lubbock (later Sir John and then Lord Avebury), the author of *Prehistoric Times*, was a banker who enjoyed an active career in politics as well as writing books on a number of other topics.[5] John Thurnham, who summarized the results of excavating a large number of barrows in Wiltshire and adjoining counties in a series of lectures given to the Society of Antiquaries and published in *Archaeologia*[6], was a medical doctor. John Evans on the other hand had to write his massive works on the stone and bronze antiquities of Britain[7] in the intervals of a demanding paper-making business.[8] Although Evans hardly ventured beyond describing, illustrating and comparing artefacts, the very quantity of material he displayed aroused emulation and fired the imagination of many who later made their mark on archaeology. It is a sign of the times that Evans, who made a point of acknowledging the sources of his information, addressed his thanks to individuals rather than to the institutions they in many cases served.

Along with Lubbock, Thurnham and others Evans used the Three Period System developed in Scandinavia, where public museums had long taken the lead in prehistoric research. C. J. Thomsen devised the system,[9] which played such a key role in the emergence of prehistory as an intelligible subject, in a guide intended to help visitors to the National Museum at Copenhagen opened in 1819. His book received a widespread welcome. It was soon translated into German and in 1849 appeared in English. Across the Öresund, Sven Nilsson, Professor of Zoology at Lund, adopted the Three Age System, though he preferred to present the university's archaeological collections in broadly anthropological terms.[10] One result of interpreting their collections in terms of historical processes and social change is that in Scandinavia museum men were early called upon to provide university teaching.[11] At Copenhagen J. J. A. Worsaae taught in Copenhagen University while serving in the National Museum before succeeding Thomsen as director in 1865. Sophus Müller was called upon in turn to lecture to the university, though he soon preferred to devote his full attention to the museum. It was left to a later member of the museum staff, Johannes Brøndsted, to resume teaching. This he did to such good effect that, following the appearance of his three-volume exposition of Danish prehistory,[12] he was appointed Professor of Scandinavian Archaeology and European Prehistory in 1941. A close link between the museum service and university teaching existed also in Norway and Sweden. The first chair of archaeology in Norway was founded in 1875 in Oslo where the university appointed O. Rygh, Professor of History and director of the university's Museum of Archaeology. The only other chair of archaeology in that country was established at Bergen in 1914. Here again a museum man was appointed in the person of Haakon Shetelig of the University Museum. In Sweden Oscar Montelius earned his European reputation developing the typological method as a means of sub-dividing the Bronze Age in different provinces while serving in the State Historical Museum at Stockholm. When Lund University established a chair of prehistoric and medieval archaeology in 1912 it appointed Otto Rydbeck, director of its museum. Uppsala followed suit in 1914 by calling upon Oscar Almgren who had already been teaching archaeology in the university privately during his tenure at the State Historical Museum to serve as Professor of Archaeology. In recent times Scandinavian universities have shown a greater independence in developing teaching and research in prehistoric archaeology, though they still maintain close links with the museum profession.

The link has never been so close in Britain. With the outstanding exception of the British Museum, public museums never enjoyed the same prestige as they have long done in Scandinavia. The British Museum has indeed played a crucial part in enhancing the standing of archaeology. The Museum's concentration on antiquities has come about in part by a contraction or elimination of other responsibilities. When founded by Act of Parliament in 1753 the British Museum embraced natural history, the fine arts, books and manuscripts, as well as antiquities.[13] Ample provision has since been made elsewhere for painting and sculpture. The National Gallery was moved to its present location in 1833, a National Portrait Gallery was erected next door in 1886 and a National Gallery of Modern Art, known since 1909 as the Tate Gallery, was opened in 1897. Although the British Museum retains its Department of Prints and Drawings, it is no longer the centre of national concern with the fine arts. The natural history collections were removed to a separate Museum of Natural History at South Kensington in 1886. An even more drastic curtailment is now being realized through the movement of the British Library from Bloomsbury to St Pancras. The effect of these changes has been to concentrate on the Museum's unrivalled collections of antiquities. Apart from the indigenous material housed in the Departments of Prehistoric and Roman and Medieval and later Antiquities, it includes departments dealing with the archaeology of every part of the globe. The Museum anticipated British universities in its appreciation of the educational value of archaeology. The official guides to the Stone, Bronze and Early Iron Age collections issued between 1902 and 1905 established the basis on which museums and individuals could build. Even more decisive, because brought to bear directly on those carrying out and guiding original research, was the influence exerted by the various Keepers and their assistants. In respect of British archaeology the Keeper of British and Medieval Antiquities, Reginald Smith, acted as Director of the Society of Antiquaries and briefly as President of the Prehistoric Society of East Anglia, as well as counselling a broad range of amateurs and writing the 'Early Man' chapters for a succession of volumes of the *Victoria County History*. The influence of the department was greatly enhanced after the war by the appointment of two assistant keepers of exceptional brilliance. The book prepared by T. D. Kendrick and C. F. C. Hawkes[14] put a respectable front on British archaeology in time for the International Congress of Pre- and Proto-historic Sciences held in London in 1932 as well as nourishing generations of Cambridge undergraduates. It is significant of their quality that Kendrick later became Director of the British Museum and that Hawkes was appointed foundation Professor of European Archaeology at Oxford. Comparable departments manned by specialists helped materially to further British scholarship in the archaeology of Egypt and the Orient. Antiquities from Australasia, the Pacific and the New World were included in the Department of Ethnology which, though at present housed in the Museum of Man, still forms an integral part of the British Museum. It was largely through the Keeper, T. A. Joyce, that British interest in New World archaeology kindled by A. P. Maudslay was maintained, to take a place, albeit an extremely modest one, in British academic teaching.

Although by far the most important, the British Museum was not the only one in England, let alone Scotland and Wales, to promote archaeological research of a high scholarly standard. This was particularly true of Oxford. The Ashmolean Museum, the oldest in the country, stemmed from the cabinet of curiosities[15] formed by John Tradescant, who died in 1638. It was transferred to Oxford in 1675 by Elias Ashmole who enlarged it and bequeathed it to the university. The building erected to house the original Ashmolean collection still survives at Oxford, though long used for other purposes. The archaeological material was transferred to new buildings constructed elsewhere in Oxford between 1841–5 and since extended on more than one occasion. The creation of the existing department of antiquities was largely the work of Arthur Evans. When he retired in 1909 he had the satisfaction of having realized his aim since his appointment in 1884 of turning the museum into one of the main centres, though not as it happened the only one of archaeology at Oxford. It must have given him particular satisfaction to include his father's collection of Anglo-Saxon and Teutonic material, of which Thurlow Leeds was later to make such excellent use, as well to display a cross-section of his own Minoan finds. Today the museum exhibits British archaeology, as well as European material with a special emphasis on the East Mediterranean, and rich displays from Egypt, Western Asia and China. The Ashmolean caters for a wide range of interests in British prehistory and in the antecedents of the major civilizations of the Old World.

The Ashmolean was and still is complemented by the Pitt Rivers Museum founded in Oxford in 1884 to house the ethnological collections originally built up by Col. Augustus Lane-Fox before he changed his name on inheriting the Cranborne Chase estate in 1880.[16] The prime object of the Pitt Rivers is to illustrate the evolution of technology among the non-literate peoples who still flourished over extensive parts of the world when these were first penetrated by ethnologists. The museum was from the outset the home for Oxford anthropology, developed by Edward (later Sir Edward) Tylor, the very father of the subject in Britain. Since as long ago as 1871 Tylor had proclaimed in his great book[17] that 'the master key to the investigation of man's primeval condition is held by Prehistoric Archaeology', it is hardly surprising that the Pitt Rivers has from the outset been a focus of early prehistoric studies in Oxford. It was entirely appropriate that when the Baden-Powell Quaternary Research Centre was set up under Donald Baden-Powell's will it was incorporated in the sphere of the Pitt Rivers Museum.

Although beyond question British archaeology stemmed from antiquarian interests concerned with the antecedents of our native history, the concept of early prehistory was a product of the radical change in scientific thought embodied in the idea of evolution. The notion that the earth and the manifold species of animals and plants which inhabit it were the outcome of natural processes unfolding over immense periods of time not merely transformed geology and biology, but radically altered man's view of his own history. Transformist ideas began to affect archaeology long before Charles Darwin published *The Origin of Species*. Already in 1797 John Frere had reported to the Society of Antiquaries that he had found flint implements at Hoxne, Suffolk, in deposits that might tempt one to refer them 'to a very remote period indeed; even beyond that of the present world'.[18] In 1823 Dean Buckland, Professor of geology at Oxford, excavated what has since been recognized as a ceremonial burial of Upper Palaeolithic age in the stratified cave of Paviland, South Wales, and two years later a Roman Catholic chaplain, the Rev. J. M. McEnery, discovered flint implements along with traces of extinct animals in Kent's Cavern, near Torquay.[19] In 1847 the French customs official Boucher de Perthes claimed to have recovered worked flints in alluvial deposits in the Somme Valley and in 1858 the English geologist H. Falconer concluded that the Frenchman's claims ought to be taken seriously. The next year John Evans and a geological colleague Sir John Prestwich, checked the Somme valley sites and convinced themselves that Boucher de Perthes was indeed correct. The appearance of Darwin's book gave an immense stimulus to anthropology, despite the fact that Darwin himself refrained from stressing the implications of his hypothesis for man. T. H. Huxley showed no such compunction. In his *Evidence of Man's Place in Nature* he emphasized that man himself was as much the product of evolution as other forms of life and indeed as the earth itself. It followed that he must have undergone development over periods of time of geological duration. His prehistory could be understood only in the context of geology, palaeontology and anthropology. Acceptance of evolution effectively broke down the frontiers between archaeology and natural history. It certainly did so at a personal level. John Lubbock's family had settled within three miles of Darwin's home at Downe in Kent and the boy had helped the great man with his zoology. As a young man he was proposed for the fellowship of the Geological Society by Charles Lyell whose *Principles of Geology* (1830–3) had established the doctrine of uniformitarianism. Lubbock published *Prehistoric Times*, in which he divided the Stone Age into the Palaeolithic and Neolithic ages, in 1865 and it met such a need that it reached a sixth edition in 1913, the year he died.

The Palaeolithic sequence was first established in France, but in the wake of Darwin and Huxley it is not surprising that an English banker, Henry Christy, in company with Edward Lartet, a French lawyer turned palaeontologist, should have played a leading part in the scientific exploration of the caves of the Dordogne. The results of their joint excavations were published in a lavish style in *Reliquiae Aquitanicae* (1865–75). The work of excavating the infill of caves and rock-shelters proceeded so rapidly in France that in 1881 Gabriel de Mortillet was in a position to tabulate the cultural succession which, because it was the first established for the palaeolithic, served for some years as a standard until the appearance of the Abbé Breuil's definitive paper in 1912.[20] The time was ripe to make the results of the French pioneers more generally available. The first summary to appear in English was *Ancient Hunters*,[21] written by W. J. Sollas, Professor of Geology at Oxford, following a visit to France in company with R. R. Marett. This was followed in 1912 by *Der Mensch der Vorzeit* from the pen of the German Hugo Obermaier, a fellow professor with Henri Breuil in the Institute of Human Palaeontology founded by the Prince of Monaco in Paris in 1910. The German contribution was further emphasized in 1912 by R. R. Schmidt's monograph *Die diluviale Vorzeit Deutschlands* and the geographical basis was further broadened by the appearance in 1916 of Obermaier's *El Hombre Fósil*, a book which appeared in English in 1925. The revival of scholarly activity after the First World War was marked by several works that set out to summarise knowledge about the Palaeolithic derived from excavation in France and neighbouring countries. 1921 alone saw the publication of three works which between them made it possible to teach Palaeolithic archaeology as an organized body of knowledge. These included Marcellin Boule's *Les Hommes Fossiles*, the first – and as it proved the only – volume of R. A. S. Macalister's *A Text-Book of European Archaeology*, and M. C. Burkitt's *Prehistory*, the text on which Cambridge teaching was initially based. The chorus was further swollen by Grant MacCurdy's *Human Origins* from Yale.

By contrast the later stages of prehistory had been sadly neglected in Britain unless as a field for collecting and the accumulation of data by excavation. As Kendrick noted in *The Axe Age*,[22] understanding of the Neolithic was still in much the same state in 1925 as it had been when Thurnham summarised the outcome of barrow-digging far back in the nineteenth century. As it turned out Kendrick wrote at a dramatic turning point. 1925 saw the beginning of systematic excavation at Windmill Hill, Avebury, which began a veritable surge of research into Neolithic Britain. Even more decisively it saw the publication of V. Gordon Childe's *The Dawn of European Civilization*, which set Neolithic and Bronze Age Britain in the context of European prehistory. Only three years later the same author, by then installed as Abercromby Professor at Edinburgh, published *The Most Ancient East*, which set Europe in the perspective of Egypt and Western Asia. This meant that texts suitable for undergraduates were available for later as well as early prehistory.

Already in the latter half of the nineteenth century archaeology had been recognized as a vital source of information for anyone concerned with early civilization. This is shown not only by the literature but by the formation of research funds and schools to promote archaeological studies overseas. The Palestine Exploration Fund led the way in 1865 and this was followed in 1883 by the Egypt Exploration Fund and in 1887 by the British School of

Archaeology at Athens. Similar steps were taken by other European nations as well as by the United States. In 1887 the University of Pennsylvania Museum was founded with the aim of promoting archaeological research into early Old World civilizations, followed in 1919 by the Oriental Institute of Chicago. One of the things people most wanted to know about early civilizations was how and when they first developed. The desire to learn more about the earliest literate civilizations was in fact one of the main driving forces behind the advance of prehistoric archaeology. Already in the opening volume of the *Annual of the British School at Athens* the Director took note of the continuing excavations at Mycenae by Tsountas, of Dörpfeld's recovery of Mycenaean pottery from Hissarlik (Troy) and not least of Arthur Evans' activities in Crete. By the ninth volume (1902–3) prehistoric archaeology took the lion's share of the *Annual*: the first 153 pages were taken by Evans' excavations at the palace of Minos at Knossos, and pages 274–387 were needed for Bosanquet's dig at Palaikastro. Mainland Greece, the Aegean islands and Crete, not to mention Cyprus, have ever since been among the world's most exciting fields of prehistoric research. Already before the First World War Alan Wace had revealed the Neolithic succession in Thessaly in company with M. S. Thompson. Later, as Director of the British School, Wace undertook his brilliant campaigns at Mycenae. When in 1935 he succeeded to the Lawrence chair of Classical archaeology at Cambridge he symbolized the triumph of Ridgeway's claim that the Greek, like any other civilization, could only be fully appreciated in the context of its own prehistory. When Ventris and Chadwick deciphered the Mycenaean Linear B script as Greek this confirmed Ridgeway's contention that the makers of Mycenaean pottery must have spoken Greek. None of this impaired the integrity or independence of Classical archaeology at Cambridge or elsewhere. It merely served to underline the need to commit greater resources to investigating the prehistoric antecedents of Classical civilization.

Whenever archaeologists have been drawn to a region on account of its historical renown or the splendour of its ancient monuments, they have inevitably been led to probe its prehistory. Egypt is only another example. The man first appointed to direct the Egypt Exploration Fund, Flinders (later Sir Flinders) Petrie, had won his spurs by making an outstandingly accurate survey of Stonehenge.[23] There is a certain irony in the fact that the first holder of the Edwards chair of Egyptology at University College, London, attained eminence for his achievements as a prehistorian. When he came upon the scene Egyptologists had already pieced together Dynastic history by reading the hieroglyphs inscribed on monuments and written on papyri. Wilkinson's *Manners of the Ancient Egyptians* was already widely read. Looted Egyptian obelisks stood in European capitals as trophies, and London architects exploited Egyptian styles. What Petrie set out to do was to uncover the foundations rather than add details to the superstructure of Dynastic Egypt. This he did by meticulously excavating early cemeteries and tracing their development over centuries by devising his system of sequence dating. In this way he revealed a lengthy Predynastic phase in Egyptian history and at the same time showed how the Dynastic period came into being. One of those he initiated into prehistoric archaeology at a late stage in his career was Gertrude Caton Thompson, who proceeded in turn to uncover the antecedents of her teacher's Predynastic by revealing not only Neolithic but in due course traces of Palaeolithic settlement in Egypt.

Similar results accrued wherever excavators probed beneath the civilizations of the ancient world. Palestine and Jordan which early attracted the attention of Biblical scholars, proved to be of crucial importance to prehistorians in respect both of the transition from a Palaeolithic to a Neolithic way of life, and much earlier from a Middle to an Upper Palaeolithic. Similarly when archaeologists took advantage of the overthrow of the Ottoman Empire they lost no time in probing beneath the dynastic phase of Mesopotamian history. When the Oriental Institute of Chicago entered the fray it took as one of its main priorities the genesis of settled life based on farming. Again, one of John Marshall's great discoveries when sent as a young man to revive the Directorate of Archaeology in India was the urban but still basically prehistoric culture of the Indus Valley, which later work has shown to have been crucial to subsequent developments of culture in the sub-continent. The theme could be developed in greater detail. Enough has been said to show that the appearance of literate civilizations in whatever part of the world inevitably posed the question of their prehistoric origins and called for research by prehistoric archaeologists.

When Arthur Evans first heard rumours that the university might appoint a Professor of Archaeology, he assumed bitterly but correctly that it intended to do so in the sphere of literary studies. Since Joan Evans has described her half-brother as 'a halting, involved and inaudible speaker',[24] it is perhaps as well that things went the way they did. When Percy Gardner duly entered on his duties as Professor of Classical Archaeology and Art[25] one of his early pupils was J. L. Myres. Ironically Myres spent most of his time while a student at the British School at Athens (1892–5) on prehistoric sites, and in later life went on to revive the International Congress of Pre- and Protohistoric Sciences as well as maintaining the prehistoric interests of the Royal Anthropological Institute. It was only when Evans retired from the Ashmolean in 1909 that he was accorded the title of Extraordinary Professor of Prehistoric Archaeology, though at a nominal salary and with few duties. In this way the university made graceful acknowledgement of Evans' eminence as a prehistoric archaeologist without committing itself to the academic advancement of the subject, still less to making it a subject for examination by undergraduates. Meanwhile the archaeology of Roman Britain, which marched on the frontiers of prehistoric Britain, was put on a scholarly basis by two Oxford academics holding posts in other fields, successively F. J. Haverfield, Camden Professor of Ancient History and R. G. Collingwood, Waynflete Professor of Metaphysical Philosophy.[26] When in 1946 Oxford established a chair for the Archaeology of the Roman Empire, it appointed I. A. (later Sir Ian) Richmond, who had attended Haverfield's lectures as an undergraduate.

Teaching in prehistoric archaeology in fact began at Oxford as it had at Cambridge under the aegis of Anthropology.[27] Efforts made to include anthropology for undergraduate examination in the Honours School of Natural Science had failed in 1895. Ten years later the subject won acceptance, though only as a postgraduate diploma. The syllabus drawn up under E. B. Tylor recognized two main spheres. Physical anthropology was deemed to cover the study of man and his fossil remains by means of zoology, palaeontology and ethnology, whereas cultural anthropology dealt with prehistoric archaeology, cultural ethnology and sociology. As at Cambridge, one of the reasons for accepting the Diploma was that it might have practical value for intending colonial administrators. The inclusion of prehistory, even if only as a small part of a postgraduate diploma, played a significant role in the development of the subject. For instance when T. D. Kendrick, later to become director of the British Museum, decided to give up a medical career as a result of war wounds he made the change to archaeology by taking the Oxford Diploma in Archaeology. Again, it was in reading for the diploma after the war, when her parents settled in Oxford, that Dorothy Garrod discovered an interest in prehistory under the supervision of R. R. Marett. Marett himself[28] played a key role in the growth of anthropology at Oxford. He spent twenty years as secretary of the Committee for Anthropology and from 1910 until his appointment as Rector of Exeter in 1928 held the Readership. As a native of Jersey Marett excavated at the Cotte de St Brelade before the war and had previously gained the esteem of French prehistorians by inviting Cartailhac to lecture in Oxford. Understandably when Dorothy Garrod had secured her diploma she headed for the Institute of Human Palaeontology at Paris for more specialized training under the Abbé Breuil. The fact that Oxford anthropology was based on the Pitt-Rivers made this, as it still is, the natural focus for early prehistory in the university.

When Oxford did establish a chair of European Archaeology in 1946, it tacitly recognized the division by providing that the new professor should begin his field of teaching and research with the introduction of agriculture.[29] The new chair was intended to throw light on the barbarian antecedents, post-Roman as well as pre-Roman, of European civilization. By confining its range in this way the university ensured that the new professor would not embark on any large view of world prehistory. His status was made all the plainer by housing him with the Professor of the Archaeology of the Roman

Empire, hard by but separate from the Ashmolean Museum. It was perhaps superfluous for the foundation professor to assure the audience at his inaugural lecture that he found it impossible to imagine the university setting up an Honours School of Archaeology.[30] Oxford had no intention of doing so. Archaeology was fragmented and designedly reserved for postgraduate work. The contrast with Cambridge is palpable. Whether it is also culpable[31] is perhaps another question. There is merit in diversity. If the present holder of the chair of European Archaeology began his contribution to a recent hand-book with the bleak sentence 'There is no undergraduate degree in archaeology at Oxford',[32] he was stating only the blunt truth. This does not alter the fact that Oxford houses more archaeological scholarship than any other centre in Britain and a rich variety of archaeological institutions, including since 1969 the prestigious Research Laboratory for Archaeology and the History of Art.

One of the earliest and most ambitious efforts to establish archaeology in a university setting was made at Liverpool. The Institute of Archaeology was established there in 1904 with a flourish. It was opened under the patronage of H. R. H. Princess Henry of Battenberg and the joint presidency of Lord and Lady Derby. Among the vice-presidents were two private benefactors, Sir John Brunner, M.P., and John Rankin, flanked by such scholars as Boyd Dawkins, Arthur Evans, William Ridgeway and A. H. Sayce. The staff comprised Professors of Classical Archaeology, Egyptology, the Methods and Practice of Archaeology, Social Anthropology and Medieval Archaeology, and lecturers in Assyriology, classical geography, numismatics, and central European archaeology. A prime aim of the Institute was to sponsor excavation in Greece and the ancient East. To ensure prompt and adequate publication of the results J. L. Myres, who then held a chair in the university, founded and edited the *Annals of Archaeology and Anthropology*. Although the Institute concentrated on the archaeology of literate societies, it is significant that the chair for the Methods and Practice of Archaeology was held by a prehistorian, John Garstang, the excavator in due time of Mersin, who also acted as Secretary of the Institute. Although neither the *Annals*[33] nor the Institute in its full glory survived the war, the university still maintains a school of Archaeological and Oriental Studies. The Rankin Lecturer is still a prehistorian and undergraduates at Liverpool as at so many other British universities since the Second World War can qualify for a primary degree in the subject.

The founding of the Abercromby chair of Prehistoric Archaeology at Edinburgh in 1926 marked a more permanent step in the academic acceptance of the subject. Immediately, it also provided Gordon Childe with an assured post at the most productive period of his career and enabled him to exert a more powerful influence than he would otherwise have been able to do. Although he was conscientious in teaching, it has to be admitted that during his time at Edinburgh he only turned out one honours graduate. The fact is that Childe was far more effective as a writer than as a lecturer. His books earned him a European reputation and attracted a stream of distinguished visitors to Edinburgh. His specialist books covering the later prehistory of Europe and adjacent parts of the ancient East were indispensible to students, not least at Cambridge. Those he addressed to a wider readership[34] did much to mould opinion favourable to the adoption of prehistoric archaeology as a subject for teaching and research at universities. Moreover his experience at Edinburgh prepared Childe to take over the Directorship of the London University Institute of Archaeology in 1946.

Academic recognition of archaeology at London University came about in the first instance through the concern of two outstanding excavators to improve the competence of their assistants. Flinders Petrie, who became the first holder of the chair of Egyptology at London under the will of Amelia Edwards in 1892, was not only a passionate digger, but a natural teacher. Unquestionably it was due to him that University College first became committed to archaeology. The college remains to this day the home of the Edwards Professor, and since the war has also developed a major centre for European Dark Age archaeology. It is entirely appropriate that the College should recently have amalgamated with the neighbouring Institute of Archaeology, a brainchild of one of its former alumni.

Mortimer Wheeler was a museum man by profession. He came to London from the National Museum of Wales in Cardiff to direct the museum at Lancaster House, but he was not content to organize and display collections of artefacts. It was his ambition, in conjunction with the Society of Antiquaries of London, to put the excavation of major archaeological sites on a footing unattainable by the amateurs of the time. His prime reason for digging at Verulamium and Maiden Castle was to advance knowledge, but he also set great store by training young people to emulate General Pitt-Rivers. During each of the four seasons at Maiden Castle (1934–7) he disciplined around a hundred assistants and students in the rigours of scrupulous excavation, as he was to do as Director-General of Archaeology in India at the Taxila School. In the immediate aftermath of Maiden Castle he persuaded London University to start up an Institute of Archaeology in 1937 with himself as Honorary Director. Premises were secured in Regent's Park and a skeleton staff assembled before he had to leave for the war and in due course to serve as Director-General of Archaeology, first of all India, and later of Pakistan. One way in which the Institute contrived not merely to survive in his absence and keep in the public eye was to host conferences on the future of archaeology.[35] In retrospect this seems a crazy thing to have done in 1943 and 1944, but it worked. The exercise was of some therapeutic value to those who took part and it certainly helped the Institute to survive.

When it resumed full activity after the war Gordon Childe became the first full-time Director and combined this office with the chair of European Archaeology which he was so pre-eminently qualified to fill. The Institute profited by securing two European scholars who had found refuge in England, namely F. E. Zeuner from Germany and T. Sulimirski from Poland, each of whom took part in the conferences of 1943 and 1944. Wheeler had already spotted Zeuner's potential for the development of Quaternary chronology and the study of palaeoenvironments,[36] and Sulimirski was well equipped to provide teaching in the prehistory of Eastern Europe. The Director's interest in the ancient East led to the appointment of a Professor of West Asiatic Archaeology and a lecturer in Palestinian Archaeology. Wheeler's concern with the archaeology respectively of the Roman provinces and of India led to the coverage of each of these at a professorial level. The Institute continued to reflect Wheeler's original concern with the practice of archaeology as well as with the results of applying it to different fields. Instruction in excavation technique, survey and drawing, photography, technology and conservation have consistently featured in the syllabus. A limitation which went along with this was that the Institute was for some time confined to postgraduate students. As Childe's successor, Prof. W. F. Grimes (1955–73), noted in his inaugural lecture, too much emphasis was at first laid on technical qualification and too little on education.[37] The value of the Institute's diploma courses was not in doubt. By the end of Grimes' tenure students were being drawn from over thirty countries and there can be no question that they returned to their home countries better equipped to advance archaeology. Yet the need to broaden the Institute's teaching by including courses for undergraduates was becoming increasingly evident as a larger number of British universities instituted undergraduate teaching in archaeology. In 1968 their introduction brought London more into line with general practice and as it turned out prepared the way for the fusion with University College.

CHAPTER 2

ANTHROPOLOGY AT CAMBRIDGE, 1904–20

Formal teaching in anthropology at Cambridge began slightly more than a hundred years ago in the Department of Anatomy under Professor Alexander Macalister. While still at Dublin, where he qualified in medicine and surgery at the Royal College of Surgeons, Macalister had fallen under the spell of Charles Darwin's ideas and developed a deep interest in human evolution. He had also begun to study Egyptology as a hobby. Shortly after moving to Cambridge in 1883 to take up the chair of Anatomy he found that his lecturer in Advanced Morphology, S. J. Hickson of Downing, had become interested in anthropology while engaged in zoological field-work in Indonesia between 1883 and 1885.[1] He therefore took the opportunity of inviting him to give a course of lectures on anthropology, the first to be given in the university. In the event Hickson decided to persist with his old subject and in 1894 took the chair of Zoology at Manchester. At this point Macalister turned to A. C. Haddon, who had likewise acquired an interest in anthropology while carrying out zoological research, this time in the Torres Straits. Lecturing in anthropology for Macalister may have helped to deepen Haddon's commitment. When in 1898 he led a second expedition to the Torres Straits it was specifically to pursue anthropological research. At this juncture Macalister decided to establish physical anthropology in his department. To this end he secured the appointment of a University Lecturer in this branch of Anthropology, namely W. L. H. Duckworth, who was later promoted to a Readership in the same subject. While this ensured the future of the aspect of anthropology most closely related to human anatomy, it helped to precipitate a crisis for Haddon when he returned from the expedition which effectively marked the beginning of the scientific study of other aspects of anthropology in this country.

Haddon was by no means the first man to turn from zoology to anthropology. His Oxford friend and colleague Henry Balfour was another. Again, Baldwin Spencer, who achieved fame for his anthropological studies of the aborigines of Central and Northern Australia,[2] had originally migrated to Australia to take up the foundation chair of Zoology at Melbourne, which he continued to hold until retirement.[3] It is of interest to recall also that Baron Anatole von Hügel, who in effect founded the University Museum of Archaeology and Ethnology, first took to anthropology while observing

bird-life in Fiji.[4] The progression from animal to human life came naturally
enough at a time when the implications of *The Origin of Species* were still
dominant. While a third year undergraduate at Christ's,[5] which his father is
said to have found less expensive than keeping him in the family business,
Haddon had shared in the festivities which marked the visit to Cambridge of
its old member, Charles Darwin, to receive an honorary Ll.D from the
University in 1871. T. H. Huxley's speech at the dinner held in Christ's to
celebrate the occasion made such an impression on Haddon that he decided
to seek his advice at crucial junctures of his own career. It is probably
through Huxley that Haddon gained his appointment as Professor of
Zoology at the Royal College of Science at Dublin at the early age of
twenty-five. Certainly it was with Huxley's approval that he chose the Torres
Straits as a likely base for studying corals and their faunas in their natural
surroundings. On this first expedition to the Torres Straits in 1888 Haddon's
attention had already begun to stray from sea anemones to men as subjects
for research. He was first attracted by the skills of the native fishermen as
they guided him in their boats to gather his specimens. In time he became
interested in the way the indigenous people at large regulated their lives. His
interest was heightened as he came to realize that the Torres Straits islanders
were themselves an endangered species. Unless they were observed and
recorded their unique way of life was likely to disappear as if it had never
been under the pressure of European intruders. This sense of urgency, which
goaded him to action for the rest of his life, was heightened by the visit he
paid to the Rev. W. W. Gill in New South Wales. Gill, whom he had first met
in parental non-conformist circles as a South Seas missionary, impressed on
him the speed with which the aboriginal population and its way of life had
been disappearing since he had settled in Australia. While still engaged in
zoological research in the Torres Straits Haddon had already taken notes on
the local ethnology and had even assembled a collection of ethnological
specimens. Although on his return Haddon's first obligation was to work on
his zoological findings, he found time to send reports on the customs and
beliefs of the Torres Straits islanders to the British Association and to *Nature*.
The resulting publications caught the eye of J. G. (later Sir James) Frazer,
who wrote to congratulate him, and in this way began a life-long friendship.
Furthermore, Haddon spent two months in London, mainly in the British
Museum, identifying the specimens he had brought home.

    During this spell in London Sir William Flower, Director of the British
Museum of Natural History, suggested that he might care to consider
transferring from zoology to anthropology. Haddon must have been temp-
ted, but he was mindful of his family responsibilities. For the time being he
accepted Huxley's advice to stay with a subject that gave him a living. He
continued to publish papers on zoology until 1893 and retained his chair for
another three years. Yet he had already made up his mind to change over

when circumstances allowed. In 1893 he had moved his household to Cambridge and for some years combined his anthropology lectures in the Cambridge anatomy department with discharging his duties as a Professor of Zoology in Dublin.

The keener his interest in anthropology the more concerned he became to engage in field research. Just as with zoology, lecturing about people was no substitute for seeing and experiencing them in the field, all the more so that their way of life was under threat of rapid extinction. Haddon therefore determined to undertake a second expedition to the Torres Straits, this time to study the indigenous people in their native environment. Professor Macalister who headed the appeal to raise money for the expedition, found it more difficult to get funds for studying the human outcome of the evolutionary process than he would have done if he was seeking them to investigate the lowlier forms of life studied by zoologists. For financial and logistic reasons Haddon had to keep his party small, and he aimed to complement his own particular interests. He weighted his choice in favour of psychology because of the need to understand the reactions and thought processes of the indigenous people he hoped to investigate. In practice the

1   A. C. Haddon, by Lazlo, 1925

proportion of psychologists proved to be greater than he had planned. His first choice, W. H. R. Rivers, a fellow of St John's, agreed to come only when his two prize pupils, C. S. Myers, an accomplished musician, later Professor of Psychology at King's College, London, and W. McDougal, a pioneer of social psychology who later took a chair at Duke University in the United States, had already accepted. A competent linguist with special knowledge of Melanesian languages proved more difficult to find, and it was only through several intermediaries that one such was secured in the person of S. H. Ray, an elementary school-teacher at Battersea. The party was completed by Anthony Wilkin, who as a King's undergraduate had attended Haddon's lectures and who made himself particularly useful as a photographer on the expedition, and at the last moment by C. G. Seligman, a medical man with research interests in tropical diseases. Although Wilkin was to die at a tragically early age in 1901 in Cairo from dysentery contracted while digging in the Kharga Oasis under Flinders Petrie, his name has been perpetuated by the research studentship founded in his memory. Seligman, who was taken on only at his own insistence, was converted to anthropology as a result. In return he later made outstanding contributions to the subject ranging over its cultural, physical and social dimensions as well as holding the first chair of ethnology at the London School of Economics for over twenty years.

The success of the second Torres Straits expedition posed a number of problems. First there was the question how to establish Haddon, who was elected a Fellow of the Royal Society the year after his return, in Cambridge, and second how anthropology could be established as an integral part of the teaching and research activities of the university. According to Mrs Hingston Quiggin, his biographer, a leading part in the task of persuading the university to create a post for Haddon was played by Frazer, but Haddon himself emphasized that it was William Ridgeway who contributed the main driving force behind the establishment of anthropology at Cambridge. The fact is that the university was moved to act only because of the wide measure of support behind the movement. Those who signed the memorial to the General Board urging that action be taken to recognize anthropology included, in addition to several heads of houses, the Professors of several natural sciences, including Anatomy, Astronomy, Geology, Physiology and Zoology, as well as the Professors of Greek, Archaeology and Fine Arts. Despite the weight of opinion marshalled by Ridgeway and his supporters the response of the university was minimal. Yet the establishment in May 1900 of a Lectureship in Ethnology, even at the derisory salary of £50 per annum, marked a beginning. Among other things it gave a signal to which Christ's was not slow to respond. Election to a fellowship of his college, even if only for an initial period of three years, allowed Haddon to take the risk of resigning his Dublin chair in 1901. As Mrs Quiggin makes so plain in *Haddon the Head-Hunter*, he was compelled, with children to educate, to supplement his income by giving extension lectures in London and the provinces as well as by the vigorous use of his pen. Even so he was now free to devote a substantial part of his energies to publishing research and establishing anthropology in the working life of the university.

In establishing anthropology and (non-Classical) archaeology in the university curriculum the leading role was unquestionably played by William Ridgeway,[6] who never forgot that he stemmed from the Irish Pale and was

2   William Ridgeway, from a drawing by Frances Cornford, 1908

always vigorous when fighting for causes close to his heart. Ridgeway was also a man of wide-ranging academic sympathies who did not hesitate to advance his ideas by delivering lectures wherever he could find an audience. In addition to the Board of Classical Studies, to which he belonged as Brereton Reader, he also lectured for the Board of History and Archaeology, the predecessor of the modern Faculty of History. Few Cambridge historians today remember that the old Board presided over two sections, A for History and B for Art and Archaeology. Since his appointment as Reader in Classical Archaeology in 1892 Charles Walstein had for years supplied the only courses under Section B, namely ones devoted to the History of Greek Art, the History of Greek Sculpture and Archaeological Illustrations of Greek History. In 1900–1 Ridgeway advertised in addition courses on Greek and Roman religion, Greek and Roman Numismatics and Precious Stones, and the Ancients. Even more significantly Haddon was advertised by the same Board to lecture on 'The Races of Man, Evolution in the Light of Simple Societies and the Evolution of Decorative Art', thus covering aspects of what we would now term Physical Anthropology, Social Anthropology and Ethnology. Still, it was one thing to advertise lectures for young historians and classicists, quite another to establish anthropology as a subject in its own right. Ridgeway appreciated that this could be achieved only if Anthropology was granted its own Board. It was largely due to his efforts that the Board of Anthropology was officially constituted in 1904. To begin with the Vice-Chancellor acted as chairman. Its members included the Disney Professor of Archaeology (Ridgeway), the University Lecturers in Physical Anthropology and Psychology (Duckworth and Rivers) and among others H. M. Chadwick of Clare, the future Professor of Anglo-Saxon, as well as Alexander Macalister, who had been the first to mount lectures in the subject which were held in the Department of Anatomy.

In the meantime Haddon continued to strengthen the cause of anthropology by steady progress in publication and teaching. He pressed ahead with the publication of the *Reports of the Cambridge Anthropological Expedition to the Torres Straits*. By 1913 volumes II to VI, the first in two parts, had issued from the University Press under his editorship, and the appearance of each one further enhanced his own reputation and the commitment of the university to anthropology. Haddon was no less active in teaching. Like Ridgeway he lectured for the Boards of Classics, of History and Archaeology and latterly also of Anthropology. Again he sought to provide teaching and to persuade the university of the importance of teaching anthropology to future administrators, civil servants and missionaries expecting to work in overseas territories. Added pressure came from below. In 1907 Indian Civil Service probationers requested a course, and in 1908 one was provided for Sudan probationers at the insistence of the Governor, Sir Reginald Wingate. Appreciation of the practical value of the subject helped to bring about the establishment of a Diploma of Anthropology in 1908 even though it could at first be obtained only by thesis. In 1909 Haddon, already in his fifties and an F.R.S. of ten years' standing, was advanced to a Readership in Ethnology and a stipend of £200 a year. It is significant that Haddon's promotion was confirmed by the Board of History and Archaeology and that the Reader in Ethnology became a member of that Board *ex officio*. Another feature of this period was the beginning of a trend towards specific recognition of archaeology as a dimension of anthropology. The lecture-list for 1909–10 issued by the Board of Anthropology included a declaration by Dr Chadwick of his readiness to direct studies in Northern Ethnology. Dr A. B. Cook advertised a course on Greek vase-painting to be given in the Museum of Classical Archaeology and courses were also offered by orientalists on the archaeology of Assyria and Babylonia, Egypt and Palestine.

The teaching provided by the Board of Anthropology turned out only a handful of graduates to adopt the subject as a profession, but each of these was to make his mark. The deepest imprint was unquestionably left by A. R. Radcliffe-Brown who went up to Trinity in 1901 to read Mental and Moral Science. Radcliffe-Brown first began to develop a keep interest in anthropology under W. H. R. Rivers. Two years later his career turned a decisive corner when he was elected to the Anthony Wilkin Studentship founded in memory of Haddon's young assistant on the Torres Straits expedition. Following the example set by Haddon, Radcliffe-Brown decided to use this opportunity to study the anthropology of a particular community occupying a restricted habitat. This was in stark contrast to the practice of a life fellow of his own college, J. G. Frazer, who constructed books from data abstracted without regard to time or place. In order to make sure of studying a community relatively detached from history, Radcliffe-Brown chose to conduct his field-work on the Andaman Islands, situated in the south-eastern part of the Bay of Bengal, sufficiently remote from the mainland to serve as a repository for convicts. The dissertation he worked up from his field-notes won him in 1908 a research fellowship at Trinity which set him on his way to a dazzling career. A further tenure of the studentship in 1910–12 allowed him to complete the field-work he needed to finish *The Andaman Islanders.*[7] Although this epoch-making book was finished in 1913, as a result of the war it was not published until 1922. Along with Bronislav Malinowski's *Argonauts in the Pacific*[8] published that same year Radcliffe-Brown's book set the agenda for the next generation of anthropological research not merely in Cambridge but in the English-speaking world as a whole. His influence stemmed fundamentally from the cogency and originality of his views and the clarity and consistency with which he expounded them.[9] The extent to which they gained such world-wide acceptance was certainly not diminished by the fact that he went on to hold chairs of Anthropology, generally as foundation professor, in all six continents. In addition to inaugurating social anthropology at the Universities of Cape Town (1921–6), Sydney (1926–31), Oxford (1937–46) and the Farouk University, Alexandria, he also held a chair of Anthropology at Chicago (1931–7) and served as Visiting Professor at Yenching University, China, and at São Paulo, Brazil (1942–4).

That Radcliffe-Brown should have devised the functional approach to social anthropology in the same college from which Frazer was sending out new branches from *The Golden Bough* in aid of pseudo-history calls for less remark when account is taken of the difference in their ages. More surprising is the fact that another of Rivers's pupils, W. J. Perry, grew up to be the arch-apostle of another kind of pseudo-history and leading exponent of diffusion as the key to the understanding of the societies studied by anthropologists.[10] In dedicating his first book *The Megalithic Culture of Indonesia*[11] to Rivers, Perry acknowledged that the source of his inspiration was the address given by Rivers as president of the anthropology section of the British Association in 1911. To have launched pupils on courses as divergent, not to say contradictory, as those of Radcliffe-Brown and Perry, can be taken as a tribute to a great teacher or as pointing to a flaw in his genius, according to taste. What is sure is that it reflects on the still unformed state of anthropology as an academic discipline. The cure for the conjectural history on which Radcliffe-Brown poured so much scorn and which Frazer and Perry continued to propagate, was not to ignore the historical process, but rather to substitute fact for fiction. As the accepted father of British anthropology, E. B. Tylor, had maintained as far back as 1871, 'the master-key to the investigation of man's primeval condition is held by Prehistoric Archaeology'.

The third of Haddon's early pupils to adopt anthropology as a profession was a New Zealander, H. D. Skinner,[12] who had acquired an interest in the Maori from his father, a surveyor in the New Zealand Lands Department. In 1915 Skinner found himself in London, invalided from the Gallipoli campaign. While there he married a New Zealand girl. A chance encounter with Boyd Dawkins at breakfast in a London hotel next morning led to an introduction to Arthur Keith. As a result he soon joined the Royal Anthropological Institute as a fellow and in 1916 gave a paper on 'Evolution in Maori Art'. Since he had decided to equip himself for a career in anthropology on his return to New Zealand, Skinner and his wife moved to Cambridge to secure the Diploma under Haddon. Skinner himself joined Haddon's own college as a postgraduate student, having already taken a first degree at Wellington University. Although Cambridge was at a low ebb in the depth of the war, Skinner determined to make the most of his opportunity. He was happy to tap the special knowledge of Fiji and its arts of his director of studies, Baron von Hügel, the founder curator of the University Museum of Archaeology and Ethnology. He gained a sound general training in the classification of artefacts and the evolution of decorative arts from Haddon. Since he regarded archaeology as an essential part of cultural anthropology, he made a point of attending, even though he was the sole member of the audience, the course of lectures on the early civilization of Greece in the light of Arthur Evans' recent excavations in Crete given by William Ridgeway.

On his return to New Zealand equipped with the Cambridge Diploma in Anthropology, Skinner accepted an appointment as assistant curator in the museum and as lecturer in ethnology in the University of Otago. He thus filled the first teaching post in anthropology established in Australasia, anticipating by more than a decade Radcliffe-Brown's appointment to the Sydney chair. At the same time he marked the beginning of a long series of exchanges in personnel between the Australasian universities and Cambridge which operated to the advantage of both in the years to come.

One of the preconditions for the growth of an effective Faculty of Archaeology and Ethnology at Cambridge was the construction of a museum to house and display the collections needed for teaching and research. When the university built the Museum of Classical Archaeology in 1883 on land leased from Peterhouse most of the space was used for the library and the collection of casts of classical statuary supervised by the Fitzwilliam Museum. Part on the other hand was reserved to house the collection of General and Local Archaeology controlled by the University Antiquarian Committee. The curator appointed to look after this latter collection, which formed the basis of the University Museum of Archaeology and Ethnology, was Baron Anatole von Hügel (1851–1928). Von Hügel had been born in Florence, the son of an Austrian baron distinguished for his services to the imperial army, diplomacy and science. He had settled in Britain in 1867, but in 1874 had been sent to Australia on doctor's orders. It was on an ornithological trip to Fiji that he acquired what was to prove an abiding interest in ethnology. When appointed curator, von Hügel was still in his early thirties, but he continued to serve the university in this capacity throughout his working life. When he retired in 1921 he left behind a museum which not merely displayed collections but exerted a pervasive influence on all who gave and sought instruction in both archaeology and anthropology, and helped to give Cambridge achievement in these fields its unique character. Although naturally a gentle person von Hügel manfully shouldered the task of raising the funds needed to bring the new museum into being and render it fully functional. It may be guessed that he needed all his charm to guide a team of men as strong-minded as Haddon and Ridgeway, particularly when account is taken of the disparate and sometimes unwieldly nature of some of the principal exhibits. The quality of von Hügel's personality was reflected in the garden which brought him much solace and in the deep religious faith which helped him to consolidate the Catholic community in Cambridge. The foundation stone of the new museum was laid on 14 May 1910, by his wife, Eliza Margaret, Baroness von Hügel. Two years later the Syndicate was able to report to the University that Block 1, providing rooms for the Curator, the Disney Professor and the Reader in Ethnology, together with a temporary lecture room and library, was nearly complete. At the same time estimates were submitted for Block 2, designed to provide exhibition halls for the collections previously stored under cramped conditions in the Museum of Classical Archaeology.

As its name indicates the new museum housed antiquities alongside the material culture of peoples who were still practising their traditional ways of life when first observed by traders, missionaries and anthropologists. Prominent among the archaeological exhibits were those formed by the Cambridge Antiquarian Society, which had been founded in 1840 'For the encouragement of the study of the History and Antiquities of the University, County and Town of Cambridge'. The housing of this collection in the Museum made available for teaching and research a range of antiquities extending from the Old Stone Age to the medieval period. Among the archaeological material from further afield mention may be made of the Murray collection of Irish antiquities which came to the university largely through the good offices of

3   Baron Anatole von Hügel, by Lazlo

Sir William Ridgeway. On the ethnological side pride of place went to the Fiji collection assembled by von Hügel and the extensive collection brought home by the Cambridge Expedition to the Torres Straits under the leadership of A. C. Haddon. Other prominent features included a lofty totem pole from

4   Main gallery of the University Museum of Archaeology and Ethnology, Cambridge, as originally displayed

Canada and casts of two magnificent Maya stelae made from moulds taken at
Copan in the tropical forests of Honduras by A. P. Maudslay.[13]

The formation of the Board of Archaeological and Anthropological Studies
in 1920 was brought about by amalgamating the Antiquarian Committee,
which since 1883 had been responsible for the university's collection of
General and Local Archaeology, with the Board of Anthropological Studies
set up in 1904. Its ostensible object was to ensure that the museum collections
were fully used for teaching and research. At the same time it marked a
decisive step in the recognition of archaeology other than as an adjunct of
Classics. As already noted, archaeology had begun to feature in the lecture-
lists published by the old Board of Anthropology. Indeed William Ridgeway
and other Cambridge figures of that time drew no clear line between
archaeology and anthropology: the distinction was only drawn sharply as
each began to fashion its own theoretical aims and the techniques necessary
to achieve them. Ridgeway himself cheerfully offered the same courses to the
Boards of Anthropology, History and Archaeology and Classics. The
presidential address he gave to the Royal Anthropological Institute on 'The
Relations of Anthropology to Classical Studies'[14] made the same basic points
and indeed used much the same language as his equally famous lecture on
'The Relationship of Archaeology to Classical Studies'.[15] In the latter he even
went so far as to state that the two were in all essentials the same:

In the use of the term archaeology, which appears in the title of this lecture I do not
restrict it to the narrow sense of pots and pans with which it is too much bound up in
many people's minds, but rather in the wider connotation of what are called in
classical instruction antiquities and which is better expressed by the term anthropology, which embraces not only the material productions of man, but also all that
appertains to his sociology and to his religion.

Ridgeway cultivated archaeology first and foremost as a way of enhancing
his understanding of classical texts, but also because it could be used to test
and often support the testimony of ancient historians. He took particular
pleasure in the way 'the influence of archaeology is silently and steadily
lessening the pettifogging spirit of scepticism'. In praising Ridgeway for
having shown himself a true classic, A. B. Cook in his inaugural lecture as
Laurence Professor of Classical Archaeology shrewdly observed that he
nevertheless preferred Science to Letters when proceeding to his own
doctorate. In insisting that to understand the Classical world it was necessary
to look to its prehistoric antecedents Ridgeway was in effect emphasizing the
need to develop prehistoric archaeology. In his address to the Royal
Anthropological Institute he poured scorn on those who failed to appreciate
this:

To have suggested that Greek art could ever have had an early stage comparable to that of modern savages had never entered the head of any student of classical archaeology and still less of any professor of fine art.

Ridgeway's insistence that to understand Greek religion it was necessary to identify and examine successive layers had a powerful influence on the thought of Jane Ellen Harrison, who gave a vivid impression of him as a teacher in her contribution to his *Festchrift*.[16] Ridgeway would lecture in the library of the Museum of Classical Archaeology, his students seated round the table. He taught them to 'go back to the ultimate authority for proof' and, as she added, 'proof was largely found in the collection of coins and other objects in his own pockets'. According to her, 'Though unscrupulous in his methods, Ridgeway was concrete in his approach to problems. He had no use for Frazer's *Golden Bough*.' Ridgeway never practised prehistoric archaeology but he showed no doubt about its value in his writings and most notably in *The Early Age of Greece*.[17] In contrasting the Mycenaeans with the Achaeans of the Homeric poems he relied on features recoverable from archaeological or iconographic sources, above all on such features as hair-styles, dress and fastenings, weapons, shields and helmets. In his famous article of 1896 'Who made the Objects called Mycenaean?'[18] he had used arguments based on similar evidence to support his view that the Mycenaeans, so far from being the first Aryan invaders of Greece, were indigenous to the Aegean and what is more spoke Greek. It is revealing that Ridgeway cited the collection of 'ancient and medieval coins, precious stones, Greek, Roman, Anglo-Saxon and medieval objects', and 'prehistoric and Savage implements' among his recreations listed in *Who's Who*. Again, it is entirely in keeping that the formal portrait now in Caius College shows him in the scarlet gown of a Doctor of Science holding a British socketed bronze axe-head, probably one of those from the Cambridgeshire fens bequeathed in his will to the University Museum of Archaeology and Ethnology. When he died in 1926 the Regius Professor of Greek wrote of him[19] that

In a Cambridge crowd he looked like a stranger from some older and mightier race, one whose sword not ten men of modern breed could lift.

It was in large measure the weight of Ridgeway's sword and the power of the personality behind it that established archaeology alongside anthropology at Cambridge.

Yet, though he lived to a good age, Ridgeway experienced only the first-fruits of victory. If in 1920 'archaeology' was included for the first time in the title of the Board, it was not until the Faculty system came into effect that the Disney chair of Archaeology[20] was put on the same footing as others in the university. The Disney chair, which he held for a third of a century, was subject to re-election every five years and was so ill-rewarded – its endowment produced less than £100 a year until the university made it up to

£200 – that from 1901 he had to hold it concurrently with the Brereton Readership in Classics. It is hardly surprising that the Disney Professor had no staff of lecturers, even unpaid ones like those attached to the Reader in Ethnology. The one advantage Ridgeway had was that, whether by oversight or prescience, the scope of his chair had never been closely defined. The founder, John Disney, a Peterhouse graduate, was an amateur of Classical archaeology. He indulged his hobby by forming a collection of Classical

5 John Disney, by an unknown sculptor

statuary at his home at Ingatestone, Essex. After publishing this in his three-volume *Museum Disneianum* he presented it to the university and in 1851 endowed the chair which perpetuates his name. Disney reserved the right to appoint the first holder and he chose Canon John Marsden of St John's, who shared his own interests. After being re-elected twice Marsden was succeeded by Churchill Babington who held the chair from 1865 to 1879. Babington also came from a Classical background, but fortunately declared himself 'in a manner bound by the tenure of his office to treat every branch of archaeology with honour and respect'. His successor, Percy Gardner, was a man whose interests are apparent from the fact that in 1887 he resigned to take the chair of Classical Archaeology at Oxford. The next holder, G. F. Browne, was an Anglo-Saxon scholar who left after a single tenure to become bishop of Bristol. When Ridgeway was elected in 1892 he was free in theory to range as widely as he chose over the field of archaeology, though in practice starved of the means to do so.

The formation in 1920 of a new Board of Archaeology and Anthropology offered the promise of advancing the standard of non-Classical archaeology at Cambridge, but progress necessarily had to wait on a new generation of men and not least on radical changes in the structure of the university itself. The pioneers were aging. Baron von Hügel ceased to be able to attend the museum in 1920 and retired in 1921. Haddon retired from his Readership in 1925 on reaching the age of seventy, and Ridgeway after suffering from impaired eyesight for some years died in 1926. The lack of adequate teaching staff – Haddon complained in 1923 that none of his three lecturers was paid a salary – meant that there were few candidates for the Anthropology Tripos. Between 1921 and 1925 only sixteen secured honours, little more than three a year on average and as low as one in 1923. The Tripos first came to life in 1926 when eleven men obtained honours including two who were to achieve distinction in the profession, Gregory Bateson in social anthropology and Louis Leakey in prehistory.

CHAPTER 3

PREHISTORIC ARCHAEOLOGY AT CAMBRIDGE, 1920–39

Approval by the King in Council of the statutes stemming from the report of the royal commission appointed after the war to review the working of Oxford and Cambridge universities resulted in the introduction to Cambridge of the faculty system. The Faculty of Archaeology and Anthropology which replaced the Board of that name in 1926 was able for the first time to recruit a salaried staff to provide teaching for what was to be a one-part Tripos until after the Second World War. The basic needs of anthropology were met by the appointment in succession to Haddon of a retired Indian Civil Service official, Col. T. C. Hodson, who had been introduced to Cambridge by Haddon himself to take a course in Indian anthropology during his own absence on leave. With the recognition of social anthropology as such Hodson took over the newly founded William Wyse chair in 1932. When he originally succeeded Haddon as Reader in Ethnology his post was complemented by the appointment of R. U. Sayce from Manchester. Sayce was required to provide basic teaching in physical anthropology as well as in the technology and material culture of non-industrial societies. The staffing of archaeology took a little longer. At the University Lecturer level there was no problem. Miles Burkitt had been providing teaching in prehistory throughout the life of the Board of Archaeology and Anthropology without pay and was author of the first modern text-book on prehistory in the English language.[1] His appointment as University Lecturer, a post he continued to hold until he retired in 1958, was almost a foregone conclusion. The problem presented by the need for a senior post in archaeology was met by upgrading the Disney chair vacated by Ridgeway's death in 1926 and assigning to it the standard stipend and tenure. The person chosen to fill the reconstituted Disney chair of Archaeology in 1927 was Dr Ellis H. Minns, fellow of Pembroke, University Lecturer in Palaeography and author of the standard work on the archaeology of the Russian Empire.[2]

Like previous Disney Professors Minns was a Classical scholar by training, but his archaeological interests extended far beyond the Graeco-Roman world.[3] Coming up to Pembroke from Charterhouse he qualified for research by taking firsts in both parts of the Classical Tripos. He then opted for Slavonic rather than Classical studies and set about acquiring Russian.

6 Miles Burkitt (left) and family with the Comte Henri Bégouën

7 Ellis Hovell Minns

This he did in Paris under Prof. Paul Bayer at the École des Langues Orientales Vivantes. Next he headed for Russia where he spent 1898–1901. From his place in the library of the Imperial Archaeological Commission at St Petersburg he mastered the literature of Russian archaeology on which he was able to build for the rest of his life. At the same time he took every opportunity to study the archaeological material housed in the Hermitage, the Historical Museum at Moscow and in museums in Kazan, Kiev, Odessa and smaller centres in other parts of Russia. He also visited key archaeological sites and in the course of his travels obtained the understanding of Russian topography that informed his lectures and writing notably and enhanced his appreciation of Russian archaeology. In the course of these activities Minns acquired many friends among Russian colleagues and with these he was careful to maintain contact by exchanging letters and publications. Thus, although he never revisited Russia, he was able to keep track not merely of new discoveries but of changes of opinion among Russian scholars. His regard for his hosts was warmly reciprocated. He continued to receive leading periodicals and was granted many honours by learned societies and universities in Russia. His own love for the people transcended the Revolution. Much as he deplored the event, he always maintained that it affected the basic character of the Russians and their way of life much less than was commonly supposed in the west. For him Russia remained Russia whatever the regime. He found no difficulty in accepting Corresponding Membership of the Institute for the History of Material Culture and he regarded it as a signal honour in his retirement to be called upon to compose the inscription for the sword of honour presented by King George VI to the heroic citizens of Stalingrad.

On returning to Cambridge from his studies in Russia, Minns must have been disappointed when the university established a post in Slavonic Studies and chose someone else to fill it. Instead Minns was appointed to a University lectureship in Palaeography in the Department of Classics, a post he continued to hold until he was elected to the Disney chair. It fell to his college to recognize and encourage his particular bent by appointing him Librarian and College Lecturer in Slavonic Studies. Although scrupulous in fulfilling his obligations to Pembroke and the university, Minns now had the secure background he needed to compose and illustrate his magnum opus, *Scythians and Greeks*, published by the University Press in 1913. This noble volume on which his international reputation was founded gave him a claim hardly to be overlooked when the Disney Professorship was placed on a proper footing in 1927. As an archaeologist Minns explored no new territories. Still less did he undertake excavations of his own. Nor was he concerned to devise new methods of obtaining, dating or interpreting archaeological data. He was content to study and inform his readers about what was known of 'the archaeology, ethnology and history of the region between the Carpathians and the Caucasus'. In the course of time he extended his range to include the nomadic peoples of Eurasia as a whole and not least the relations established between these and the settled civilizations of Greece, Iran and China. To open windows onto a vast territory little known in the west was in itself invaluable to his pupils. Even more precious was the quality of his scholarship.

One of Minns's most attractive qualities was his attitude to colleagues. Whereas some academics find it necessary to criticize or even deride their fellows in order to hold the attention of their juvenile classes, Minns was invariably courteous and used differences of opinion not to score points but to bring home the necessarily provisional nature of what we can learn about remote antiquity. He aimed above all to emphasize the need for more evidence and was at pains to remind us of the advantage to be gained by advancing knowledge in concert with rather than at the expense of colleagues. In short he aimed to generate in his pupils a sense of the republic of learning and an appreciation of the need for cooperation in the task of advancing knowledge of ancient societies through a study of their archaeological traces. He did so not by abstraction and generalization, but by reference, as Haddon had done in the Torres Straits, to particular peoples occupying definable territories over specific periods of time. At all times he taught a deep respect for cultural usage. He reverenced artefacts not merely for their utility but as embodiments of the values of particular groups. Nor did he lose sight of the fact that of their very nature they were the work of individual craftsmen. Just as in his work as a palaeographer he sought to reproduce ancient scripts in his own hand, so when studying objects he was ready to go to great trouble to understand how they were made. To test the idea that the style of gold work featuring slanting planes meeting to form an arris displayed by the famous deer from Kostromskya had been inspired by wood-carving, he set about shaping a wooden version for himself. Again, he was a great believer in drawing objects as a way of understanding them. He found this particularly useful in unravelling the intricate design of bronzes cast in the animal style beloved of the northern nomads, as witnessed by illustrations he drew for his Academy lecture of 1942 on 'The Art of the Northern Nomads'.[4] Some of Minns's lessons called for moral qualities beyond the scope of some of us. The value of handling, scrutinizing and drawing specimens of ancient craftsmanship as a key to understanding them, was more within reach. It was certainly a lesson I took to heart myself when confronted with the flint, antler and bone artefacts of early man.

Minns set great store by the special volume of *Eurasia Septentrionalis* dedicated to him to mark his sixtieth birthday in 1934. The volume was presented in the library of Pembroke College, of which he had been put in charge on his return from Russia over thirty years previously. It was edited by A. M. Tallgren, Professor of Archaeology at Helsingfors, and contributed

to by thirty-two scholars drawn from seventeen countries, in itself a tribute
to the international character of his scholarship. The range was also wide,
extending from the Old Stone Age to the medieval period over a territory
from Western Europe to China. Although the volume was overwhelmingly
archaeological and art-historical in orientation, two of the contributions
reflect Minns's interest in the actual peoples of the region, one a brief note on
Mongolian folk-lore, the other on bow and arrow symbolism by C. G.
Seligman, a former member of Haddon's anthropological expedition to the
Torres Straits and for over twenty years Professor of Ethnology at the
London School of Economics.

It was not merely his conscientiousness that led Minns as chairman of the
Faculty Board of Archaeology and Anthropology to take such a close interest
in its schedule. As he had long proclaimed in the preface to his great book he
had a deep interest in ethnology. His classical background disposed him to
interpret archaeology in terms of people. Like William Ridgeway he found
himself in close sympathy with Haddon's approach. He was interested not in
man as a concept so much as in men as they could be studied in the flesh by
ethnology or recalled from the past by archaeology. The Schedule for the
Archaeological and Anthropological Tripos agreed for 1927 comprised:

1. Principles, including physical anthropology
2. Social anthropology
3. Archaeology (restricted to the Stone and early metal ages of Europe and
   the Mediterranean) and technology (or material culture)

Since it was a one-part Tripos designed to be taken as a rule as a second part,
and considering the limitation of staff, it follows that the ground could be
covered only at an elementary level.

As Minns confined his formal lecturing to a single course he had to rely
heavily on his only University Lecturer, Miles Burkitt, son of F. C. Burkitt,
the first layman to hold a chair of Divinity at Cambridge. Miles was himself a
graduate in Geology and it was in the Sedgwick Museum that he first became
interested in archaeology. The Woodwardian Professor of Geology,
McKenny Hughes, was a keen amateur of archaeology and a close associate
of Haddon and Ridgeway. Burkitt acknowledged in the preface to his first
book, *Prehistory*, that his interest in prehistoric archaeology had first been
inspired by his professor. Another influence was Dr J. E. Marr, Hughes'
lecturer and successor. Marr himself had been ensnared in prehistory by Reid
Moir, an Ipswich amateur who in 1910 had recovered what he took to be
humanly worked flints from a deposit of apparently Late Tertiary age. To
check the geological age of the flints Reid Moir consulted two professionals,
one of whom was Marr. In return he submitted samples of his flints to the
Sedgwick Museum. Dr Marr enlisted his pupil to help scrutinize them.
Whether or not it was this which deflected Burkitt from geology to
prehistory, it is certain that the question how to recognize the earliest

objective clues to the emergence of man as a tool-maker was one that long influenced his teaching in archaeology.

The contact with Moir which eventuated was important for two main reasons. It brought Burkitt into immediate connection with the Prehistoric Society of East Anglia, which although at that time a local body of amateurs was to develop rapidly into one internationally acclaimed for its part in promoting world prehistory.[5] Second it brought him into fruitful contact with the Abbé Breuil and so with the most important exponent of the French science of prehistory. Breuil first came to East Anglia together with M. Boule, head of the Institut de Paléontologie Humaine in 1912 following the publication of a powerful endorsement of Moir's claims in the *Philosophical Transactions of the Royal Society*.[6] When Breuil next visited England Burkitt took the opportunity of being a fellow luncheon guest at Haddon's home in Cambridge to ask directly whether he would accept him as a pupil. Breuil agreed and Burkitt spent 1913–14 in France and Spain. He began by joining Breuil's fellow professor in the Institut, the Bavarian Hugo Obermaier, in

8 T. McKenny Hughes

excavating the unrivalled series of Stone Age deposits in the Cantabrian cave of Castillo, ranging from the Middle Palaeolithic through the Upper Palaeolithic sequence to the Neolithic. After this experience of cave stratigraphy he learned under Breuil's supervision how to classify Stone Age assemblages by tackling the material recovered from Laussel in the Dordogne by Gaston Lalanne. In the summer of 1913 he assisted Breuil in excavating the painted cave of Gargas in the Hautes-Pyrénées. In 1914 he joined Breuil in an expedition to Andalusia to make an original study of the prehistoric rock-art of the province. This involved living rough, traversing dry riverbeds and sheltering in the primitive dwellings of modern pastoralists, on occasion even in the caves or rock-shelters of prehistoric man.

9   The Abbé Breuil (centre) outside the Senate House in Cambridge, where he received
    an honorary degree in 1920. In front of him are (left) Earl Jellicoe and
    (right) Earl Haig

On returning for a spell to Cambridge, before setting off to study the rock-art of middle Sweden and Finland with Gustaf Hallström, Miles Burkitt was anxious to share his excitement over the work being done in France and Spain. Significantly it was the Woodwardian Professor who gave him the opportunity. He duly advertised lectures on 'The Further Exploration of the Caves of France and Spain' to be given by Mr Miles Burkitt, B.A., of Trinity College on 12 and 14 May in the Sedgwick Museum. These were the first lectures on prehistory to be delivered formally to the university. One result was that when the Board of Anthropology announced its lectures for 1915–16 they included three by Miles Burkitt on 'Prehistoric Archaeology and Primitive Art'. The first lecture-list advertised by the new Board of Archaeology and Anthropology in 1920 provided for a larger number of lectures on the same topic and in 1921 Burkitt further enhanced his position by publishing what proved to be his most substantial book, *Prehistory*. His standing at Cambridge was finally established when he was appointed a University Lecturer in 1926.

In 1927 the Faculty was reinforced not only by the election of the first full-time Disney Professor of Archaeology, but also by the transference of Section B from Modern and Medieval Languages under H. M. Chadwick, Elrington and Bosworth Professor of Anglo-Saxon. Chadwick made the change because he looked for a quieter atmosphere to develop his concerns than he might expect to find in the new Faculty of English. Section B was readily accommodated in the structure of its new home by the simple expedient of grouping anthropology and prehistoric archaeology in Section A. Although it remained numerically small, Section B brought many advantages to its new host. Although largely complementary in that whereas Section A was exclusively prehistoric in its archaeological dimension, Section B was primarily concerned with the protohistory of the Celtic, Anglo-Saxon and Norse-speaking peoples of northern Europe, there was also a useful overlap. Chadwick and his group were concerned with the prehistoric antecedents of the peoples with whom they were particularly engaged. This meant that students reading for section A were able to take advantage of the courses on Bronze Age and Early Iron Age Europe provided by Chadwick's University Lecturer, J. M. de Navarro. There was a further advantage. The fact that Sections A and B were substantially complementary meant that candidates could qualify for an honours degree by taking them successively, a course followed with notable success by among others, Glyn Daniel, a future Disney Professor, and John Brailsford, later Keeper of British and Medieval Antiquities at the British Museum.

Chadwick himself, like Ridgeway and Minns, had achieved distinction in the Classical Tripos only to shift his research interests to another field.[7] Whereas Ridgeway had been seduced by anthropology and Minns by Slavonic studies, Chadwick had been attracted to northern studies. What caught his imagination in the first instance was a chance encounter with du Chaillou's *Viking Age*, a striking testimony to what an essentially amateur book can achieve if addressed to an important theme and presented in an attractive style. After his election to a fellowship at Clare in 1893, Chadwick sought experience on the continent by following courses at the University of Fribourg. On returning to Cambridge he embarked on teaching for Section B of the former Medieval and Modern Languages Tripos and wrote the books[8] concerned with Anglo-Saxon history, tradition and mythology that helped

10   Hector Munro Chadwick receiving an honorary degree at Oxford

him win a University Lectureship in 1910 followed by election to the chair of Anglo-Saxon in 1912. The same year he had published in *The Heroic Age* a book which brought him closer to Ridgeway by the comparisons he drew between early Teutonic and Homeric poetry. In the course of the First World War Chadwick widened his interests to include the history, traditions, religion, literature and archaeology of the Celtic as well as of the Teutonic peoples. The growth in his interests is reflected in the lecture-lists published by the Board of Anthropology and its successor. Whereas in that for 1909–10 he merely signified his willingness to direct the reading of anyone wishing to study 'Northern Ethnology', in that for 1913–14 he offered courses on 'The Early History of the North' and on 'Northern Mythology'. The first list issued by the Board of Archaeology and Anthropology in 1920 advertised a course on the archaeology of the period from La Tène to Viking in addition to his lectures on history, life and literature before the period 925–1066. It is significant that by 1924 Chadwick's name appeared along with those of Minns and Burkitt among those nominated for the Board of Studies in Archaeology and Anthropology. When the Board was replaced by the Faculty in 1926 the Professor of Anglo-Saxon Studies was named a member *ex-officio* along with the Disney Professor and the Reader in Ethnology. The transference of Section B was thus a logical outcome of a progressive development in Chadwick's scholarly interests.

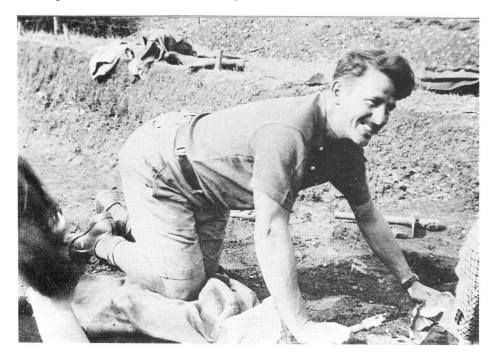

11   J. M. de Navarro

J. M. de Navarro had been appointed to his University Lectureship in 1926 while still assigned to the English Faculty. 'Toty', as he was known to his friends, was the son of a wealthy New Yorker and of Mary Anderson who before her marriage had been an ornament of the London stage. Although he remained an American citizen throughout his life, he was educated in England and grew up deeply attached to European culture with a ready access to continental museums and literature. He began his scholarly career by defining the routes by which amber passed during the Bronze Age from its sources in the Baltic zone to the head of the Adriatic and beyond[9] and won a research fellowship at Trinity on a dissertation devoted to this topic. He next turned to the archaeology of the Early Iron Age Celts, on which he contributed a chapter to the *Cambridge Ancient History* (1928). Thereafter he wrote little until, years after his retirement, he published a volume[10] embodying a meticulous study of the swords and scabbards from the classic site of La Tène. His classes were always small, but those who attended them were taught to handle archaeological material with accuracy and to show restraint in its interpretation.

The new Faculty was housed in the University Museum of Archaeology and Ethnology. Many supervisions and some small classes were held in college rooms or private homes, but the main lectures, at least for Section A, were given in the Museum. The library was formed by Haddon while he was acting curator during von Hügel's incapacity. He did this by amalgamating the Curator's private collection of ethnological literature with the Cambridge Antiquarian Society's archaeological books and the periodicals received in exchange for its own publications. The library was housed on the ground floor and effectively supervised by Miss E. S. Fegan. After only a short interval the university was fortunate to secure Louis Clarke, who had taken the Diploma of Anthropology at Oxford and had since travelled extensively in Central and South America and several parts of Africa including Abyssinia, as well as excavating in Hungary and New Mexico. Louis was one of the great Cambridge characters of his time. He was distinguished for his catholic and discriminating taste, for his generosity, and not least for the outspokenness to which he was prepared to give expression with a blithe disregard for the self-importance of his victim. He never undertook formal teaching and was happy to leave publication to others. This left him free to devote himself to improving the museum's collections so as to make them reflect to the fullest extent the diversity of human cultural expression over the full range of time and space. The hospitality he dispensed in Cambridge to visiting scholars from overseas, combined with his own taste for exotic travel and his foresight in helping young men to conduct research in territories as far afield as Arctic Canada combined to enrich the collections at no cost to the University Chest. When to this is added his zeal for collecting and his flair in the sale-room, it is no wonder that under his care the university's collections of archaeological and ethnological artefacts were so notably enriched. Not the least of his services was to secure an Assistant Curator in the person of Maureen O'Reilly to help in cataloguing and making accessible the increasing wealth of material.

Another resource should be mentioned. The contribution of the Cambridge Antiquarian Society in making over its collections of antiquities and its library was recognized by giving it formal representation on the Faculty, as previously on the Board. This was not the end of the matter. The Society's lecture programme, which the Disney professor was able to influence as an ex-officio member of its Council, brought distinguished archaeologists to Cambridge as well as giving publicity to its own activities in research and at the same time providing a useful platform for Faculty members and their research students. Further, the Society's Director of Excavations, for many years T. C. Lethbridge, gave opportunities for field activities not at first provided by the Faculty.

12   Louis Clarke, by Lazlo, 1927

The stimulus to learning in a collegiate university extends far beyond what is provided by its official establishment, and this was especially true before inflation and political changes had transformed the relations between the university and colleges. A special weakness of the teaching provided for Section A of the Archaeological and Anthropological Tripos was that before the Second World War none of the teaching officers in archaeology were (with the single exception of a Faculty Assistant Lecturer appointed in 1935),

13   T. C. Lethbridge studying material excavated by the Cambridge Antiquarian Society

themselves engaged in primary research. So far as students were concerned the situation was only mitigated by local excavations conducted by Tom Lethbridge and the off-stage activities of people like Louis Leakey of St John's and Gertrude Caton Thompson and Dorothy Garrod of Newnham, who opened windows on a wider scene and advertised both the needs and the gains of research in prehistory.

Louis Leakey[11] had come to Cambridge from Kenya where his father had worked as a missionary among the Kikuyu. After taking firsts in modern languages and in anthropology, in the latter of which he concentrated on technology and prehistoric archaeology, Leakey made off for a three-year spell in Kenya as leader of the East African Archaeological Expedition (1926–9). On his return his college, St John's, elected him to a fellowship to make it possible to work up his results. During this period he influenced archaeological teaching at Cambridge in part by supervising undergraduates in his college rooms stuffed with packing cases and Palaeolithic implements, but not least by exemplifying the need for research. In the preface of his first book[12] he made only scant reference to his Cambridge teacher. Instead he acknowledged help in working up his results from Breuil, Caton Thompson and Garrod, as well as offering warm thanks to Haddon and Arthur Keith. He made his rivalry with Miles Burkitt even more overt by following up the former's text-book *The Old Stone Age*[13] the very next year by his own *Adam's Ancestors*.[14] In 1934 he published the anthropological findings of his expedition[15] and in 1936 gave the Munro Lectures at Edinburgh. These he published in his brief but highly effective *Stone Age Africa: an Outline in Prehistory in Africa*,[16] a book which not only advertised what had already been achieved since Burkitt's *Africa's Past in Stone and Paint*[17] but stimulated thought about future research. Before leaving for Kenya in 1937 to undertake intensive study of the Kikuyu, Leakey had brought home to Cambridge students and others the local and provisional nature of the old prehistory and the imperative need to engage in purposive new research overseas.

Leakey was not the first prehistorian based in Cambridge to bring home the potential of prehistoric research in Africa. Before he ever reached Cambridge, Gertrude Caton Thompson[18] had already embarked on intensive work on the later Stone Age occupation of Egypt. Although she took her first steps under the wing of Flinders Petrie, whose home base was University College London, her investigation of the Fayum between 1924 and 1928 brought her to Newnham first as Associate and in due course as Research Fellow. Gertrude Caton Thompson showed no interest in teaching, though she was always ready to give an occasional lecture and the example she set of scientific field research was by no means lost on those who read the Cambridge Tripos between the wars. Her partnership with a fellow Associate of Newnham, E. W. Gardner, the geologist, who applied herself to the physiographic development of the Fayum basin during prehistoric times as well as carrying out all the necessary survey work, was particularly instructive in emphasizing the value of conducting prehistoric fieldwork in the context of Quaternary Research. Not least of the lessons which she preferred to teach by example rather than by precept was the need to publish the findings of fieldwork promptly, comprehensively and with full illustrations.[19]

It was the gentlest of the three, Dorothy Garrod,[20] who in the end exerted by far the greatest influence on the advance of prehistoric studies at Cambridge. Dorothy came of Suffolk family which in the course of the

14   Gertrude Caton Thompson, 1939

previous two generations had attained eminence in medicine. After taking an honours degree in history at Newnham, she enrolled in the Catholic Women's League for service in France. The war took a heavy toll, including the loss of all three brothers, and it was while resting in Malta where her father was in charge of wartime hospitals that she first discovered an interest in archaeology. When her father moved to Oxford as Regius Professor of Medicine in 1920 she decided to sit for the Oxford Diploma in Anthropology under Marett, the excavator of La Cotte de St Brelade, and duly obtained it with distinction. This success encouraged her to head for the Institut de Paléontologie Humaine in Paris, as Miles Burkitt had done before her, and sit at the feet of the Abbé Breuil. It was Breuil's encouragement to test a narrow

15   Dorothy Garrod, 1962

fissure at the foot of the Devil's Tower, Gibraltar, in 1925–6 that launched her on her career of research. Her discovery of the remains of a Neanderthal child in deposits that had earlier yielded Mousterian flints came at a time when F. Turville Petre of the British School at Jerusalem had just found traces of a young Neanderthal adult with similar cultural material in a cave by the Sea of Galilee. The coincidence was not lost on George Grant MacCurdy who happened to be attending an international archaeological congress at Jerusalem and Beirut in 1926. He realized that here was a superb opportunity for the American School of Prehistoric Research to test the extent of Neanderthal man and Mousterian culture in south-western Asia. He fully appreciated his good fortune in having Dorothy Garrod ready to hand.

Research was directed to two regions, northern Iraq and Palestine. In February 1928 Dorothy Garrod identified a Mousterian industry in the Kirkuk region of Kurdistan.[21] Returning in the autumn she excavated two caves in the same area, one of which, Hazar Merd, near Sulaimanieh, yielded the first evidence for a Mousterian industry in a stratified deposit, one overlaid moreover by an industry of Upper Palaeolithic type. During the intervening season the expedition returned to Palestine and under the auspices of the British School in Jerusalem Miss Garrod made a promising beginning by sectioning the cave of Shukbah in Judaea and revealing traces of Mousterian occupation overlaid by a rich Mesolithic deposit of previously unknown type accompanied by human remains of *sapiens* type. As things turned out she did not resume work at Shukbar when her second expedition returned from Kurdistan. Instead attention was focussed on the caves of the Wady el-Mughara, Mount Carmel, where the threat of quarrying operations for the harbour works at Haifa was only dispelled in time by the Director of Antiquities. Soundings in the Mugh[a]ret el-Wad by the Department of Public Works gave convincing proof of the archaeological importance of the valley and at the same time alerted the American School of Prehistoric Research and the British School of Archaeology in Jerusalem to its possibilities for prehistoric research. Dorothy Garrod found herself committed as director to carrying through what proved to be one of the most productive research projects ever mounted in Palaeolithic studies. Between 1929 and 1934 she directed six seasons of field-work with never more than four assistants. One of these was Jacquetta Hopkins (Mrs Christopher Hawkes and later Mrs J. B. Priestley), who later wrote on the Channel Islands and on prehistoric sites in the British Isles as well as becoming a discerning critic of prehistorical writing in general.[22] Another, Hallam J. Movius Jr of Harvard, went on to take a Cambridge Ph.D. In all, including the season directed by the American human palaeontologist Theodore McCown, some twenty-one and a half months were spent in the field under canvas. Three caves were excavated. Between them they yielded a finely stratified sequence extending from the close of the Lower Palaeolithic to the Mesolithic, all this in a territory where the very existence of these phases of prehistory was previously barely known. The documentation was unusually complete. Successive lithic industries were accompanied by a wealth of animal refuse capable, in the hands of Dorothea Bate of the British Museum of Natural History, of yielding information about the course of ecological change as well as about the economic activities of early man. The excavations were also remarkable for yielding exceptionally rich human skeletal material, notably the Neanderthal cemetery uncovered at the Mugharet es-Skhūl appropriately enough by Theodore McCown, the human palaeontologist who with Sir Arthur Keith wrote the second volume of the report.

Her old college, Newnham, had recognized the importance of the task on which Dorothy Garrod had embarked by electing her to a research fellowship for 1929–32 and several Cambridge institutions made available space for working on her finds, notably the Department of Physiology and the University Museum of Archaeology and Ethnology. Her identification with Cambridge was further strengthened when her parents decided to retire there from Oxford. To have achieved the substantive publication of a material as complex, massive and novel as that recovered from Mount Carmel within so short a space of time – her own volume written with Dorothea Bate covering the archaeological and zoological evidence appeared in 1937, to be followed in 1939 by that on the fossil human remains by Theodore McCown and

16   Dorothy Garrod's camp at Mount Carmel

Arthur Keith[23] – called for the same disciplined and organized effort as that displayed in the excavations themselves. Further, the Mount Carmel project gave ample evidence of her capacity for sustained abstract thought. As early as 1928 Dorothy Garrod had already anticipated Gordon Childe by seven years in calling for an end to the notion endlessly repeated in text-books that archaeological data could sensibly be treated in the same terms as geological fossils.[24] The validity of the conventional sequence was in reality limited to those parts of western Europe where it had been devised on the basis of stratigraphy. The pattern of cultural development approximated much more to the phyla devised by palaeontologists. To obtain the evidence needed to reconstruct the cultural history of mankind it was needful as a first step to conduct excavations in the vast regions outside Europe hitherto neglected.

Others to influence prehistory before the Second World War were two of the earliest to take Ph.D degrees in archaeology at Cambridge. The first was Cyril Fox who came up to Magdalene immediately after the First World War as a mature student to qualify himself for a career in archaeology. Fox began by attending Section B lectures while these were still being given under the aegis of the English Tripos, but Professor Chadwick soon realized that having interested himself in the local archaeology since 1914 Fox was ready to embark on research. Since he was not yet a graduate, it needed the drive and skills of Chadwick and Ridgeway, aided by the exceptional nature of the times, to secure his registration for the newly instituted Ph.D. This he duly secured in 1922 for what must rank among the most mature and original dissertations presented in this field in Cambridge. After a brief spell assisting in the University Museum Fox was recruited by Mortimer Wheeler as Keeper in Antiquities at the National Museum of Wales, of which he soon became Director when Wheeler himself moved to London. If Fox himself was lost to Cambridge, his book, *The Archaeology of the Cambridge Region*,[25] remained to give meaning to the local collections in the University Museum. His treatment of archaeological finds as clues to human settlement attracted the attention of leading historians, among them Sir Alfred Clapham and G. M. Trevelyan, and helped to enhance the esteem in which archaeology was held. In the university it also gave direction to archaeological research in particular by emphasizing the role of surface geology and geography. By plotting finds from successive phases from Neolithic to Anglo-Saxon onto physical base maps over an area some forty-four miles square centred on Cambridge, he was able to demonstrate the expansion of human settlement from a primary zone, which he supposed to have carried relatively open vegetation, to a secondary one of heavier soils carrying forest with dense undergrowth. In the Cambridge region the Romans were shown to have penetrated and the Anglo-Saxons to have occupied on an increasing scale territories calling for a heavy investment in labour without immediate return. Fox's work gave an immediate impetus to the study of geographical distributions, and before long persuaded archaeologists of the need to recover the contemporary environments of different phases of settlement by means of palaeoecological research.

Another to influence students of prehistory was Hugh O'Neill Hencken, a Princeton man who came up to St John's, Cambridge, took a first in Section B of the English Tripos and gained his Ph.D in 1930 for a thesis on the archaeology of Cornwall and Scilly. The book published under this title[26] was widely acknowledged as setting a new standard in regional archaeology, and the author was soon appointed Director of the Harvard Expedition to

17 Cyril Fox, 1931

Ireland. This resulted between 1932 and 1936 in a series of brilliant excavations of sites, notably the timber crannogs of Ballinderry and Lagore,[27] which revealed the potential of wetland environments for the conservation of antiquities of a kind which could only be recovered if at all on dryland sites in the form of traces.

Undergraduates reading archaeology before the war were also open to external stimuli, notably by taking part in archaeological excavations. Although as a rule these were conducted by amateurs there was usually a choice of ones of a high level of technical excellence. In my own case I learned the basic skills of excavation on the chalk downs of Sussex under Dr E. C. Curwen, a medical practitioner of Hove who applied methods perfected by the legendary General Pitt Rivers on his Dorset estates. The party assembled in 1928 in bell-tents under the lee of the Iron Age rampart of the Trundle, Goodwood, to test the Neolithic features in the interior, including myself, a Cambridge undergraduate, Charles Phillips, the future excavator of Sutton Hoo, and Stuart Piggott, already engaged on assembling his corpus of British Neolithic pottery. One of the skills most easily picked up in the field was the ability to read air photographs. Curwen organized excavations at the Trundle only to test features which first appeared on routine air photographs taken of the encircling Iron Age hill-fort.

18   C. W. Phillips in the burial chamber of the Sutton Hoo ship; Stuart Piggott at work on the left

Museums and not least the University Museum of Archaeology were important for documenting and reifying the data on which archaeology was based, as well as exerting a powerful aesthetic influence which helped to attract and mould the interests of those who visited or, in the case of Cambridge students, constantly passed through their collections. An even more powerful influence was exerted by books and periodical literature. As already indicated many of these were written by archaeologists based in or stemming from Cambridge, but others, including some of the most potent, came from outside. Until the subject was more widely studied in universities

19   Teamwork at Sutton Hoo, July 1939: clockwise, from bottom left, C.W. Phillips, T.D. Kendrick, Basil Brown, Sir John Forsdyke, Stuart Piggott, W.F. Grimes

archaeological publications in Britain were largely concerned with the excavation and description of structures and artefacts or with their classification. Students were splendidly served by the research reports and periodicals issued by the Society of Antiquaries of London and a number of county societies, but if British archaeology before the Second World War was long on fact it was miserably short on thought and narrow in perspective. One of the few institutions to mitigate this situation was the British Museum, whose Department of British and Medieval Antiquities contained three outstandingly productive Oxford graduates. If the Keeper, Reginald Smith, dominated Lower and Middle Palaeolithic studies in Britain, the book produced by his Assistant Keepers, Kendrick and Hawkes,[29] in time for the London Congress of 1932 was a guiding light to students of later prehistoric and protohistoric times.

Whereas the early prehistory which formed the basis of Burkitt's teaching was avowedly French in origin and under Garrod and Leakey's influence increasingly came to be thought of as embracing the Old World as a whole, British archaeology, so long as it was mainly amateur, remained largely insular. Undergraduates studying early prehistory were accustomed to reading foreign books,[30] but de Navarro was the only prehistoric archaeologist in the Cambridge faculty who directed attention to European scholarship in relation to later prehistory. Burkitt's *Our Early Ancestors*[31] was couched at too elementary a level to compete with *The Dawn of European Civilization*, published a year previously by Gordon Childe[32] who in the following year took the newly founded Abercromby chair of Prehistoric archaeology at Edinburgh. Within the next three years Childe produced three more books[33] which together with *The Dawn* not only depicted Britain as a province in a highly variegated continent but presented prehistoric Europe as both peripheral to the ancient civilizations of Egypt and south-west Asia and as itself the cradle of the western civilization that was ultimately to dominate world history.

Compared with all but a handful of disciplines archaeology and anthropology attracted relatively few undergraduates until the Tripos was expanded after the Second World War to provide a full degree for those taking Section A. Even so, by comparison with Section B, which averaged between three and four between 1928 and 1939, the number graduating in Section A increased nearly six-fold during the same period, with a marked upturn after archaeology received its first increase in staff in 1935. During the pre-war decade nine of those who graduated in Section A went on to pursue archaeology as a profession, seven of them since 1935. Thurstan Shaw, Desmond Clark and Bernard Fagg began their careers in Africa, and another three took official posts in Britain, John Brailsford in the British Museum, John Hamilton in the Inspectorate of Ancient Monuments and H. G. Wakefield in the Victoria and Albert Museum. Three others, Grahame Clark,

Glyn Daniel and Charles McBurney, successively embarked on postgraduate research at Cambridge. The ability to generate its own staff was crucial at a time when the Cambridge faculty was the only one in Britain producing a flow of honours graduates in prehistoric archaeology. Before the state made provision for research students a decisive role was played by colleges. Without their patronage prehistory could hardly have emerged as an academic subject at Cambridge. The opportunities provided by Christ's, Pembroke, Clare and Trinity for Haddon, Minns, Chadwick and de Navarro have already been noted. The build-up to a full two-part Tripos could hardly have been realized in respect of archaeology without the election of Clark, Daniel and McBurney to fellowships at Peterhouse, St John's and King's.

As the first candidate registered for research in archaeology since the Faculty had been constituted I was encouraged to chose a broad topic. My supervisor, Miles Burkitt, though always helpful, notably in making me free of his off-print library, left me very much to my own devices. The basis from which I began to research on the Mesolithic phase in British prehistory was the ten-page treatment of what Dorothy Garrod termed 'epi-palaeolithic' cultures in her book on *The Upper Palaeolithic Age in Britain*.[34] Like Miss Garrod I had no other recourse at that time than to rely on typological comparisons between British assemblages and ones assigned by continental prehistorians in their own countries to the period intermediate between their Upper Palaeolithic and Neolithic phases. Where we differed was in the much greater stress I laid on comparisons with Mesolithic material across the North Sea. This was given added point by a dramatic discovery in the North Sea itself made just in time to be incorporated in my book.[35] This occurred when the skipper of the trawler *Colinda* broke a lump of moorlog trawled from between the Leman and Ower Banks at a depth of some nineteen fathoms below the surface. The finely barbed antler point which clattered out was displayed to a meeting of the Prehistoric Society of East Anglia at Norwich in February 1932. It was immediately seen to resemble in form and technique of production specimens previously found in Holderness and at many sites on the north European plain extending as far east as Estonia. The fact that the Leman and Ower specimen was recovered from a freshwater deposit from such a depth below sea-level excited intense interest since comparable specimens in the context of Maglemosian assemblages had been assigned by Danish and Swedish investigators to a period when sea-levels were still low, pending a further melting of the Pleistocene ice-sheets, and the Baltic was still occupied by the Ancylus Lake. The North Sea find did far more than confirm the emphasis laid on the Maglemosian contribution to the Mesolithic settlement of Britain. It opened up two distinct but complementary lines of research. For one thing it pointed to the need to look more closely into the methods used by colleagues in north Germany and Scandinavia to advance knowledge of early Post-glacial settlement by collaborating with geologists and palaeontologists in the concert of Quaternary Research.[36] For another it inspired a desire to emulate them by applying similar interdisciplinary research in Britain.

As it happened Dr (later Professor Sir) Harry Godwin and his wife Margaret, when embarking on an ambitious study of the history of the British flora, had taken A. G. Tansley's advice and gone to Sweden to acquire a mastery of pollen analysis from Lennart von Post.[37] They returned to Britain equipped to zone deposits and thus to emulate their colleagues in northern Europe by effecting precise correlations between climatic, geographical, faunal, botanical and archaeological sequences. The fact that the Leman and Ower antler point was embedded in a lump of freshwater peat gave the Godwins an opportunity to demonstrate the value of pollen analysis to prehistorians.[38] In the event their readings agreed closely with those obtained by the Swedish investigator Erdtman from similar samples. Both were consistent with the attribution of the point to an early phase of the Maglemosian culture. For their part it proved the value of archaeology for providing independent markers.

The most convenient territory to begin the task of tracing the history of

20   Professor Sir Harry Godwin and Sir Albert Seward examining a large yew exposed at Isleham Fen, Cambridge, c. 1935

British vegetation since the Ice Age and correlating this with geographical change and human settlement was offered by the Fenland Basin, essentially an extension of the North Sea in which waterlogged deposits had accumulated during Post-glacial times. Palaeobotany was not alone in beckoning to the fens. Geology also pointed in the same direction. Research had been at a low ebb since the appearance of Skertchley's magisterial memoir in 1877.[39] One of the first to stimulate interest was a vigorous and determined layman, Major Gordon Fowler, at that time Transport Manager of the Ely Beet-sugar Factory. Fowler was the first to draw attention to the meandering banks of marine silt, locally known as 'roddons', which were becoming increasingly prominent as modern drainage was causing the upper peat to waste away. Air photographs combined with surface survey convinced him that what he had found represented remains of the natural waterways of the fenland. Apart from their interest to geographers and geologists, the roddons were of vital relevance to archaeologists since in a flat region like the fens waterways have always been a prime focus of human settlement. In *The Archaeology of the Cambridge Region* Cyril Fox had emphasized the importance of the geographical approach to a study of human settlement. What he was not in a position to do when he wrote his book was to relate early settlement patterns to their contemporary physical environments. That information was contained in the waterlogged deposits which occupied much of the northern part of his area, but it could not be extracted until pollen analysis had been effectively introduced to Britain.[41]

The time was obviously ripe to apply the expertise available in Cambridge to the adjacent fenland sequence. The best way to achieve this was to form an interdisciplinary committee. This was done on 7 June 1932 when the Fenland Research Committee[42] was instituted in the Upper Parlour at Peterhouse. The committee was exceptionally fortunate to secure Sir Albert Seward, Master of Downing and Professor of Botany in the university, as chairman. Sir Albert had made his career in palaeobotany and was accustomed to pursuing botany in the context of geology. His genial and wise personality ensured that a proper measure of cooperation was forthcoming between the several disciplines involved in the committee's work. It wisely appointed Gordon Fowler as vice-president. Apart from his special knowledge of the ancient waterways of the region, Fowler was exceptionally well placed because of his job to keep track of new finds and secure the goodwill of the farmers on whose lands we would need to work. Academics working in the Departments of Archaeology and Anthropology, Botany, Geography and Geology at Cambridge formed the majority of the Committee, but it was greatly strengthened on the archaeological side by O. G. S. Crawford, Christopher Hawkes and Stuart Piggott. When it met it combined elements of a research seminar, a practical working committee and a convivial group which habitually dined together in one or other of the Cambridge colleges.

A measure of the Committee's success is the way in which it shared in publishing prompt accounts of its work. All four of the reports dealing with the fens, the first of thirteen 'Studies of Post-glacial History' published by Harry Godwin in preparation for his Classic *History of the British Flora*,[43] were communicated to the Royal Society by Sir Albert Seward in 1938[44] and 1940.[45] In these Godwin cited references to the work of ten other members of the committee. Again, the five reports dealing with the archaeological excavations that established the archaeological succession, published in the *Antiquaries Journal* and the *Proceedings of the Prehistoric Society of East Anglia*, were signed in all by five members of the Committee.[46] Another indication of the Committee's worth is that, although it did not survive the war under its own name, it inspired the formation in 1948 of the University Sub-department of Quaternary Research. Although the work of the Sub-department is now world-wide in scope, it still reports to the heads of the Departments of Archaeology, Botany and Earth Sciences at Cambridge.

Tenure of a bye-fellowship at Peterhouse gave me a chance to press ahead with the research promoted by the Fenland Research Committee and above all to establish the stratigraphic context of successive phases of prehistoric settlement in the Ely fens. It also allowed me to study at first hand the outcome of applying Quaternary Research to early Post-glacial settlement in the West Baltic area and at the same time to obtain a firmer grasp of the later prehistory of temperate Europe. At this time I also gained a closer insight into the traditional methods of British field archaeology from Charles Phillips,[47] who was then a fellow of Selwyn engaged in teaching history. On Sundays in full term we would board his upright Austin, commanding a generous view of the country, and speed across the then almost empty roads to the Lincolnshire wolds, armed with air photographs and Ordnance Survey maps. Among his early triumphs was the discovery of a new group of long barrows and the excavation of one of them, Giant's Hills, Skendleby.[48] My first chance to tackle an ancient monument on my own account came in 1935 when I was invited to test an air photograph of what appeared to be a 'henge' at Arminghall near Norwich.[49]

The year 1935 proved to be important for more lasting reasons. For one thing it witnessed the formal transformation of the provincial Prehistoric Society of East Anglia into the national Prehistoric Society.[50] Since the *Proceedings* were already being edited at Cambridge this put prehistoric archaeology there in a strong position to influence the course of the subject. It helped young prehistorians to obtain rapid publication of their results from as far afield as Africa and Australasia, and at the same time widened the basis of the Society's interests and strengthened the influence of its *Proceedings*. For another the Cambridge Faculty was able to enlarge its teaching staff by recruiting a Faculty Assistant Lecturer who thanks to the threat, and ultimately the outbreak of war found himself frozen in that grade until being

21 Excavations through the Little Ouse river channel at Peacock's Farm, Shippea Hill, Cambridgeshire, 1934. Grahame Clark stands in the channel bed, Gordon Fowler seated above

demobilized in 1946. As was only to be expected he lectured on his own special field, the Mesolithic settlement of Northern Europe. Of greater interest for the future, he also chose to lecture on the aims and methods of prehistoric archaeology as such. After spending his last two years as an undergraduate studying prehistory alongside social anthropology it is hardly to be wondered at that he was dissatisfied with conventional archaeology. The writings of Gordon Childe, even before he had published more explicit works for the general reader, had made it evident that prehistorians had something to say as well as things to find, classify and date. A more explicit prompting came from the editor of Minns's *Festschrift*, A. M. Tallgren. In an article printed in English in *Antiquity*[51] he complained that archaeology had got itself into something of a cul-de-sac, that it had come to consist 'merely of a comparison of forms and of systematization' and that its practitioners had too often come to regard 'forms and types, that is products . . . as more real and alive than the society which created them and whose needs determined their manifestations of life'. Tallgren concluded that archaeology was not a natural but an 'economic-social, historical science'. His advice to archaeologists was that they should concentrate more on the function of artefacts than on their classification as forms. The message of the Cambridge lectures was that prehistorians should recover their evidence and seek to interpret it for the insights it could afford into the lives of the communities represented. The tenor was suggested by the title of the ensuing book, *Archaeology and Society*, which originally appeared in 1939.[52]

The outbreak of war later that year and the absorption of myself, the Disney Professor and the two younger Cambridge prehistorians, Glyn Daniel and Charles McBurney, who were later to help in its development in the context of a full-scale Tripos, meant that Cambridge prehistory was put in abeyance until 1946.

CHAPTER 4

PREHISTORY AT CAMBRIDGE, 1946–74: EXPANSION OF THE SYLLABUS AND PROVISION FOR EXCAVATION

Although the war, by diverting faculty members to national service and severely reducing student numbers, made cruel inroads into Dorothy Garrod's tenure of the Disney chair, it had its compensations. For those who served in Britain within at least occasional reach of literature it allowed some time for reflection, and for those who went overseas it brought expanded horizons. More important the euphoria which greeted victory, however misplaced, greatly increased the funds available to universities and made possible decisions for new developments which would otherwise have been much delayed. Within two years the Archaeological and Anthropological Tripos had been expanded to comprise two parts, and within these to allow a considerable degree of choice. Before she took early retirement in 1952 to pursue her own research Dorothy Garrod had succeeded in designing, winning acceptance for and implementing a Part II which gave archaeological candidates a notable range of options. This she did by drawing on the resources of Classics and Oriental Languages which from an early stage had been involved with the teaching of archaeology and anthropology at Cambridge. By gaining cooperation with these two faculties and ensuring that archaeology was taught in the same Tripos as anthropology, students were not only given a wider choice than could otherwise have been provided, but they were encouraged to study their chosen fields in the context of world prehistory.

In the previous chapter the importance of producing and retaining an academic staff capable of teaching the subject to full Tripos standard was emphasized. In this respect the faculty was fortunate not to sustain serious loss during the war. The Disney Professor herself returned from war service ready to give substance to her vision of prehistory as a subject far transcending the European continent in which it first developed. Miles Burkitt remained at Cambridge and continued to capture the interest of newcomers to prehistory, a role he went on to discharge effectively for the Part I of the new Tripos until he retired in 1958. I myself returned as a university lecturer after being frozen in the grade of faculty assistant lecturer since 1935. Glyn Daniel, who had given his first course in 1938, was appointed an assistant lecturer when he returned and was made a full University Lecturer in 1948. Charles McBurney resumed his research fellowship at King's and in 1951 shared a course with Dorothy Garrod. In 1952 his position was fully established when he was appointed to a University Lectureship.

The Museum also saw changes. T. T. Paterson, who had succeeded Louis Clarke as Curator before the war, resigned the post to take up a position

22   G. H. S. Bushnell

elsewhere in social psychology. Meanwhile Geoffrey Bushnell, who had taken on the acting curatorship during Paterson's leave of absence, was appointed Curator in 1948, an office he continued to hold until he retired in 1970. Although as an undergraduate Bushnell had read geology, he knew the museum well because of the visits he used to make to it when he consulted the collection of brass-rubbings presided over by Dr Ralph Griffin. Indeed it was in passing through the main gallery with its Mesoamerican and Peruvian antiquities that he gained the interest in New World archaeology that stood him in good stead in later life. When as a young recruit he was posted by his oil company to Ecuador this interest proved a godsend for his leisure hours. The systematic excavations he made in an ancient cemetery of the Santa Elena peninsula on the south-west coast of Ecuador provided the material which he later used for his Ph.D thesis.[1] Although as it turned out the university never made provision for an option in New World archaeology, Geoffrey Bushnell kept the subject in play to such good effect that Cambridge in fact turned out two men who later became distinguished Americanists, Warwick Bray and Norman Hammond. He did so by keeping abreast of and reviewing the literature, by writing books himself,[2] by lecturing and not least by attracting a steady stream of Americanists to Cambridge. In this regard Bushnell built on the reputation established in his field by Maudslay and Louis Clarke and displayed in the exceptionally rich collections of New World antiquities in the Museum.

In the growth of a new faculty the quality of its teaching officers was a matter of crucial importance. What was needed even more was a body of knowledge acquired by definable disciplines and therefore capable of indefinite extension. Until prehistory began to be studied systematically it was, like anthropology, to a large extent deficient in the qualities needed to validate its claims for academic acceptance. Even in the case of mature subjects like Classics or History the transmission of existing knowledge was at university level only a small part of their contribution. In the case of a subject at such a primitive stage of development as prehistoric archaeology it was all the more necessary to bring home the precarious nature of existing knowledge and further the appetite for research. So long as candidates were required to cover the entire range of anthropology envisaged by Haddon, including physical anthropology and social anthropology, prehistoric archaeology could be taught only at a Part I standard. When Archaeology and Anthropology became a full Tripos in 1948, candidates for Part II were required to take an initial paper on the aims, methods and objectives of archaeology, which had already been taught in outline before the war.[3] In addition they were required to take two papers in each of two options drawn from nine on offer. One of the merits of this scheme was that while insisting on a common framework it opened up a number of different areas of research and ultimate employment. Another was that it could be implemented relatively cheaply by drawing on the teaching resources of a number of university departments.

As we have already noted Classics and Oriental Languages both contributed to Part II of the archaeological part of the Archaeological and Anthropological Tripos. In addition teaching for the compulsory first paper received important contributions from biology, geology and geography. Although as it happens no candidate chose the option available from the Classical Tripos, two members of that faculty in particular contributed notably to the teaching of other options. Frank Stubbings[4] provided teaching for the Mediterranean option, and Jocelyn Toynbee[5] for Roman Britain in that stemming from the old Section B which covered the archaeology and protohistory of north-western Europe and the British Isles. As we shall see the glamour of Wace's work[6] at Mycenae and the decipherment of the Linear B tablets by Michael Ventris and John Chadwick, confirming Ridgeway's inference that the Mycenaeans spoke Greek, were enough to ensure that prehistoric Greece exerted a powerful influence on Cambridge prehistorians. The contribution to Greek prehistory made by products of the Department of Archaeology and Ethnology would have been relished by Ridgeway as a vindication of his interest in the prehistoric background of the Classical world. An early illustration was provided by one of the earliest recruits to the newly constituted Part II of the Archaeological and Anthropological Tripos. Lord William Taylour, after taking the Mediterranean option in the Tripos, went on to acquire a Ph.D on Mycenaean pottery in Italy and has since devoted his life to the prehistory of Greece. Two of the most brilliant performers in the Tripos, John Evans and Colin Renfrew, devoted much attention to Aegean studies. The Department was also responsible for opening up the earlier prehistory of Greece, through the early Neolithic excavations at Nea Nikomedeia, and later by the still continuing exploration of the Palaeolithic occupation of Epirus, initiated by Eric Higgs and currently being carried forward by Geoff Bailey.

Teaching for the options covering Egypt, Mesopotamia and Asia Minor as well as for India and the Far East was provided by the Faculty of Oriental Languages. In respect of Egypt we were well served by successive holders of the Herbert Thompson chair of Egyptology, Stephen Glanville[7] and from 1957 Martin Plumley,[8] each of whom served for a period as chairman of the Faculty Board of Archaeology and Anthropology. Teaching for the Indian sub-continent was given by Mrs van Lohuizen before she left Cambridge to take up a chair at Leiden. In 1959 she was replaced at Cambridge by Raymond Allchin who with his wife Bridget has carried out extensive research across the whole span of South Asian prehistory.[9] In respect of China we were able to call upon Cheng Te-K'un[10] who held a University Lectureship in Far Eastern Art and Archaeology and was an acknowledged authority on early Chinese ceramics.

The fact remains that the great majority of undergraduates chose to take options wholly or at least mainly taught by our own Faculty. That covering the Palaeolithic and Mesolithic of Europe and the Mediterranean area was defined in such a way as to include the territories studied by Dorothy Garrod in Palestine and Iraq and Charles McBurney in Libya, as well as European territories from Iberia to the Soviet Union. In respect of the Mesolithic I was able to contribute the results of personal work in Scandinavia as well as in Britain, notably at Star Carr, as well as a general knowledge acquired largely through reading and museum study of relevent material from other parts of the region. The later prehistory of Europe was divided into two options, those covering the Mediterranean and Temperate zones. Through his special interest in megalithic tombs Glyn Daniel[11] contributed to both, though the main weight of his teaching rested on the Mediterranean, in which he was joined in respect of Greece and the Aegean by Frank Stubbings. In the Temperate zone my own interests were concentrated on the Neolithic and much of the teaching for the Bronze and Early Iron Ages was given at first by J. M. de Navarro and subsequently by John Coles. Coles himself had come to Cambridge as an affiliated student from Toronto. On taking the Cambridge Diploma he moved to Edinburgh to study for his Ph.D under Stuart Piggott

23   Glyn Daniel and the Irish archaeologist Sean P. Ó'Ríordáin before the entrance stone at Newgrange, Co. Meath, 1962

with the Late Bronze Age in Scotland as the subject of his dissertation.[12] Once established in Cambridge Coles earned rapid promotion, culminating in a personal professorship in 1980. He did so by unremitting scholarly productivity and a notable widening in the range of his teaching.[13]

The European section was rounded off by an option covering the Archaeology and Protohistory of north-western Europe and the British Isles. This reflected and perpetuated the archaeological interests which H. M. Chadwick had combined with his concern for the history and literature of the Celtic, Anglo-Saxon and Teutonic peoples. Appropriately enough much of the teaching was given by members of Section B, notably by de Navarro and Peter Hunter-Blair, though Glyn Daniel also contributed, as did Jocelyn Toynbee, and for a period Brian Hope-Taylor.[14]

The initial paper, entitled 'Advanced Prehistory', was designed to test the understanding by candidates of the evidence on which prehistory depends. It is based on the premise that prehistoric societies can only be approached directly through material traces. It followed that archaeologists needed to understand how these could be located, excavated and interpreted. This still applies where help can be had from adjacent literate traditions or even in the case of civilizations with their own historical records. To an overwhelming extent the archaeology of early societies can only be recovered from the soil and apprehended from the excavation reports. The value of these depended not merely on their technical competence but on the theoretical basis on which they operated. The only excavations capable of advancing a knowledge of prehistory in a significant way are those addressed to questions worth answering. In this connection the history of archaeology, that is the history of why our predecessors engaged in archaeology and what they hoped to learn by doing so, was, as Glyn Daniel emphasized,[15] of crucial importance. In teaching young archaeologists it was certainly important to emphasize the need to improve techniques in the recovery of data, but even more to explore the aims and consider the purpose of archaeological activity. This could be done in part by precept through lectures, personal teaching or publications, but to an important degree, as the present chapter shows, by providing opportunities to assist at excavations and share in the study of finds and the preparation of reports.

To the initial task of reconnaissance Cambridge made a notable contribution by promoting aerial photography. As a way of discovering sites and surveying terrain the method was already familiar to the Disney Professor and her staff. When Kenneth St Joseph sought how to establish aerial photography in the university after the war he received a warm welcome from archaeology, as from other subjects likely to benefit from its development. St Joseph had begun his career at Cambridge as a geologist and his early interest focussed on fossil brachiopods. His interest in aerial photography had first been aroused by a chance encounter with O. G. S. Crawford before the war.[16] They first met in 1932 in Cambridge at a time when Crawford then was a frequent visitor as a member of the Fenland Research Committee. Crawford waxed so eloquent about the merits of aerial survey that St Joseph decided to accompany him on his first flying expedition to Scotland in 1939. His concern was further enhanced by his wartime service in Operational Research in Bomber Command. On returning to Cambridge he persuaded the university to explore the potential of aerial photography as a way of advancing academic research. When a committee was appointed in 1948 to offer advice, Classics, Geology and Geography, and History were represented as well as Archaeology and Anthropology. The Commitee's

24   J. K. St Joseph during the filming of Anglia Television's *Frontiers of Discovery*

report led directly to St Joseph's transference from geology and his appointment that same year as Curator in Aerial Photography, a post subsequently upgraded to Director and then Professor. His duties were deemed to include securing aerial photographs for teaching and research and the maintenance of the university's collection as an archive for reference. Initially he had to depend on Royal Air Force training flights to obtain new photographic cover. It was only later that the unit was able to secure an aircraft of its own and in this way gain greater control over targets for reconnaissance. Its first aircraft was an Auster, but due to the generosity of the Nuffield Foundation it was later able to secure a Cessna Skymaster. This made it possible to extend the range to include the whole of the United Kingdom, northern France, the Netherlands and Denmark. The fact that the unit operated from Cambridge and that St Joseph himself lectured on the application of aerial photography to archaeology meant that its capabilities and achievements were well advertised. Moreover the Cambridge University Press ensured that the results were widely appreciated by publishing a series of *Cambridge Air Surveys*. Not surprisingly the Cambridge unit was frequently called upon to support the Royal Commission on Historical Monuments and the Inspectorate for Ancient Monuments.

The crux of archaeology is excavation, since it is from the soil that archaeologists have to obtain the bulk of their documents. Whether they excavate themselves or depend on the reports of others, it is plain that command of archaeological evidence must depend first and foremost on understanding the processes involved in excavation. To learn about or teach archaeology without experiencing excavation would be tantamount to trying to understand biology, chemistry or physics without being involved at some stage with the discipline of working in a laboratory. How a university can best provide such experience is another matter. Scientific experiments can be repeated at will so long as adequate premises are available on the campus. Archaeology, on the other hand, addresses questions which because they are historical can never be exactly repeated and need to be answered whenever and wherever the opportunity arises. To some extent the underlying principles can be explained in the lecture-room, but real understanding can only come with practical experience in the field. Up till 1960 this was mainly supplied within daily reach of Cambridge or on excavations carried on by faculty members further afield during vacations. As early as 1951 Cambridge students were digging as far afield as North Africa, and ten years later opportunities were provided in Greece and south-west Asia.

Until a two-part Tripos was established in 1948 little could be done, but it is a sign of the importance of providing field experience that a beginning was made during the long vacation of 1947. The site chosen was at Bullock's Haste on the Car Dyke at Cottenham, within easy reach of Cambridge, and the aim was to establish the date and purpose of the Dyke.[17] Excavations by

T. C. Lethbridge at Waterbeach a few miles to the south in 1926 had already shown that the dyke had been cut before the existence of an Anglo-Saxon settlement. The choice of a site occupied during the Roman period offered the possibility of refining on this date. Excavation in fact showed that the dyke had been cut during an early phase of the Roman occupation and the profile suggested that it might have served as a canal. The dig provided some three hundred and fifty man-days of field experience including ancillary work on the adjacent settlement. Among the students assisting in the dig was John Evans, then a refugee from the English Tripos. The party was reinforced for a week by a group of three young Swedes under the aegis of the British Council, including Berta Stjernquist, presently Professor of Archaeology at Lund, Eric Cinthio, the art historian of the same university, and Erik Lundberg, who did important work on the antiquities of the island of Gotland. At a time when Europeans could visit Britain after the war it was gratifying to be able to welcome to the excavations Prof. A. E. van Giffen, Director of the Archaeological-Biological Institute at Groningen, and Sune Lindqvist, Professor of Archaeology at Uppsala. Another happy outcome was the formation of the Cambridge Field Archaeology Club. Although it served to attract lectures from outside Cambridge, its role was also to focus interest on archaeological field-work and encourage recruits for more ambitious operations in the future.

An exceptional opportunity occurred in 1949 just one year after the new Tripos had got into its stride and the Sub-department of Quaternary Research had taken shape under Harry Godwin. The discovery of worked flints of distinctively Maglemosian character along with antler and bone in a drainage ditch on the northern margin of the Vale of Pickering near Scarborough offered an opportunity for recovering a Mesolithic assemblage along with animal refuse and fossil pollen much on the lines already known from the West Baltic region. This was something we could not afford to miss. The discovery by John Moore offered a chance to substantiate the strength of the West Baltic component of the British Mesolithic and at the same time to engage in a joint enterprise with the Sub-department of Quaternary Research. Excavations during the summers of 1949–51 were undertaken primarily to advance research. At the same time they served the purposes of teaching. They provided immediate experience to volunteers and they built up capital for the future by amassing invaluable material for lectures and museum exhibits. Not least they provided rich material for publication, an ancillary purpose which was to stimulate further research and engage the interest of colleagues and students. The General Board even made a grant of fifty pounds to the Faculty Board of Archaeology and Anthropology towards the cost of providing instruction in field archaeology. In the event ten Cambridge students gained experience during the 1949 season, eighteen in that of 1950 and sixteen in 1951. Undergraduates were especially valuable under the particular conditions at Star Carr, which needed critical observation and a readiness to observe new small-scale features. The students themselves were fortunate to have the experience of working alongside members of the Sub-department of Quaternary Research, the Director of which took part in person during the first season and visited later ones. His assistants included the future foundation Professor of Biogeography at the Australian National University, Donald Walker, and a future Professor of Botany at the Queen's University, Belfast, and subsequently at Cardiff, A. G. Smith. We also had the advantage during the two later seasons of having a technician from the British Museum of Natural History on the site to conserve the bone and antler finds as they were made. Around half the undergraduates who took part in the excavation became professional archaeologists, including each of the half dozen who helped during all three

25   Grahame Clark, by Ruskin Spear, 1953

seasons. Prominent among those who attended were John Evans, successor of Gordon Childe in the chair of Prehistoric Archaeology at the London Institute of Archaeology and later its Director, Jack Golson, who became foundation Professor of Prehistory in the School of Pacific Studies at the Australian National University, Gale Sieveking, who later became Deputy Keeper of the Department of Prehistoric and Romano-British Antiquities at the British Museum, and John Hurst, who played a conspicuous part in the recording and interpretation of deserted medieval villages in the Inspectorate of Ancient Monuments.

From a research point of view the excavations at Star Carr gave the fullest picture of a Mesolithic site in Britain and did so in a context peculiarly favourable for the deployment of pollen analysis and radiocarbon dating. It produced a flint industry in mint condition, and many of the antler and bone artefacts associated with it were new to Britain, notably the stag antler frontlets and the mattock-heads of elk bone and antler. Other forms, like the barbed antler points, were found in over thirty times the numbers previously known from the entire country. Evidence for the vegetation prevailing during early Post-glacial times was available in both microscopic and macroscopic

26 Star Carr, 1950: Grahame Clark holding a stag frontlet; on the right, in black hat, Professor V. Gordon Childe. On the left is John D. Evans, who later succeeded Childe in the chair of Prehistoric Archaeology at London University

form, and there was a rich assemblage of animal antlers and bones which gave a good idea both of the prevailing ecological conditions and of the culling policy of the Mesolithic people. The discovery was reported without delay. The Prehistoric Society published the results of the first two seasons during the same calendar years as the excavations themselves,[18] and the University Press ensured that a full illustrated account of all three seasons, including drawings of around three hundred and fifty objects, many from three aspects, appeared in 1954.[19]

In 1948 we had been invited by the Norfolk Research Committee to investigate two circular enclosures on Micklemoor Hill, West Harling, in advance of threatened afforestation. The original investigator had confined himself to quarrying the ditches and recovering quantities of Early Iron Age sherds. We decided to concentrate on structures rather than merely to accumulate potsherds. In the course of three seasons we managed to recover the plans of two structures. One was evidently a substantial dwelling with fire-places in the interior. The other was built on a single circle of wooden posts and probably served an ancillary purpose. One of the students who took part in this excavation was David Stronach, who later became Director of the British Institute of Persian Studies at Tehran. The fact that neither structure showed signs of having been rebuilt suggested a comparatively short life for the site, and this made it worth while for Clare Fell, then assistant Curator of the University Museum, who also took a valuable part in the excavations, to undertake a definitive study of the 530 vessels represented among our finds. These Miss Fell dated to the period around 400 B.C.[20]

The next site to be tackled was located in Hurst Fen, close to the fenland margin near Mildenhall in Suffolk. The locality had been identified by a local antiquary as the source of Neolithic pottery and flints, and seemed to offer an opportunity to recover useful information about the nature of the settlement and hopefully about the structure of individual houses. Work began in 1954 and was resumed in 1957–8. It took the form of stripping some 20,000 square feet, removing the topsoil and scraping clean the underlying sand. Many hollows were found including a number containing more or less complete pots, showing that the site had evidently been occupied rather than merely visited. The recovery of querns pointed to the same conclusion. Unfortunately, although signs of neolithic activity were clearly visible in the form of well defined discolourations, no evidence was found of structures. It could well be that surface erosion in the course of four millennia had removed all signs of these. We were therefore left with a large assemblage of flints and sherds, all traces of organic material other than charcoal having disappeared. Analysis of the flint-work showed that apart from residual Mesolithic pieces we were confronted by a distinctive regional group marked by large bifacially flaked laurel-leaves alongside the usual leaf-shaped arrowheads and polished flint and stone axes. Ian Longworth's analysis of the pottery disclosed around three hundred vessels, about one quarter of which were decorated mainly by incised lines on rim and neck and by impressions on the shoulder zone. The assemblage as a whole resembled others in southern England of the same Middle Neolithic phase, notably at Abingdon and Whiteleaf.[21]

Help in supervising the later stages of the excavations was given by a new recruit to the Faculty, Eric Higgs, who came up to Magdalene as a mature affiliated student to read for a Diploma in Prehistoric Archaeology. Having secured this in 1953, Higgs remained in Cambridge and was appointed to the recently established Assistantship in Research when this fell vacant in 1956. Already in 1955 Higgs had taken part in Charles McBurney's final season in North Africa. In 1957 he undertook excavations of his own on the Mesolithic hut site at Downton near Salisbury.[22] On that occasion he showed his judgement of men in his choice of assistants. These included Ian Longworth, later of the British Museum, Richard Wright, who now holds a chair at Sydney, and Brian Fagan, currently Professor at Santa Barbara. Eric Higgs was to play a significant part in the development of prehistoric research at Cambridge, first by opening up the Palaeolithic of Epirus, and later by serving as Director of the Early History of Agriculture Project.

In 1960 the opportunity was taken to open up a new section at Peacock's Farm, Shippea Hill, to confirm the stratigraphy in the lower peat and to obtain samples for radiocarbon assay of the Mesolithic and Neolithic levels. Harry Godwin took a fresh series of pollen samples and others were taken for radiocarbon tests by E. W. Willis of the Sub-department of Quaternary Research.[23] The determinations made by Willis confirmed that the Neolithic phase in England had begun a thousand years earlier than leading archaeologists had recently been prepared to admit.

On the Palaeolithic front the lead was naturally taken by Charles McBurney. In the intervals of his major campaign in Cyrenaica he carried out work at Hoxne, Suffolk, in conjunction with Richard West. The aim was to establish the Lower Palaeolithic hand-axes which had been known from the site since the later eighteenth century in their correct Pleistocene context. West was interested in the flints as markers in the geological sequence, whereas McBurney was primarily concerned with fixing the stratigraphy of series of worked flints having close analogues in France.[24]

In 1958 McBurney was urged by the Prehistoric Society to try and secure better correlations between the British Upper Palaeolithic and episodes in the Upper Pleistocene. Eleven weeks were spent testing a number of sites in Mendip and South Wales, including a substantial excavation in the Cathole, Gower. Although in his report[25] McBurney referred to his student helpers a trifle austerely as providers of 'labour in the field' and mentioned none of them by name, the fact remains that they gave essential help voluntarily, sufficient indication that they appreciated the value of gaining first-hand experience from a master of his craft. The notion that students should be paid to attend excavations of this kind was as alien to the ethos of the time as the idea that academics should be paid for giving up their vacations in the interest of research and setting an example to their students. Although archaeology was already in the process of becoming professional, the notion that advancing prehistory was a privilege in itself remained a key incentive. No one who reported on excavations expected to be paid for doing so. The Prehistoric Society, in whose *Proceedings* many of the early Cambridge excavations appeared, was, and for that matter still is, administered on an honorary basis.

McBurney's most ambitious contribution to British archaeology was his investigation of the stratigraphy of the Cotte de St Brelade in Jersey. His chance came when Father Burdo retired and placed his collection and manuscript notes in the University Museum at Cambridge. As we know from McBurney himself, he mounted campaigns from Cambridge in 1961 and 1962 and again in 1967 and 1969 'partly as a research project and partly as field training for third year and research students'.[26] The attraction from a research standpoint was the opportunity of establishing the precise context of Middle Palaeolithic assemblages in the sequence of climatic and sea-level changes during the Pleistocene. This required in the first place meticulously controlled excavation, including the collection and documentation of archaeological and palaeontological samples. Secondly it involved prolonged and patient work in the laboratory which as well as being vital to the research itself served to introduce students to the rigours of intensive and prolonged work in the laboratory in the aftermath of excavation. As things turned out the definitive report did not appear until some years after the excavator's death.[27]

McBurney's concern with North Africa stemmed from his war-time experiences in Libya. His first published paper[28] recorded the results of surface prospection covering some thirty sites between 1942 and 1943 and featuring in the main Lower to Middle Palaeolithic and microlithic assemblages. In 1948 he decided to undertake further reconnaissance directed on that occasion specifically to the ancient shorelines of the Mediterranean. It was on the final day of this expedition that one of his helpers, C. T. Houlder, then a freshman, drew decisive attention to the archaeological possibilities of the great cave of Haua Fteah situated at the foot of the northern escarpment of the Gebel el Akhdar range in Cyrenaican Libya, half a mile or so from the present shore of the Mediterranean. This turned out to be a key site and the objective of expeditions between 1951 and 1955. In the first season McBurney took three students, and in 1952, when he was accompanied by the Cambridge geologist Richard Hey,[29] he took four, including John Mulvaney, who later became the virtual founder of modern Australian prehistory. In 1955, he took a larger party, including Ray Inskeep, now of the Pitt Rivers Museum, Oxford, and Jacques Nenquin who at the present time holds the chair of Archaeology at Ghent. It is significant that the person who took effective control of the faunal remains at this time was Eric Higgs. Only a comparatively small part of the cave was investigated, but the fourteen metres of deposit revealed in the section were so evenly stratified that we may be sure that McBurney's samples effectively mirrored the complete history of its prehistoric occupation. This proved to extend from the Middle Palaeolithic up to the Neolithic. The material brought back to Cambridge for closer study included half a million lithic artefacts, twelve thousand identifiable animal bones, parts of two Neanderthal men and quantities of snails as well as a series of carefully chosen samples for radiocarbon dating. Analysis of this material gave invaluable experience to students and colleagues at Cambridge, but proved to be a slow process. When the book was finally issued by the University Press in 1967,[30] providing a definitive account of the Haua excavations and using the results to review the situation in the Mediterranean as a whole, it was hailed as the most important single contribution made to the prehistory of northern Africa. It is doubly appropriate that the book should have been dedicated to Dorothy Garrod. For one thing, she had taught McBurney by precept as well as by example. For another, it was her invitation to share her course in 1951 that prepared the way for his own appointment as a University Lecturer on her retirement from the Disney chair the following year.

27   The massive cave of the Haua Fteah, Libya

The third territory to which McBurney directed his attention extended into south-west Asia as far as Afghanistan and the Soviet Union. His object was to test the hypothesis that modern man and his associated blade and burin flint industries had originated in south-west Asia. He began by making a six-week reconnaissance into north-east Iran in 1962, followed in 1964 by excavations in the cave of Ali Tappeh close to the south-eastern shore of the Caspian at the foot of the Elburz mountains.[31] In doing so he paid special attention to the micro-stratigraphy of deposits, taking particular care to ensure that artefacts and fauna remains were collected systematically in correct stratigraphical context. For this reason he was able to test the extent to which cultural changes from one deposit to another equated with

28   Charles McBurney briefing journalists during excavations at La Cotte de St Brelade

variations in animal remains. At the same time this gave him a good control of radiocarbon determinations. In 1971 he extended his investigations further into Asia by testing the cave of Karar Kamar near Samongam in Afghanistan. Finally, although he was never able to undertake independent research on his own account in the Soviet Union, he was able as the holder of a Visiting Fellowship to the Academy of Sciences to gain a remarkably complete overview of the outstanding advances achieved by Soviet colleagues in investigating the Palaeolithic settlement of their country. What fascinated him above all was the geographical extension of Middle and Upper Palaeolithic settlement over vast expanses of Eurasia documented by excavation backed by radiocarbon dating. He succeeded in conveying this to his Cambridge students as well as to the world of scholarship at large in his richly documented and superbly illustrated Reckitt Lecture before the British Academy.[32]

In the meantime the department had embarked on the prehistory of Greece. This began with excavations at the Early Neolithic site of Nea Nikomedeia on the southern margin of the plain of Macedon. The site had first attracted attention when Bob Rodden, who had come to Cambridge as an affiliated student from Harvard to study for a Ph.D degree, and David Clarke had noticed pottery exposed in a road quarry cut into a settlement mound. The pottery attracted their special attention because it seemed to have affinities with early wares both in Thessaly and in Bulgaria and Yugoslavia to the north. Fuller investigation was called for and in 1961 excavations were mounted from Cambridge under the aegis of the British School in Athens and the Greek authorities. Systematic excavations were carried out under the direction of Bob Rodden on that part of the mound into which quarries had been cut in order to investigate the lowermost levels. Traces of substantial rectangular dwellings were recovered together with pottery, including distinctive painted wares and human figurines, stone and bone artefacts and animal skeletal remains. The only radiocarbon date available at the time of the interim publication[33] confirmed the Early Neolithic date of the first phase of settlement. The expedition included R. W. Hutchinson, the former curator of Knossos and subsequently lecturer in the Classics Faculty at Cambridge, the Disney Professor, and Eric Higgs, who characteristically preferred to camp in the adjacent mountains rather than stay with the rest of the party in Verroia. Among the students who later became professional archaeologists were John Nandris and Colin Renfrew, the future Disney Professor.

Responsibility for opening up the earlier prehistory of Greece fell to Eric Higgs, who had been introduced to the Palaeolithic by Charles McBurney in North Africa. A few artefacts of Palaeolithic character had been found in Greece, notably during wartime occupation by the Germans, but to all intents and purposes the early Stone Age was still virtually an unknown quantity. In 1962 Higgs set about remedying this by making a reconnaissance in western Macedonia. This produced among other things a well made hand-axe from Palaiokastro, but it was not until he crossed the Pindhos mountains in 1963 into Epirus that an abundant Palaeolithic industry was found in a well defined geological deposit. The recovery of an abundant lithic industry of Middle Palaeolithic character at Kokkinopilos,[34] close by the Louros Gorge, surmounted by traces of an Upper Palaeolithic industry laid the basis for a programme of research which is still after some interval proceeding. Richard Hey brought his geological knowledge to bear on the Kokkinopilos red clay. The expedition also included two Cambridge under-graduates, Charles Higham and Rhys Jones, who went on to make names for themselves in New Zealand and Australia. The discovery and partial excavation of the cave of Asprochaliko in the Louros Gorge in 1964 confirmed and amplified the sequence noted in the red clay.[35] Excavation showed that a basal Middle Palaeolithic was overlaid by successive industries

29   Nea Nikomedeia from the air

of micro-Mousterian and Upper Palaeolithic character. Finally in 1966 the
Kastritsa cave was discovered at the south-eastern end of the lake of
Ioannina.[36] Radiocarbon dates showed that this was occupied from twenty to
ten thousand years ago and was broadly contemporary with the last of the
three occupations of Asprochaliko.

Since during his final decade Higgs became preoccupied with the Early
History of Agriculture Project described in the next chapter, study of the
Palaeolithic of Epirus went temporarily into abeyance. It was not until after
Higgs' death that research was resumed on this problem under the lead of
Geoff Bailey, one of Charles McBurney's ablest pupils. Other members of
Bailey's team included P. L. Carter, Assistant Curator of the Museum of
Archaeology at Cambridge, and Mrs H. P. Higgs, both of whom had taken
part in the earlier work in Epirus. C. S. Gamble, a more recent graduate of
the Cambridge Department and now a lecturer at Southampton, also took
part in the operations led by Bailey. These involved analysing the substantial
body of material excavated by Higgs, including animal remains as well as
artefacts, re-examining the stratigraphy of the caves and obtaining additional
samples for radiocarbon dating. This served to clear the ground for further

30   Eric Higgs during excavations at Kastritsa, Epirus

excavations, at present going forward in the cave of Klithi on the right bank of the Voidomatis River, not far from the Albanian frontier.

It is appropriate that Geoff Bailey and another of Charles McBurney's pupils, Paul Callow, should have co-edited the volume of studies recently dedicated to his memory.[37] Nearly all the contributors were former pupils, whether as undergraduates or postgraduates or both. Together they embody one of the strongest traditions in Cambridge prehistoric studies stemming by way of Miles Burkitt and Dorothy Garrod to the Abbé Breuil, an honorary doctor of the university. Geoff Bailey, like Paul Mellars, is a present member of the Cambridge teaching staff. Other contributors included university teachers based on two African, three Australian, one Canadian and four United States universities. As might be expected – Charles McBurney was himself an American citizen until at the height of the war he took British nationality – there were close links with the United States, and this led to some interchange. For example, Nicholas David, who graduated at Cambridge in 1960, undertook his doctoral research under Hallam Movius, an old friend of Cambridge, spending four seasons at the Abri Pataud excavations in the Dordogne and taking his Ph.D at Harvard for a dissertation[38] on a phase of the Perigordian in Western Europe. Nicholas David now teaches at Calgary. One of those contributing to the memorial volume was Alan Bilsborough, who when he wrote his essay was lecturing in physical anthropology in the Duckworth Laboratory at Cambridge, but has since been appointed to the chair of Physical Anthropology at Durham. Bilsborough's contribution reflects McBurney's strong concern with human palaeontology,[39] an interest which goes back to the very origins of anthropology at Cambridge. Characteristically Bilsborough's successor in the Duckworth Laboratory, Robert Foley,[40] who graduated in 1974 at Cambridge was another former pupil of Charles McBurney.

CHAPTER 5

PREHISTORY AT CAMBRIDGE, 1946–74: QUATERNARY RESEARCH AND ECONOMIC PREHISTORY

If at Cambridge prehistory sprang from anthropology and classics, it drew also consistently on the natural sciences for many of its methods and procedures. This was particularly true of dating. From the outset it took stratigraphy, the prime means of establishing sequence, directly from geology. This does not mean that it was a parasite of the earth sciences. For the Quaternary period artefacts provided zone fossils of crucial importance for geology. This was recognized in so many words as early as 1920 when J. E. Marr, the Woodward Professor of the day, maintained in his presidential address to the Prehistoric Society of East Anglia that 'flint implements were the true fossils of the gravels'.[1] Although Marr's research interests were in earlier periods, he still found time to watch the Traveller's Rest pit off the Huntingdon Road exit from Cambridge and establish the context of two sets of palaeolithic implements in the Pleistocene succession. Anyone who attended Miles Burkitt's course[2] will remember the store he set by this sequence. Marr's successor, O. T. Jones, actively supported the Fenland Research Committee and his successor, W. B. R. King (1943–55), was able to play a useful part in the development of prehistory at Cambridge. While still at University College, London, he had combined with Kenneth Oakley of the British Museum of Natural History to present a masterly review of the Pleistocene sequence in the middle and lower parts of the Thames Valley in an early issue of the new *Proceedings of the Prehistoric Society*.[3] Both authors stressed the crucial importance of flint artefacts as zone fossils. They further accepted the nomenclature established by the Abbé Breuil in his recent papers on the ground that the stratigraphy and implement types in southern England were closely similar to those in northern France. In the same paper they duly acknowledged the work by Reginald Smith of the British Museum concerned with the geological context of assemblages of flint artefacts from southern Britain. They also referred to the results obtained in East Anglia and the Thames Valley by such stalwart amateurs as J. P. T. Burchell, R. R. C. Chandler, Reid Moir and Hazzledine Warren, members of the former Prehistoric Society of East Anglia. It was because their findings were mutually beneficial that the alliance between prehistoric archaeology and Quaternary geology proved so enduring. Although Professor King did not in the event engage very actively in Quaternary Research at Cambridge he did not hesitate to promote a close association of his department with research and teaching in prehistory. The collaboration of one of his lecturers, Richard Hey, with Charles McBurney in working out the context of Palaeolithic assemblages in Cyrenaica in the sequence of climatic and sea-level changes has already been mentioned. Hey also played an important part in opening up the Palaeolithic settlement of Epirus under the lead of Eric Higgs.

Since fossils of biological species, plant as well as animal, survive only by being incorporated in geological deposits, and since they can live only by accommodating to geographical circumstances, it follows that they can be effectively studied only in conjunction with the earth sciences. This applies as much to archaeology as to botanical and zoological fossils. Human societies can exist only by occupying territory which in turn underwent changes recoverable by geologists. The Fenland Research Committee in its day had had to make its first objective the establishment of successive phases of human occupation in the stratigraphy of the region. Sir Albert Seward, who had served as its president, was himself a palaeobotanist whose prime interest lay in the Carboniferous period. As a schoolboy he had first been attracted to geology by attending a university extension lecture[4] given by J. E. Marr in person. Similarly the botanist (later Sir Harry) Godwin, who later directed the Sub-department of Quaternary Research and came to the chair of Botany at Cambridge, retained a keen awareness of the importance in the development of vegetation of topography, land-drainage and fluctuations of land and sea levels.

As Godwin recalled in his autobiography, the Sub-department of Quaternary Research at Cambridge stemmed ultimately from the Fenland Research Committee. A scheme for the development of Quaternary Research at Cambridge had indeed been submitted to the General Board as early as 1938. It was discussed in 1939 only to be postponed until after the war. The Sub-department was not finally approved by the university until 1948, to run from 1 October of that year.[5] The importance of geology appeared in the first report covering the work of the Sub-department for the period 1948–50. One of its first research students, Donald Walker, was cited as having carried out the pollen analysis of Inter-glacial samples, including one collected by Professor King from Histon Road, Cambridge. Further, Richard West, who in 1966 succeeded Godwin, proceeded to write an important text-book on the Pleistocene[6] and to make his personal reputation by differentiating the British Inter-glacial phases through their fossil pollen.[7] The fact remains that, like Godwin himself, whom he succeeded in the chair of that name, West adhered fundamentally to the discipline of botany. At the same time he went out of his way to pay some regard to archaeology. He cooperated with Gale Sieveking at High Lodge and with John Wymer at Hoxne, though in the latter case he was careful to avoid deciding whether the decline of forest trees was an invitation to Palaeolithic man or on the contrary was an outcome of his activities.

One result of putting Quaternary Research on a professional basis at Cambridge instead of relying on the voluntary cooperation of fully stretched teaching officers was to multiply the techniques and methods at its disposal and extend the sphere of their application from the Cambridge region to the world. The advantage which accrued to prehistorians based in Cambridge hardly needs to be stressed. Conversely, the Sub-department was able to take advantage of the many opportunities opened up by the excavations carried out by Cambridge archaeologists and their pupils.

The technique most widely used to investigate the palaeoecology of the Quaternary period in different parts of Britain was pollen analysis. Originally developed on a substantial scale in Sweden, the technique had first been effectively introduced from that country to Britain by Dr and Mrs Godwin and was first intensively applied to the postglacial deposits of the southern fenland. When as early as 1936–7 Godwin began to employ it in the Somerset Levels he followed the practice of the Fenland Research Committee in seeking archaeological markers. He began by operating in the proximity of the Meare lake village in consultation with the excavators Arthur Bulleid and H. St George Gray. He next made wider contacts in the region and investigated further prehistoric timber trackways in the area.[9] These provided opportunities for effecting correlations between archaeology and palaeobotany which Godwin was quick to appreciate. They were constructed at times when the onset of flooding threatened to cut established routes, and they were preserved for later investigators by the waterlogging and peat formation that ensued. It soon became apparent that this occurred twice on an extensive scale, once in the lower part of zone VIIb of Godwin's Post-glacial forest sequence as defined by pollen analysis and once just before the beginning of zone VII. The fact that the tracks were made and used by prehistoric man meant that by following them when they were exposed in modern peat-working an observer like H. L. Dewar[10] could recover sufficient archaeological evidence in the form of artefacts to assign them to their proper cultural context. In such terms the earlier two groups could be assigned respectively to the Neolithic and the later Bronze Age. Two of Dewar's most sensational finds, the halves of two bow-staves of Neolithic age from Ashcott and Meare, were brought to Cambridge for conservation by the technical staff. There they were made the basis of a comprehensive study of prehistoric archery in north-western Europe as a whole.[11] In conjunction with Godwin's basic work on the stratigraphy and palaeoecology of the region this led in effect to the prehistory of the Somerset Levels passing for a time into the hands of Cambridge. Responsibility for this area of research fell upon John Coles, a graduate of Toronto who first came to Cambridge to secure a Diploma in Prehistoric Archaeology and returned in 1960 to take up an Assistant

31 The Sweet Track, one of the prehistoric wooden trackways across the Somerset Levels excavated by John and Bryony Coles

Lectureship, in the meantime having secured a Ph.D at Edinburgh for research into the Bronze Age of northern Britain. Coles, who in due course was promoted to a University Lectureship, a Readership and a personal Professorship at Cambridge, began to undertake field-work in the Somerset Levels in 1966.[12] His opportunities were notably enhanced by sharing the work with F. A. Hibbert of the Sub-department of Quarternary Research at Cambridge. It soon became apparent that conditions would still further be improved by forging a working link with Exeter University. In 1971 the project received the adherence of Bryony Orme, who held a lectureship in archaeology in the Department of History at the University. It soon became apparent that due to increasing mechanization of the process of peat-extraction and the speeding up of discoveries, the task could be adequately met only by employing full-time workers to maintain a close watch on the workings and ensure that archaeological findings could be recorded and where possible salvaged before they were destroyed. This was something the universities could hardly be expected to match. In the meantime, thanks to the prompt and effective publication of discoveries in a number of archaeological and biological journals, the importance of the evidence likely to be destroyed unless adequate steps were taken to ensure its recording were becoming manifest and widely known. The situation was saved by the Department of the Environment stepping in and treating the Somerset Levels as an area qualifying for treatment under rescue archaeology. In 1973 the Somerset Levels Project was formally constituted and the necessary officers appointed. The effectiveness of the new arrangements has been consistently demonstrated by Coles and Orme in their extremely productive series of *Somerset Levels Papers* which have appeared annually since 1975. Between them these have brought new awareness of the potentialities of wetland sites, a topic to which Coles has recently given pointed expression.[13] Coles also found time to make an important advance in our knowledge of Mesolithic Scotland through his excavations at Morton, Fife.

A further outcome of the pioneer work of the Fenland Research Committee deserves a mention even if its implementation falls beyond the time span of the present book, namely the formation in 1982 of the Fenland Project. Like the Somerset Levels Project this was also supported by the Historic Buildings and Monuments Commission, which, at this time of high personal taxation and the high cost of labour, alone makes it possible to conduct long-term field research in archaeology in Britain. The new Project is concerned less with stratigraphy and much more with the spacing and nature of human settlement. It aims further to cover the fenland basin as a whole instead of merely a part of it. Its objective was clearly defined at a successful one day conference held at the Society of Antiquaries of London on 11 October 1985, at which the results were summarized of work already carried out in south Lincolnshire and the Peterborough area. One of the points to emerge was the opportunity this gave to the British Museum and the University Museum at Cambridge.

For a generation pollen analysis had already been systematically applied to zone deposits in Britain and to correlate the archaeological, botanical and geological evidence they contained. It had for instance been of key importance in providing a framework for the Mesolithic settlement of north-western Europe as well as zoning the deposits formed there during the Late-glacial and Post-glacial periods and, latterly, for distinguishing deposits formed during different interglacials. From a purely chronological standpoint on the other hand it had lost some of its importance. By comparison with radiocarbon dating it is time-consuming, local and imprecise. From a botanical standpoint radiocarbon provided a better chronological check than archaeology itself. No wonder that palaeobotanists were quite as eager as archaeologists to avail themselves of the new method.

Radiocarbon dating stemmed from a suggestion first expressed in 1946 by W. F. Libby of the Chicago Institute of Nuclear Physics.[14] Libby and his colleagues held that radiocarbon, a substance generated at high altitudes through the reaction of cosmic ray neutrons with atmospheric nitrogen, ought to be detectable in living matter, since atoms entered into the carbon dioxide of the atmosphere on which living organisms depended for building their tissues. In 1947 Libby and his team found that methane from petroleum had virtually disappeared, whereas contemporary Baltimore sewage yielded radiocarbon in the predicted amount. The inference was that whereas in life there was an exact balance between the intake and disintegration of radiocarbon, on death disintegration proceeded unchecked.[15] It only remained to measure how fast this occurred, and in the case of a particular sample to measure the amount still remaining. After many checks Chicago came up with a half-life for radiocarbon, that is the time it took for it to lose half its radioactivity, of 5,568 ± 30 years.[16] As a first check the amount of radiocarbon remaining in samples of known age, notably from ancient Egyptian burials and from trees datable by counting their annual growth-rings, was measured. It was the general agreement between the known age of such samples and the age calculated from their residual radiocarbon that convinced the Chicago physicists. In 1949 they published the three-page article that was to shake the world.[17]

Cambridge was fortunate to have a Sub-department[18] ready to make an early response. Already in October 1949 its Director Harry Godwin forwarded a dozen samples to Chicago. Apart from a couple of old samples from the British Museum and a specimen from one of the ritual holes at Stonehenge, these comprised samples collected by the Sub-department itself, including one from Star Carr. Radiocarbon was discussed by the Cambridge Philosophical Society in 1950 and Professor O. R. Frisch supervised the building of a modified plant in the Cavendish Laboratory. Setting up an effective working station for radiocarbon assay proved to be a more difficult matter. Help was offered by A. G. Maddock, then Assistant Director of Research in Radio-Chemistry, and it was on his advice that E. W. Willis, a graduate of King's College, London, was chosen to design and erect the necessary apparatus for the Sub-department with the aid of a five-year grant from the Nuffield Foundation. In those early days the various European centres anxious to emulate those already set up in North America lent each other generous aid. One way of ensuring mutual support was to hold a series of symposia.[19] The first was organized by Hilde Levi and held in November 1954 in Copenhagen, whose laboratory was among the first to operate in Europe and indeed in the Old World. Not surprisingly the Copenhagen Laboratory was chaired by Therkel Mathiassen, the prehistorian, and fed with samples already zoned by pollen-analysis. The Copenhagen symposium was exclusively European and included members from seven different countries. At the same time the need was expressed to establish contact with

32   Dr Eric Willis placing a counter inside a lead casket in the apparatus developed for radiocarbon assays by the Botany School, University of Cambridge, in the mid-1950s

laboratories in North America. The symposium held at Cambridge under Godwin's lead in the following year welcomed nineteen laboratories, fully functional or, like the one at Cambridge itself, still in the preparatory stages. It was notable above all for receiving a number of delegates from North America funded by the Wenner-Gren Foundation of New York. So far as Cambridge is concerned the occasion was notable in persuading Willis to change from counting in acetylene to carbon dioxide. The symposium strongly emphasised the need to publish the results of radiocarbon assay and make the results available internationally. It is significant that in 1955 *Radiocarbon* began publication to do just that. The symposium held at Andover, Massachusetts, in 1957 under the lead of Fred Johnson was characteristically practical and aimed to meet the needs of potential users. Among representatives to attend were archaeologists, botanists, geochemists, geologists, physicists, oceanographers and soil scientists. The symposium held in September 1959 at Groningen under the joint lead of Hl. de Vries of the Natural Sciences Laboratory and H. T. Waterbolk of the Archaeological–Biological Institute showed that radiocarbon assay was by then accepted as an essential tool of research. Delegates attended from Africa, Asia, Australasia, South America and the Soviet Union, as well as from Europe and North America. By the time the symposium met for the second time at Cambridge in 1962 a number of laboratories had published results in *Radiocarbon*. After some discussion and disagreement it was agreed to adhere for the time being to Libby's original half-life of 5,568 ± 30, rather than adopt the new figure of 5,730 ± 40: in the meantime anyone wishing to adopt the new finding (which might itself be superseded) had only to multiply existing dates by 1.03.

Although our Sub-department at Cambridge understandably directed its radiocarbon capability primarily to dating the boundaries of zones established by pollen analysis, it still contributed in a variety of ways to the general advance of prehistory. It gave immense help to the excavations at Star Carr. The director had himself been drawn to archaeology by the Mesolithic barbed point from between the Leman and Ower Banks away back in 1931. He took part eagerly in the excavation of a site which yielded a number of such objects from waterlogged deposits which promised well for pollen analysis and he ensured that a crucial sample was among those sent in the first batch to Chicago. One of his research team in the Sub-department, Donald Walker, took an active part in collecting samples and undertaking the necessary pollen analysis, and together with Harry Godwin contributed a vital chapter to the definitive report. It was thanks to the work of the Sub-department that the human occupation of the site was fixed securely in the early history of the Vale of Pickering and the Post-glacial sequence generally. An added bonus came from Dr E. J. H. Corner of the Botany Department, who identified as *Fomes fomentarius* the large bracket fungus which abounded in the cultural layer.[20] Godwin further collaborated with the present writer in June 1960 when excavations were renewed at Peacock's Farm, Shippea Hill, with the object of obtaining radiocarbon dates for the Mesolithic and Neolithic levels established twenty-five years previously.[21] Acceptable and mutually compatible dates were obtained for each and the latter was shown to be around a millennium earlier than archaeological opinion had until recently been prepared to accept. From the point of view of Quaternary Research the investigation was of interest for bringing out a discrepancy between the radiocarbon assays obtained for charcoals from the Neolithic level and peat samples from the same position which gave dates more than three hundred years earlier. The Cambridge laboratory also contributed to the prehistory of the Somerset Levels. It dated the bow staves from Ashcott and Meare and in this way precipitated the study of prehistoric archery in Europe.[22] Since then radiocarbon dating has also been systematically applied to the timber causeways which over the years have proved to be the most persistent artefacts revealed in the peat working. Again, Dr D. M. Churchill took critical care in obtaining samples for the radiocarbon dating of boats found by E. V. Wright at North Ferriby.[23] The demonstration by the Cambridge laboratory that these dated from between 1500 and 1200 B.C. opened up the whole question of the diffusion of the sewn boat.

Overseas the Sub-department encouraged the excavators of the Early Neolithic site of Nea Nikomedeia in Greek Macedonia by determining a date of 6,230 ± 150 B.C.[24] Again, when Eric Higgs began to excavate Palaeolithic sites in Epirus, Dr N. J. Shackleton collected stalagmitic material. Certainly Cambridge excavators were made to feel that wherever they dug they were likely to receive backing from the Sub-department. This did not mean they had to depend on Cambridge. Higgs obtained his dates from Isotopes Inc. of New Jersey[25] and Charles McBurney turned to the National Physical Laboratory, Washington, and Groningen for the Oranian, Dabban and Mousterian levels in the Haua Fteah respectively.[26]

The influence of radiocarbon dating extended well beyond excavations and the dating of individual finds. It encouraged thinking on wider themes. The degree of statistical uncertainty endemic to the method suggested that patterns were more significant than individual dates. Problems like the intrusion and spread of man in the New World or the expansion of farming across Europe involved the correlation of large numbers of radiocarbon dates and could be resolved only when a sufficient number of dates had been determined and made public. The early date for the Neolithic occupation at Peacock's Farm was mainly important for drawing attention to the high dates obtained elsewhere in Britain and Ireland for this phase of prehistory. In the same way the antiquity of Neolithic culture in Britain assumed importance when viewed in the context of dates obtained from sites elsewhere in Europe, in Egypt and in south-west Asia, not least at Jarmo.[27] The same applied to a consideration of world prehistory during the fifty thousand years over which radiocarbon was capable of yielding usable dates. When my *World Prehistory* first appeared in 1961, I extended the cautious welcome to radiocarbon dating to be expected of anyone who attended the early symposia at which its practitioners expressed their difficulties as well as their hopes. By 1969 when the second edition had appeared the number of determinations had increased sufficiently to furnish tables that gave a good idea of the patterns that were beginning to take shape. This applied even more to the current edition, dating from 1977, which for instance quotes the dates for twenty-one Mousterian sites from Europe, North Africa and south-west Asia as well as for stages in the development of Upper Palaeolithic cultures in seven different regions. The conservative stance adopted in successive editions is well seen in respect of Australia. The progress of radiocarbon dating and above all the increasing facilities in Australia itself have resulted in a progressive lengthening of Australian chronology. Whereas in 1961 it was concluded that there was 'no convincing evidence for the immigration of man into Australia before Neothermal times',[28] by 1969 it was accepted that man had arrived by 'a comparatively advanced stage of the Late Pleistocene'.[29] By 1977 it was conceded that 'man must have arrived' in his sapient form 'more than thirty thousand years ago'.[30]

Although after some hesitation in certain quarters radiocarbon dating has been widely accepted by prehistorians, it should be remembered that physicists first took archaeological samples for their own convenience. They were not immediately concerned with dating phases in the history of culture or for that matter in the history of forests. They were interested to see how far their own age-determinations agreed with those attained by other means. Yet by turning to archaeological and botanical samples they helped to link together different strands of Quaternary Research. The chairman of the first laboratory to take a lead in introducing the method to Europe was after all Therkel Mathiassen, who more than anyone had aimed to link Danish prehistory with the pollen zones established by Knud Jessen and inherited by Johs. Iversen and J. Troels-Smith. By the same token the leader in Britain was beyond doubt Harry Godwin, Director of the Sub-department of Quaternary Research at Cambridge and veteran of the Fenland Research Committee.

One result of the widespread adoption of radiocarbon dating was to reduce the role of pollen analysis for chronological purposes and to enhance its use in ecology. The first person to appreciate the full importance of the anthropogenic factor in forest composition was Johs. Iversen.[31] Unlike Godwin, who was still preoccupied with building up the zonation of British vegetation since the Late Glacial period, Iversen was fortunate to inherit the zonation of Danish deposits from Knud Jessen. He was the first pollen analyst to concentrate on the degree to which the composition of vegetation had been influenced by and was therefore a clue to human activities in past times. Although Godwin soon followed Iversen's lead,[32] he concentrated the work of his Sub-department to begin with on achieving his prime end, the zoning, in other words the history, of British vegetation since the last Ice Age. It was only in course of time that he was able to turn his attention to tracing the progress of deforestation and the creation of agricultural and pastoral landscapes.

The attention paid by Iversen to the anthropogenic factor in vegetational change certainly provided archaeologists with vital additional information about prehistoric economies. It coincided with a marked shift in archaeological thought which had begun before the war. So long as archaeology remained largely in the hands of museum officials it is natural that classification should have remained its main preoccupation. It was only as it began to be studied at the academic level that more account began to be taken of archaeology as a source of information about the behaviour of those who left behind tangible traces. This applied particularly at Cambridge where the subject was taught alongside anthropology at a time when that subject was itself entering on a phase of functional interpretation. University students were not content to be drilled in what was tantamount to a museological treatment of prehistoric archaeology. They needed to be taught typology and to learn how to classify flints, sherds and the other paraphernalia of archaeology, just as they needed to locate sites, excavate them and date them. On the other hand, well before the war they had been taught to interpret their finds and to see how prehistory contributed knowledge to the history and understanding of mankind. This aim was notably advanced by Gordon Childe through such books as *What Happened in History*.[33] The appeal of this book was if anything enhanced by its limitations. Childe concerned himself primarily with the genesis and special character of European civilization. At the same time he interpreted archaeology in accordance with the materialist interpretation of history. His successive Neolithic and Urban Revolutions, while they gave a swing to his narrative, also made a strong appeal to Marxist ideology.

The Cambridge approach was fundamentally anthropological. It advocated the interpretation of archaeological finds in social terms and in the first instance in terms of economic life.[34] Further it aimed to cover the world as a whole rather than merely Europe and the parts of north Africa and south-west Asia which contributed to the genesis of European civilization. As already stated, the view that the object of archaeology was not merely to assemble, classify and arrange in sequence the material traces recoverable by excavation, but rather to use such data as a way of gaining an insight into how ancient societies were structured and how they functioned and underwent change in time, was being cultivated and taught at Cambridge already before the war.

When activities were resumed after the war emphasis was laid on the

evidence for reconstructing prehistoric subsistence. This was first examined
for the later prehistory of north-western Europe, where organic materials
were best preserved and most carefully studied. Among the first objectives
were seal hunting, whaling, fishing and fowling,[35] but also the culling of
herbivorous animals, both wild and domesticated.[36] Attention was also
focussed on plant foods and on the equipment and methods used to secure
them. In studying animal skeletal material it was necessary to know not
merely what species were represented, but also the ages at which they were
taken, their habits and their seasonality. It was also essential to study the
biological evidence on the one hand with the prevailing climate and
geography, but on the other with indications of the methods used in their
appropriation by man. Direct evidence of the methods used in hunting could
be sought in wounds and associated gear. In the case of crops a wealth of
information could be sought in traces of cultivation, implements of tillage
and harvesting, facilities for storage and arrangements for the preparation of
food. Much help could be gained by interpreting residual data for hunting,
fishing, farming and settlement by observing the methods and practices of
recent inhabitants in terms of region.[37] Yet it was realized that ethnographic
parallels even when drawn from the same territory have their dangers. It is a
sound maxim, sometimes overlooked, that it is invariably wrong to argue
against the flow of time. Ethnology, even local ethnology, can do no more
than offer hypotheses about what happened in the past. The essential clues
can stem only from prehistory.

Prehistoric Europe: the economic basis[38] was essentially an act of propa-
ganda. It was written to show how much more information about prehistoric
economy could be gleaned from the archaeological evidence even of the
quality then available, and by inference how much more could be learned by
making purposeful investigations in the future. Beyond the immediate topic
of subsistence the book aimed to draw attention to the structures used to
shelter people, livestock and crops, the technology devised to shape and
utilize the environment, the gear designed to facilitate movement and the
evidence for moving materials and products from one territory to another. It
goes without saying that it canvassed the need to concentrate on sites where
organic materials, notably food refuse and artefacts made from wood, bark,
resin, fibre, basketry, leather and textiles were most likely to survive. This has
borne abundant fruit notably in the work of John Coles and Bryony Orme
(Mrs Coles) in the Somerset Levels.[39] The importance of correcting the bias
caused by the more widespread survival of artefacts made of mineral
substances has only recently been emphasized by Coles in his wide-ranging
book *The Archaeology of the Wetlands* and advertised world-wide in *Warp*,
the newsletter of the Wetland Archaeology Project at Exeter University.

Two of the main influences that led to an emphasis on economic prehistory
at this time, the anthropogenic factor in the shaping of the environment

detected by pollen analysis and the functional approach developed by social anthropologists, converged in the Albert Reckitt Archaeological Lecture for 1953.[40] In retrospect the subject of this lecture might better have been described as Ecological rather than Economic. Certainly it aimed to alert prehistorians to the need to pay more attention to the means by which early peoples ensured their food-supply. On the other hand it also stressed the importance of studying early cultures in the context of the environments to which they were adjusted but which at the same time they manipulated and modified. It made the most of the anthropological insight that all aspects of social life were to an important degree functionally and structurally interrelated. Human societies needed to be studied as functioning ecosystems in which every aspect of human life interacted both with each other and with the habitats and biomes of specific territories.

The other main thrust of Cambridge teaching at the time was to expand the range of prehistory to embrace the world as a whole. When originally introduced to Cambridge by Miles Burkitt prehistory was essentially French. Teaching was founded on the succession established by excavation in the caves of France and contiguous parts of the Continent. The first to recognize the parochial nature of this version of prehistory was Dorothy Garrod. We have already seen that she appreciated in the 1920s that it was necessary to extend excavation to territories far beyond those in which the subject had been founded. It was her own achievement in extending its range to Palestine and Iraq that brought her to the Disney chair at Cambridge in 1937. Already Gertrude Caton Thompson had opened up the old stone age in Egypt and Louis Leakey had devoted his research fellowship at St John's to his discoveries in East Africa. India was also being opened up as a field for palaeolithic research from Cambridge. As a fellow of Trinity T. T. Paterson had worked in Northern India and Madras in 1935 alongside Teilhard de Chardin and the American geologist de Terra, under the auspices of the Carnegie Institute at Washington.[41] When Professor Garrod resumed teaching at Cambridge after the war she entitled her course 'World Prehistory'. Although Dorothy Garrod extended prehistory from its classic base in France to Africa and Asia, she was still inclined to equate the subject with its earlier periods. It was Gordon Childe who mainly through his writings extended its temporal range up to the dawn of history and that not merely in Europe itself.

From an anthropological point of view this was still inadequate. No one brought up in a museum filled with artefacts made all over the world, including the Americas, Australasia and Oceania, as well as Europe, Africa and Asia, could remain satisfied even by conflating the visions of Garrod and Childe. What was needed was nothing less than a world prehistory embracing every territory and extending from the appearance of tool-making to the structures of literate civilizations. This first became possible with the development of geophysical dating methods and the expansion of competent excavation. Much was accomplished at or from Cambridge itself, but as shown in the following chapter it was Cambridge-trained prehistorians working overseas and notably in the English-speaking territories of the former empire, whether in antiquities services, museums or universities, who contributed most extensively. The increasing speed with which discoveries were made meant that *World Prehistory* had to be kept up to date at frequent intervals.[42] Since it first appeared in 1961 the author has had the opportunity to travel widely in North and Central America, the Near, Middle and Far East, Australasia and the Pacific. Even so the delay in publication by excavators, due in large measure to the increasing research involved in processing their finds, made it difficult to keep a work of synthesis anywhere near up to date. The dominant part played by Cambridge prehistorians in expanding the territory of prehistory can be judged from the composition of the editorial support for the new periodical *World Archaeology* started in 1969 from Southampton under the executive editorship of Colin Platt. They supplied six out of seven of the Editorial Board as well as a number of the internationally composed Advisory Board.

To cope with such a wide and rapidly growing field the teaching resources available in the university, even allowing for help from colleges, was barely adequate. This was even more so when it is remembered that prehistoric archaeology was still in a comparatively early stage of development. It was something of a vicious circle. Even in relatively spacious times the university had to pay some regard to the teacher–student ratio in different fields and the fact is that until more openings appeared the numbers reading archaeology, though showing a progressive increase, were nevertheless restrained. The appointment of John Coles to an Assistant Lectureship in 1960 marked a great advance but was about as much as could be expected at the time. Apart from providing teaching officers with leave of absence on full salary, the university as such made no provision for research, although this was an activity more than usually important in a field as undeveloped as prehistoric archaeology or for that matter anthropology in general. In a collegiate university the situation was eased by the generosity of colleges in providing or supplementing grants and awarding research studentships and fellowships. Moreover the faculty itself had certain funds of its own, notably the Crowther Beynon Fund and for south-east Asia the Evans Fund. Again, the Classics faculty might if it wished assist research into the prehistoric antecedents of the Greeks, Romans and associated peoples. Otherwise it was up to faculty members to secure what support they could from elsewhere. Perhaps this was no bad thing. It meant that a case had to be made for projects and presented in a way to pass the scrutiny of grant-giving bodies invariably short of the funds needed to meet all the calls made upon them. To an archaeologist wanting to undertake research overseas by far the most regular and substantial source of funds is the British Academy, in certain countries in association with the relevant British Institute or School. The Royal Geographical Society and increasingly the Society of Antiquaries of London are also sources of note. Then, in these days of world-wide activity, sources in the United States of America are often willing to provide important funds. Especially since the meeting of 1952 in New York, the Wenner-Gren (formerly the Viking) Foundation has been particularly generous to Cambridge archaeologists. In one way or another no teaching officer at Cambridge with clearly defined aims for archaeology has been frustrated by lack of funds. Since the funding of research students on a substantial scale by the state has become available to the academically able, the problem of turning out a sufficient number of men and women qualified for the public service, including an increasing number of universities, has been met and at the same time the basis of research has been substantially widened.

One of the bug-bears of archaeology is that some excavators find it more attractive to dig than to make their results available to others. This has been exacerbated by the onerous research now required in the aftermath of excavation and by the specialized expertise needed to extract the fullest information. Grant-giving bodies have recently set their face against excavators who have conspicuously failed to report by witholding grants. They have done so on the ground that archaeological sites are by nature unique. Excavation inevitably destroys evidence and can be justified only by full publication of the evidence. This was a lesson hammered home at Cambridge. That it was well taken is shown in the record of Cambridge prehistorians. If radical advances in theory were to be made, this depended on formulating problems and obtaining support over a period of time sufficiently long to resolve them or at least bring them into sharper focus. This is what we tried to do at Cambridge in respect of economic prehistory. When Lord Robbins in his presidential address to the British Academy in 1965 invited sections to submit proposals for major research projects, Section X, after some hesitation, took him at his word and suggested the Early History of Agriculture as an appropriate subject. A standing Committee[43] was formed and duly met in the Upper Parlour of Peterhouse on 23 April 1966, where twenty years earlier the Fenland Research Committee had been constituted. It began by electing as its first chairman Professor Sir Joseph Hutchinson, Drapers' Professor of Agriculture in the University, and followed by appointing a Cambridge committee to put the project into execution. Fortunately we had the right man at hand. Eric Higgs had been appointed Assistant in Research in 1956. As an experienced hill-farmer, he had shown a special interest in man–animal relations among prehistoric communities. To further this he had dealt with the faunal remains recovered from Charles McBurney's excavations in Cyrenaica and Iran as well as from the Cambridge campaigns at Hurst Fen and Nea Nikomedeia. In the meantime he had obtained sufficient experience of excavation himself to embark on opening up the Palaeolithic occupation of Epirus. As Director of the Early History of Agriculture Project, a position which he held from 1966 until his death in 1976, Higgs began with two assistants, M. R. Jarman, who held a fellowship funded by the Wenner-Gren Foundation and acted as Assistant Director, and Sebastian Payne, who held a fellowship funded by the Project. In addition Higgs had a number of associates based elsewhere but who nevertheless assisted the Project, including the geographer Claudio Vita-Finzi of University College, London, David Webley of the Agricultural Development and Advisory Services, Cardiff, and Jane Renfrew, then of Sheffield University. The Cambridge Project was also able to call upon a number of national bodies based in the locality, notably the Plant Breeding Institute and the National Institute of Agricultural Botany as well as the Sub-department of Quaternary Research. Above all it gained from attracting the interest of some of the keenest research students notably Graeme Barker, Robin Dennell, Tony Legge, David Sturdy and Paul Wilkinson.

In return for being given a home in the University Museum and the services of our only research officer, the Project gave a major boost to the research activities of the department. This was not merely reflected in the work of teaching officers, but was given independent expression in a number

33   Eric Higgs at the Bronze Age site at Littleport, Cambs., 1960

of exciting papers in the periodical literature, followed by three major volumes published by the Cambridge University Press.[44] Quite as important in the long run was the impact it made on research students, not least by stimulating opposition to some of its leading concepts. Further it has affected archaeological practice at two distinct levels. It has led to undergraduates being instructed in at least the elements of animal bone identification, and it has shown excavators that there is much more to be learned about the behaviour of early man from animal remains than they had been accustomed to think even since Pitt Rivers.

Higgs was accorded, and flourished upon, a marked degree of independence. He maintained a regular routine dictated in part by the university year but in large measure also by the climate. Field-work was mainly carried out during the summer and laboratory work and writing during the winter. This allowed time for teaching undergraduates and supervising research students, and gave him the maximum opportunity for impressing his ideas. These were at bottom simple. Man like other organisms required food. This he could obtain only from territory, whether fixed or shifting, which was readily accessible to him. In practice this would have meant in prehistoric times that the site catchment area must have been within a one or at most a two hour radius. This he had to exploit sufficiently effectively in competition with other groups, whether animal, vegetable or human, to leave archaeological traces behind him. This he did regardless of how future archaeologists would classify his remains. Thus it was of crucial importance to interpret archaeological sites in the context of their site catchment areas rather than in terms of environmental generalities. A prehistorian's first task was therefore to define site catchment areas and subject animal and plant remains recovered in the course of excavation to rigorous analysis. Only in this way could he expect to recover information about early modes of subsistence or settlement. To test the value of catchment area analysis Higgs and his group explored extensive parts of Europe from Portugal and Spain in the west to Bulgaria and the Soviet Union in the east and from Greece and Italy in the south to Sweden in the north. In Asia they tested localities in Anatolia and Palestine and in North America they extended to western Greenland and Alaska. Since, like the Disney professor, he rejected the rigidities of Childe's 'Neolithic Revolution', Higgs had no compunction in going well back into Late Pleistocene and forward into the ethnographic present. In more abstract terms the Project stressed the need to involve the humanities on a broad front with a wide range of natural sciences. The early history of agriculture was therefore a useful subject for the third symposium run jointly by the Royal Society and the British Academy.[45]

As Director of the Cambridge Project on the Early History of Agriculture, Eric Higgs gave a much needed prod to archaeological thought. By questioning the distinction between wild and domestic animals and plants he helped to undermine one of the pillars of orthodox prehistory, the 'Neolithic Revolution' propagated by Gordon Childe. He insisted on beginning his programme in the Late-glacial period, that is well before farming had been deemed to exist. This stimulated thought about the way Stone Age people adjusted to the transition to Neothermal conditions. Bioarchaeological thinking led among other things to a revision of the Star Carr find,[46] the interpretation of stratigraphy on a seal-hunting site on a Baltic island and the economic status of megalith builders in West Sweden. More fundamentally it led to a reappraisal of the transition between the two major phases of the Stone Age recognized by Old World prehistorians.[47] The transitional or Mesolithic cultures were treated as evidence of a basic readjustment to major ecological change. The 'Neolithic Revolution' came to be seen as a fossil of Marxist thought. The adoption of farming was shown to have been part of an overall adaptation to the world which emerged from the ice age, rather than as a mark of revolutionary change.

Higgs owed his influence partly to the simplicity of his ideas, but partly also to the sincerity with which he held them and the energy with which he took practical steps to realize them. By no means everyone in the department was prepared to accept bioarchaeology as sufficient in itself. A reductionist approach to archaeology is inadequate, even repellent, once it is remembered that archaeology is about people. Emphatically men do not live by bread alone. If they acquire their humanity by belonging to societies constituted by culture, it follows that archaeology must involve far more than researches into the means by which they manage to survive. It is true enough that, as Tallgren perceived, archaeologists of the old school had made their subject grotesque by limiting their studies to typology and classification. This is not to say that such studies are redundant. One could say that the greater the emphasis laid on the history of human, that is to say cultural, groups, the more important it is to classify artefacts as a way of defining these. Again, it is one of the distinctive features of human as distinct from non-human societies that they attach importance to shaping objects as a way of proclaiming identity rather than merely as a means of manipulating the environment.

Not surprisingly much of the Cambridge effort was devoted to defining the cultural patterns which emerged at different times and places. The definition of cultural groups offered a particularly suitable field for doctoral candidates. Two whose work was especially well known to me were Peterhouse men, Ian Longworth and David Clarke, who obtained their Ph.Ds for dissertations on British Collared Urns and Beakers respectively in 1960 and 1963. Longworth took a post in the British Museum but Clarke remained part of the Cambridge scene by obtaining a Research Fellowship at Peterhouse and in due course an Official Fellowship and Tutorship. This gave him the opportunity to develop ideas complementary to and in some cases diametrically opposed to those propagated by Higgs. David Clarke held strongly to the view that archaeology was in urgent need of being tightened up as a discipline capable of standing on its own feet. Unless archaeology was independent it could not be of great use in the task of elucidating prehistory. His masterpiece, *Analytical Archaeology*, though beyond the comprehension of many, was nevertheless internationally acclaimed as an outstanding intellectual achievement.[48] His tragically early death in 1976 deprived archaeology of a man who, however much his writing repelled those averse to mathematics and abstract thought, was himself fully convinced of the humane nature of archaeology. It is significant that when the Gulbenkian Foundation decided to sponsor the publication of an archaeological series to record and classify British archaeological data – a series unhappily now wound up – the first volume to appear was written by David Clarke[49] and the last by Ian Longworth[50] with one of the two intervening volumes by Joan Taylor, another Cambridge Ph.D.[51]

Ironically, as we have already noted, prehistory, in the pursuit of which some aspects at least of the history of preliterate communities can be recovered, only exists to the extent that it is written down and published. Cambridge was well placed in this regard. The formation of the Prehistoric Society has already been noted. Throughout the period covered by the present book, its *Proceedings* were edited from Cambridge. Their declared

34   David Clarke preparing for excavations at Great Wilbraham, 1975

object was to advance prehistory not merely in Britain but in Europe and the world at large. To that extent their aims coincided with those of Cambridge. Yet its contribution to the *Proceedings* remained a modest one until Cambridge graduates had established themselves in their various fields. It was only from 1961 that Cambridge prehistorians began to account for anything from two-fifths to half or more or the pages of original matter. Still, from the beginning the *Proceedings* were a valuable avenue for the prompt publication of faculty excavations as well as for articles by members of the teaching staff. Not least, the *Proceedings* were available to publish the work of promising research students in advance of the books they later produced. The benefits were mutual. The *Proceedings* helped to promote Cambridge research, which itself gave a useful and constantly renewed stimulus to the Society.

Another largely complementary journal published for some thirty years from Cambridge was the quarterly (latterly four-monthly) *Antiquity*, edited by Glyn Daniel. Although primarily concerned with keeping the interested public abreast of recent archaeological discovery, it was important for keeping students aware of the ongoing nature of exploration, and it sturdily maintained the world-wide coverage established by its founder, O. G. S. Crawford, in 1927, the year when the Disney chair was first put on a regular basis. The present editor, Christopher Chippindale, who took office in 1987, graduated in archaeology at Cambridge, as did five of his nine advisory editors.

Last, but by no means least, prehistoric archaeology at Cambridge has been well served by its University Press. Ever since it published Miles Burkitt's *Prehistory* in 1921 it has issued a stream of books needed for undergraduate teaching, as well as publishing an impressive list of major works of research by members of the Cambridge faculty and their pupils.

CHAPTER 6

PREHISTORIANS BEYOND CAMBRIDGE: AFRICA, AUSTRALASIA, AMERICA AND ASIA

The prime though never the sole aim of Cambridge teaching of prehistoric archaeology during the period covered in this book was to produce the professionals needed to establish prehistory as a subject widely taught in universities in Britain and elsewhere in the English-speaking world, as well as the specialists needed to salvage, conserve and display archaeological data. Before the Second World War the opportunities open to professionals were few and far between. The great expansion occurred after the war. During the thirty years following it became possible for any young graduate intent on pursuing archaeology as a career to do so provided he or she was willing if need be to work overseas.

The fact that Cambridge was the first British university to offer under-graduate courses in prehistoric archaeology meant that to begin with the only academic posts available in this subject in Britain were at Cambridge itself. By the same token Cambridge could advance teaching and research only by recruiting its own graduates. When Dorothy Garrod needed lecturers to implement the new regulations for Part II of the Archaeological and Anthropological Tripos there were three Cambridge graduates available, all of whom had undertaken postgraduate research at Cambridge. If prehistoric archaeology was to be taken up widely this could only happen to begin with through the efforts of her own department, educating undergraduates and qualifying a sufficient number for the profession by supervising their postgraduate research. At the same time the Cambridge faculty was respon-sible for making the subject acceptable to the academic community by pursuing their own researches, editing and writing their own books.

The initial scarcity of openings in Britain was undoubtedly one reason why so many Cambridge graduates specializing in prehistoric archaeology sought opportunities to work overseas. A more positive reason is that at Cambridge the subject was taught alongside Anthropology in a museum filled with antiquities from all parts of the world. The sense that prehistory was a subject of world-wide relevance was enhanced by a steady stream of visitors and not a few candidates for the tripos, the Diploma in Prehistoric Archaeology or postgraduate degrees, who converged on Cambridge from Africa, Asia, Australasia and North America. Yet the idea of world prehistory was from

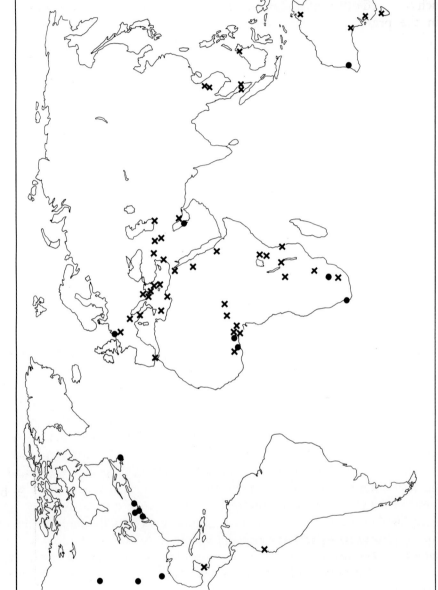

35   Map: Activities of Cambridge prehistorians overseas   x Key excavations   ● Universities

the outset balanced by a regard for the archaeology of Britain and its European setting. This was particularly true of candidates who took Section B of the tripos, but it also applied to some of the ablest taking the main Section A. Another important influence was that of the Classical Faculty which attracted others to the prehistory of Greek and Roman civilization.

In the present chapter consideration will be given to the impact of Cambridge on the prehistory most notably of Africa and Australasia. The Cambridge share in the advance of prehistory in Europe and above all in Britain, including its widespread recognition by British universities, will be considered in the one that follows.

The first person to arrive from Africa to take the Cambridge Tripos at that time still termed the Anthropology Tripos, though already providing teaching in prehistoric archaeology, was A. H. S. Goodwin. After finishing at Cambridge in 1921 Goodwin returned to teach prehistory at the University of Cape Town where he later became a professor. It was through Goodwin that Miles Burkitt was first attracted to South Africa. The impression this made on Burkitt is reflected in his book *South Africa's Past in Stone and Paint*[1] and more importantly in the interest and excitement that led him to encourage so many pupils to engage in African prehistory. Goodwin himself went some way to bridging the gap between indigenous pioneers like van Riet Lowe[2] and the kind of prehistory developed by French prehistorians that he imbibed at Cambridge. Before he died in 1959 Goodwin had made a number of forays into West Africa. In the course of these he became the first to conduct archaeological excavations at Benin. Although South Africa had a strong tradition of its own, Cape Town continued to draw on prehistorians trained at Cambridge. These included Ray Inskeep,[3] who came there after a spell with Desmond Clark at the Rhodes-Livingstone Museum and ultimately returned to Britain to join the Pitt Rivers Museum at Oxford. Another was John Parkington[4] who settled in South Africa straight after his Cambridge course and has since remained at Cape Town University. Another Cambridge graduate to begin his career in South Africa was Garth Sampson. His first assignment was to excavate rock-shelters in advance of the Orange River irrigation scheme. His promptness in excavating and publishing the results led to an appointment at the Southern Methodist University, Dallas.[5]

The most formidable character to come to Cambridge as a student of prehistory from an African background was unquestionably Louis Leakey. Leakey had been raised in Kenya by parents who worked as missionaries to the Kikuyu with the Church Missionary Society. His impact on prehistory was commensurate with his intellectual drive and personal magnetism.[6] After taking firsts in modern languages and anthropology he was elected a research fellow of St John's. He made use of this opportunity to undertake a series of expeditions to his native country. In establishing the archaeological sequence during the Upper Pleistocene he took full account of the natural environment and paid particular attention to the physical remains of the people who made and used the lithic industries recovered during his excavations. His interest in combining archaeology with Quaternary Research and human palaeontology was already manifest in his first book, *The Stone Age Cultures of Kenya Colony*, published by the Cambridge University Press in 1931. It remained with him throughout the rest of his career. In 1936 he devoted the Munro Lectures at Edinburgh to showing how African prehistory had already exposed as parochial the sequence worked out in western Europe and dispensed to his pupils at Cambridge by Miles Burkitt. When he finally returned to Kenya in 1937 he set himself as soon as the war was over to investigating the Lower and Middle Pleistocene succession exposed in the Rift Valley. With the assistance of his wife Mary and his son Richard he recovered unparalleled information about the remote prehistory of man. Apart from his success and persistence in significant research Leakey had a genius and appetite for conveying his enthusiasm to others. The founding of the Pan-African Congress of Prehistory in 1937[7] and the planning of successive conferences gave a notable impulse to research throughout the continent. Although he could be a difficult colleague Leakey was willing to help his juniors when they were prepared to stand up to him. This showed when he engaged Glynn Isaac, freshly graduated at Cambridge, to work at the palaeolithic site of Olorgesailie as Warden of Prehistoric Sites in Kenya (1963–5). Glynn came to Cambridge to read the Tripos as a graduate of Cape Town, where he had been taught by two Cambridge graduates, A. H. S. Goodwin and Monica Wilson (née Hunter), the social anthropologist. At Olorgesailie he gave so much satisfaction that he was promoted to Deputy Director of the Centre for Prehistory and Palaeontology in the National Museum at Nairobi. Isaac's success in Kenya signalled by his Cambridge doctorate earned by his research at Olorgesailie[8] led Desmond Clark to secure him for his own department at Berkeley, California. His translation in 1983 to Harvard was a further indication of the esteem in which he was held and only emphasizes the loss created by his early death in 1985 while on a professional mission to the Far East.

   Miles Burkitt's enthusiasm and persuasiveness as a teacher ensured that several of his small band of pupils before the war made their archaeological careers dealing with African prehistory. The one who influenced the course of African prehistory most comprehensively was undoubtedly Desmond Clark. Desmond gained a first in 1937 and went straight to Northern Rhodesia where he served as Director of the Rhodes-Livingstone Museum until 1961. He began this long tenure by making a rapid survey of the research potential of his wide-ranging territory. After war service in Africa he undertook an extensive study of the prehistory of the Upper Zambesi and its tributaries.[9] Having put his museum and its exhibits in order, he set about establishing the local sequence in the broader context of African prehistory. In 1955 he served as General Secretary of the Third Pan-African Congress on Prehistory. The meeting at Livingstone[10] was in itself a recognition of the standing it had already acquired as a centre for prehistoric research. Desmond Clark was soon invited to write *The Prehistory of South Africa* for Penguin Books. In 1961 he was appointed Professor in the Department of Anthropology at Berkeley, California. There, paradoxically, he was better able to pursue research in Africa and in different parts of Asia. His excavations at the

36   Louis Leakey (left) and Desmond Clark, Livingstone, 1955. Leakey had just opened the Field Museum at the Victoria Falls

Acheulian site of Kalambo Falls on the Zambian side of the Tanzanian frontier[11] was followed by field-work in Abyssinia, India and Israel. Furthermore, at Berkeley he was able to write broad syntheses of African prehistory.[12] Characteristically Desmond never forgot to acknowledge his debt to Cambridge. He dedicated *The Prehistory of Africa* to his former teacher, Miles Burkitt, whose 'teaching and enthusiasm' had led him to pursue African prehistory.[13] In the Preface to his book he acknowledged the assistance of nine colleagues. Of these six were former Cambridge students, including Thurstan Shaw who had graduated a year before him and four who had taken archaeology in the Cambridge Tripos between 1956 and 1965.

Two other early pupils of Miles Burkitt made their careers in West Africa, Thurstan Shaw and Bernard Fagg. Shaw spent two periods in West Africa separated by a spell in the Cambridgeshire Education Authority. He went first to Ghana where he was Curator of the Anthropology Museum at Achimota between 1937 and 1945. While in Ghana he made the first archaeological excavations in that country. Sectioning the substantial mound at Dawu in the East Province he recovered quantities of pipes from the upper levels showing that these must have formed since the final decades of the sixteenth century when tobacco smoking had been introduced by the

37 The Third Pan-African Congress, Livingstone, 1955. Louis Leakey demonstrating his talent for making stone tools to, among others, Miles Burkitt (second left), Gertrude Caton Thompson, Desmond Clark and Kenneth Oakley

Portuguese.[14] The next year he dug a cave near Abetifi and discovered a homogeneous accumulation containing microliths made from white quartz and a few polished stone axes overlain by a deposit of comparatively recent date with pottery and traces of iron-smelting. A detailed report on his findings appeared in the *Proceedings of the Prehistoric Society* for 1944.[15] The basic organization for the pursuit of Ghanaian archaeology was laid down after Shaw's departure by another Cambridge archaeologist, A. W. Lawrence, who gave up the chair of Classical Archaeology at Cambridge to make a blueprint for a new province of archaeology. During his tenure at

38   Thurstan Shaw measuring a section at the rock shelter of Iwo Eleru, Nigeria, 1964

what was then the University College of the Gold Coast (1951–7), during which he acted as professor and at the same time as Director of the National Museum, he not only initiated university teaching in archaeology but engaged in research[16] and established the Museums and Monuments Board to supervise the conservation and display of ancient monuments. Lawrence also commissioned Oliver Davies from Ulster to undertake a survey of prehistoric sites which he made between 1952 and 1966. Ghanaian prehistory also benefited at this time from the services of two recruits from Cambridge, Paul Ozanne and Colin Flight, the latter now on the staff of the Department of West African History at Birmingham. In 1967 Merrick Posnansky, a graduate of Nottingham who subsequently took the Cambridge Diploma in Prehistoric Archaeology, was appointed to the chair of archaeology at what had by then become the University of Ghana. In his inaugural lecture Posnansky paid tribute to the work of his immediate predecessor, Peter Shinnie, in ensuring Ghanaian participation in two international projects of major importance, namely the Volta Basic Research Project and the UNESCO campaign in Nubia. He was also able to congratulate West African states on increasing the number of professional archaeologists tenfold during the previous twenty years.[18] One of his first steps was to introduce degree courses in archaeology at Legon University, a step he rightly saw as crucial if the country was to produce its own prehistorians.

Nigeria was another West African territory to which Cambridge prehistorians made important contributions. The first to establish himself there was Bernard Fagg, who first came to Nigeria as an administrative officer and made his way into archaeology only by devoting his leaves to energetic archaeological reconnaissance. He began by searching the hills of the Bauchi Plateau in the northern part of the country for rock-shelters likely to have been occupied by prehistoric man. Having discovered a promising one at Rop he proceeded to excavate a microlithic industry which he published in the same volume as Shaw's Abetifi occurrence in the Gold Coast.[19] He next turned to the tin-workings. There he recovered human heads made of pottery which appeared to anticipate the sculptural achievements of later times, notably the bronze heads of Ife and Benin and the wooden sculptures of modern times. Fagg then defined the archaeological setting of the ceramic heads in the Nok culture which he dated to the latter part of the first millennium B.C.[20] In 1947 he was transferred to the Antiquities Service, where his first task was to construct the museum at Jos to house the new finds. When Bernard Fagg retired from Nigeria in 1964 as Head of the Antiquities Service it was to take up the Curatorship of the Pitt-Rivers Museum at Oxford.

Before Bernard Fagg withdrew, Thurstan Shaw, who had previously served in Ghana, made his first incursion into Nigerian archaeology by undertaking an initial season at Igbo-Ikwu during a spell of leave from the

Cambridgeshire Education Service. This proved a promising beginning, and in 1963 he accepted a post as Research Professor at Ibadan,[21] a post he held until 1974. He resumed the excavations at Igbo-Ikwu which revealed a royal burial and store-house dating from the final quarter of the first millennium A.D.[22] These proved to be richly furnished with bronze and copper regalia and jewellery together with a store of ivory tusks. He went on with the help of a young recruit from Cambridge, S. G. H. Daniels, who had graduated in 1961, to excavate a rock-shelter at Iwo Eleru. This yielded a rich microlithic industry overlying a human skeleton, ill-preserved but some ten thousand years old.[23] It is a tribute to Shaw's researches and teaching at Ibadan that two more young Cambridge prehistorians were attracted to Nigeria in the persons of Robert Soper[24] and Phillip Allsworth-Jones.[25] In the meantime Graham Connah, who had graduated at Cambridge in 1960, had been engaged in systematic field-work for the Federal Department of Antiquities. He began by carrying out investigations at Benin,[26] scene of the British punitive raid of 1887 that saw the looting of shrines and of royal regalia. From 1964 he turned his attention to the north-eastern part of the country and carried out deep excavations in a settlement mound at Daima, which appears to have been occupied from the sixth century B.C. until towards the

39   Bernard Fagg discussing the precise position of a fine Nok head with the Nigerian tin miner who discovered it

end of the first millennium A.D.[27] Connah continued to work on his Nigerian data after migrating to Australia.

Cambridge prehistorians have also played a predominant role in the operation of the British Institute in East Africa, founded in 1960 largely on the initiative of Sir Mortimer Wheeler when Secretary of the British Academy. The Institute was designed to cover an extensive territory from Kenya and Uganda as far south as Mozambique. To begin with it was based in Dar es Salaam with a secondary office at Kampala, but in 1964 it was concentrated on Nairobi where it has since functioned in close association with the University of Kenya. After a brief tenure by Richard Goodchild the

40   Neville Chittick in one of the stone-walled shaft tombs at Aksum in Ethiopia

Directorship was held from 1961 to 1983 by Neville Chittick, who had previously acted as Curator of the Uganda Museum at Kampala after taking the postgraduate Diploma in Prehistoric Archaeology at Cambridge. Cambridge also provided a succession of Assistant Directors. These began with Merrick Posnansky, who had begun his work in Africa as Curator at Kampala. After a period at the Institute Posnansky served as Professor at the West African University at Legon before ending up in the Department of History at Los Angeles in the University of California. He was succeeded at the Institute by Robert Soper, who had taken the Cambridge Tripos in 1961 and held the post as Assistant Director of the Institute for five years (1967–72) before leaving for Ibadan. He was followed at the Institute by David Phillipson, who later returned to Britain where he took a post in the Museum and Art Gallery at Glasgow before coming back to Cambridge as Curator of the University Museum of Archaeology and Anthropology. There he has published an admirable survey of African[28] prehistoric archaeology. The British Institute was content to leave research on early man very largely in the hands of Louis Leakey, his wife Mary and his son Richard and has concentrated its own attention on the prehistoric Iron Age in the interior

41   Glynn Isaac at Koobi Fora, Kenya

and the historic period in the coastal zone. While at Dar es Salaam the Institute focussed on Islamic activities, and the Director made his classic excavations at the trading station at Kilwa.[29] Concern with Arab commerce led the Institute to host a conference in Nairobi in 1967 on East Africa in relation to the Indian Ocean.[30] The first volume of *Azania* edited by the Director and designed to publish the findings of the Institute had begun to appear in the previous year.

Work on the prehistoric Iron Age in the interior began with a project designed to throw light particularly on the origins and migrations of the Bantu, financed largely by the Waldorf Astor Foundation of New York. This began with a pilot scheme carried out by Cambridge graduates led by Brian Fagan and concerned very largely with the southward thrust of Bantu-speaking people.[31] When Robert Soper took over the Assistant Directorship of the Institute he concentrated on the Iron Age cultures of northern Kenya.[32] During his last period at the Institute Chittick directed much of his attention to excavations at Aksum, the ancient capital of Ethiopia.[33]

Much of northern Africa was within direct reach of European pre-historians, notably from France and Italy. It also attracted, though on a smaller scale, prehistorians from Britain. The work of Gertrude Caton Thompson in Egypt and of Charles McBurney has already been dealt with. Not surprisingly the region attracted one of McBurney's brightest pupils, Angela Close, who secured a first in 1971, and took as her theme for a research degree the late palaeolithic and epipalaeolithic industries of the extensive zone between the Maghreb and the Nile Valley.[34] Before long she was invited to join the Southern Methodist University, Dallas, which had for some years been co-sponsoring the Combined Prehistoric Expedition to the Upper Nile together with the Polish Institute for the History of Material Culture and the Egyptian Geological Survey.

What Africa gained from Cambridge prehistorians both in advancing a knowledge of its past and in manning and developing the institutions and services needed to propagate this and conserve and display the archaeological evidence requires no further emphasis. It is perhaps less obvious that the benefits were reciprocal. Africa offered a superb field for research which hitherto had been tapped only in the Mediterranean zone and in South Africa. It also offered scope for professional careers in prehistoric archae-ology not so readily available elsewhere. Similarly for those who wanted to return at some stage to the temperate zone it provided qualifications of which universities were glad to avail themselves with the rise of black consciousness and the widespread recognition of world prehistory. The Pitt Rivers Museum at Oxford was glad to secure Bernard Fagg as Curator and Ray Inskeep as Assistant Curator, and Cambridge was no less happy to secure David Phillipson as Curator of its own University Museum. North American universities, faced with a need to provide more courses relevant to black studies, were glad to be able to draw on persons qualified by original work in Africa. Among Cambridge prehistorians with African experience to be recruited to the faculties of North American universities one might first cite Desmond Clark and Glynn Isaac who taught on the Berkeley campus of the University of California before Glynn moved to Harvard. Others included Brian Fagan and Merrick Posnansky who joined the Santa Barbara and Los Angeles campuses of the University of California. The Southern Methodist University, Dallas also gained by obtaining Angela Close and Garth Sampson. Grahame Connah on the other hand teaches prehistory at the University of New England at Armidale, New South Wales.

The genesis of professional archaeology in Australia and New Zealand owed even more to Cambridge. The archaeological collections housed alongside natural history exhibits and ethnographica in the great museums of cities like Adelaide, Melbourne, Perth and Sydney or Auckland, Christchurch, Dunedin and Wellington were the outcome of collecting by amateurs rather than of research by professionals. Not even the curators, who included many of outstanding ability, had themselves received university training in archaeology. Since no facilities existed in Australasia the situation could be remedied only by interchange with overseas universities.

42   H. D. Skinner, Emeritus Director of Otago Museum, 1971

In practice this meant at the time with Cambridge. As in the case of Africa, this was a two-way traffic. Some of the most valuable links were forged by Australians or New Zealanders coming to Cambridge. The chief magnet at the outset was A. C. Haddon, who ironically as a young man had been runner up to Baldwin Spencer for the foundation chair of biology at Melbourne.[35] As we have already seen a young New Zealander, H. D. Skinner, took the opportunity of being stranded as a war casualty in London to marry a fellow New Zealander and settle down in Cambridge so as to take a course in anthropology from Haddon. Shortly after his return to New Zealand, Otago University had the foresight to appoint him Assistant Curator of its museum and give him the responsibility of starting a course in anthropology. His appointment was the first of its kind in the southern hemisphere. He began his formal course,[36] which counted as a year's unit towards a B.A., in 1920. As might be expected his lectures covered what Haddon conceived to be the principal contents of anthropology, namely physical anthropology, material culture, social anthropology and prehistoric archaeology, which, like Edward Tylor himself, Skinner believed to be basic to anthropology. It is worth noting that Ridgeway had made sufficient impression on Skinner to lead him in due course to acquire for the Otago Museum the collection of Greek pottery made by A. B. Cook, the first

43   John Mulvaney at Fromm's Landing on the Murray River, 1960

Professor of Classical Archaeology at Cambridge. Towards the end of his life Haddon attracted an Australian anthropologist in the person of Donald Thompson, whose ecological approach to the subject made a profound impression on Cambridge prehistory. Donald's personality was such that his Australian colleagues found it difficult to acknowledge his work at its true value and in some respects he was his own worst enemy. Yet he knew how highly regarded his work was at Cambridge and that is probably why he consigned two of his comparatively rare scientific papers to the *Proceedings of the Prehistoric Society*.[37]

In later years Cambridge was fortunate to welcome two younger Australian graduates both of whom played important roles in advancing Australian prehistory and helping to ensure its acceptance by Australian universities, namely D. J. Mulvaney, who later became foundation Professor of Prehistory in the Faculty of Arts at the Australian National University, and Isabel McBryde, who has recently succeeded him. Mulvaney came to Cambridge as a graduate of Melbourne. He completed the Cambridge Tripos in 1953 and proceeded to a research doctorate by excavating in Australia and keeping the residence required by the regulations at Cambridge. Even so he had to spend twelve years teaching history at Melbourne while undertaking the field research he judged it necessary to accomplish before prehistory could rank as

44   Jack Golson with a colleague, Korup, on Lou Island, Papua New Guinea

a subject fit for teaching undergraduates. He began by demolishing for-
mulations based on insufficient evidence, a task he accomplished in a
masterly article published in the *Proceedings of the Prehistoric Society*.[38] He
then concentrated on acquiring the necessary data by carrying out careful
stratigraphical excavations at Fromm's Landing on the Lower Murray River,
and Kenniffs Cave, Queensland. This vital task, which was essential to
establish an acceptable sequence, was one he had to perform during his
vacations. It was not until he was freed from his teaching obligations at
Melbourne by being translated to the Australian National University as a
Senior Fellow in the Research School of Pacific Studies in 1965 that he was
able to undertake a synthesis of Australian prehistory. The publication of his
comprehensive and attractively written book in 1969[39] was soon reflected in
his appointment in 1970 as foundation Professor of Prehistory in the Faculty
of Arts. He was now free to embark on teaching a subject which he had in
large measure created himself.

The other Australian graduate to come to Cambridge at an early stage was
Isabel McBryde, who had graduated at the University of New England,
Armidale, N.S.W., where she had begun lecturing on ancient history. At
Cambridge she acquired a Diploma in Prehistoric Archaeology and on
returning to Armidale took up a lectureship in prehistory and ancient
history. This gave her the opportunity to engage in the excavation of
rock-shelters and shell-mounds in northern New South Wales as well as, in
partnership with a petrologist, R. A. Binns, in the investigation of the sources
and distribution of the different stones used in prehistoric times for the
manufacture of ground stone axes and adzes. As they made clear in their
preliminary report published in the *Proceedings of the Prehistoric Society*, this
research was clearly modelled on that previously carried out in Britain.[40]
Before leaving for Canberra to take a Readership in Mulvaney's Department,
Isabel McBryde had succeeded in having prehistory recognized as an
independent department under herself as Associate Professor. The lead in
prehistory at Armidale passed to Grahame Connah, who had moved there
from Nigeria in 1971. Connah himself then secured Iain Davidson, who had
graduated at Cambridge in 1970 and obtained his research doctorate for work
on the economy of Eastern Spain during Palaeolithic times.

If native born Australians and New Zealanders played a fundamental role
in establishing prehistory in the Antipodes, the majority of those who
developed it academically were British born and trained at Cambridge.
If we except H. D. Skinner, who had returned to New Zealand with the
Cambridge diploma in 1920, Jack Golson, who took a first in Part II of the
Archaeological and Anthropological Tripos in 1951 after graduating in
history and being subject to the influence of Michael Postan as Professor of
Economic History, was the first trained prehistorian to reach New Zealand
or for that matter Australasia. While teaching at Auckland Golson did not

publish a great deal but he made it plain that he had an essential grasp of the main problems facing prehistorians in the region.[41] His abilities were not lost on the Australian National University, which attracted him to a Research Fellowship at the School of Pacific Studies, where in due course he was promoted to a professorship. At Auckland he was succeeded by Wilfrid Shawcross[42] and later by Peter Bellwood.[43] Both at once began to excavate in the North Island, but both followed Golson in due course to Canberra. Meanwhile in the South Island Skinner was succeeded by Peter Gathercole, who had been a friend of Golson's at Peterhouse and had taken the Cambridge Tripos in 1952. At Otago, Gathercole brought anthropology[44] to the point which decided the university to establish a chair. In the event Gathercole left for research in Oceania and returned to Britain first to Oxford and later to Cambridge. Otago appointed Charles Higham, who had taken a first at Cambridge in the prestigious year 1962, as its first Professor of Anthropology. Higham decided to outflank Australia by undertaking a research programme in Thailand. This not merely attracted international recognition, but provided field experience for the Otago department as well as rich material for analysis and teaching.[45]

While at Canberra Golson's task was to develop prehistory as a field of high academic endeavour. A main problem was to recruit an adequate staff. His first step was to rescue John Mulvaney from teaching history at Melbourne and obtain him as a Senior Fellow. The appearance of *The*

45   Peter Bellwood at the Stone Age site of Tingkayu in Sabah, North Borneo; with him are members of the staff of the Sabah Museum Archaeology Division

Prehistory of Australia was a sign that the subject was ready for teaching and in the following year, 1970, the author was transferred to the Faculty of Arts and appointed foundation Professor of Prehistory to lead the teaching of undergraduates. Mulvaney in his turn attracted Isabel McBryde from the University of New England in 1974 where she was already established as Associate Professor in Prehistory. Meanwhile Golson secured Rhys Jones, another Cambridge man who had previously worked for the Department of Anthropology at Sydney and further strengthened his group by securing two Cambridge men, Shawcross and Bellwood from New Zealand. Even so the task of researching Australian prehistory from New Guinea to Tasmania and extending well back into the Late Pleistocene was a demanding one, which called for contributions from Quaternary Research and physical and social anthropology and ability to appreciate the arts. It was one that called for team-work and abstention from premature publication that might embarrass further research.

By securing Rhys Jones, Golson obtained a man who had a broad grasp of the various dimensions of Australian prehistory and at the same time was prepared to devote himself to its southernmost territory, Tasmania, as well as extending his interest to south-east Asia as the source of the aboriginal population of Australia. Since his first reconnaissance during the summer of 1963–4 Rhys Jones had focussed attention on a part of Australia which had long attracted the interests of anthropologists as a place where the aboriginal population had succumbed to the pressures of white settlement only during

46   Rhys Jones, exploring a cave on the Andrew River, Tasmania, 1984

47   Richard Wright and son beneath the rock shelter at Laura, Cape York peninsula, Australia

the first half of the nineteenth century. The lithic industries made by their forebears had already been the object of speculation since a collection had found its way to the Pitt Rivers Museum at Oxford. There they had been separately examined by Sollas and Balfour and variously compared with palaeolithic assemblages from Europe.[46] On the dubious ground that sea-faring was not practised by the aborigines in so far as their way of life could be reconstructed from highly imperfect records, it was commonly supposed that the makers of the lithic industries, forebears of the recent aboriginal population, must have arrived while Tasmania still formed part of the Australian mainland. What was plainly needed to solve such questions was systematic study of the prehistoric succession in the context of the palaeo-environment, the whole under the control of radiocarbon dating. This is precisely what Rhys Jones was equipped to do.[47] By undertaking widespread reconnaissance and excavating Beginner's Luck and Fraser Caves in the south-west of the island he was able to show that Stone Age communities were hunting wallaby and wombat between fifteen and twenty thousand years ago, at a time when Tasmania would certainly have been accessible from Australia by dry land.

Meanwhile Golson himself had shown a special interest in New Guinea, at the northern limit of his parish.[48] Ever since Haddon's historic expedition to the Torres Straits in 1898 New Guinea had been of keen interest to anthropologists, but it was not until the 1930s that the central highlands were first explored by Europeans, at a time when the inhabitants still depended on stone tools. After the war the highlands attracted many social anthropologists, but it was not until 1959,[49] by which time the people had largely gone over to metal axes, that attempts were made to investigate the production of stone ones. The initiative was taken in 1959 by Susan Bulmer, an American-trained cultural anthropologist and wife of Ralph Bulmer who had taken the Cambridge Tripos in anthropology and joined the department at Auckland. Doubtless it was through the Bulmers that an Auckland geologist, J. Chappel,[50] who subsequently migrated to the Australian National University, made the first attempt to locate the geological sources of the raw materials used for the stone axes of the New Guinea highlands. The Bulmers realized that the abundance and distribution of stone axes indicated a substantial settlement of the highlands, and cited extensive unoccupied grasslands as evidence of former cultivation. Susan Bulmer also emphasized that few highlanders obtained stone from a local source. This in turn directed attention to the factors that determined the observed patterns of distribution and gave Marilyn Strathern, a Cambridge graduate in social anthropology, a useful lead for her doctoral research on 'Ceremonial Exchange in the Mount Hagen area' which she completed in 1966.[51] The Bulmers had also gone out of their way to test the depth of prehistory in the highlands by excavating rock-shelters at Yaku and Kiowa and obtaining samples for the Yale radiocarbon laboratory indicating a time range of around ten thousand years.[52]

Plainly New Guinea at the northern margin of Australia gave rich promise for prehistoric research. When Peter White returned from Cambridge to take a research doctorate at the School of Pacific Studies, New Guinea offered him the scope he needed. After joining the Department of Anthropology at Sydney, White widened his grasp of Australian prehistory to the point at which he became co-author of the first major work on Australian prehistory since the appearance of Mulvaney's book.[53] Jack Golson also addressed himself to the problem of early cultivation in the highlands hinted at by the Bulmers. Although definitive reports are still awaited, it is already known, partly through his long-standing friend the Danish ethnologist and prehistorian Axel Steensberg,[54] that he has been able to reveal extensive areas of cultivation many thousands of years old.

Meanwhile it seems important to note that in addition to the two at Canberra and a third at Armidale, a fourth centre of archaeological teaching in prehistory in Australia had come into existence in the anthropology department at Sydney University. This was likewise started by a Cambridge graduate in prehistoric archaeology, Richard Wright. Although his prime task was to build up prehistory in the teaching of the department at Sydney, which he joined soon after taking the Cambridge Tripos in 1959, Wright, like other Cambridge prehistorians in Australasia, lost no time in undertaking excavations. As well as digging in New South Wales he ventured as far as Cape York Peninsula, where he excavated a cave and tested shell-mounds,[55] and later enhanced his reputation by his judicious examination of the Koonalda Cave on the Nullarbor Plain[56] in the extreme west of South Australia and close to the coast. Wright was able to show that this cave, whose association with prehistoric man had previously been claimed by Dr A. Gallus, had been used as a flint quarry between fifteen and twenty thousand years ago, as well as revealing enigmatic scribings on the clay wall covering. In developing the teaching of prehistory at Sydney, where he now holds the rank of Professor of Anthropology, Richard Wright was able to draw on the help of two Cambridge-trained lecturers, Peter White, and John Clegg, who had taken the tripos in 1969 and while at Sydney has published notably on prehistoric art in Australia.[57]

Prehistory has since become a popular option for students in Australia. Due to the efforts of Sylvia Hallam, who took the Cambridge Tripos and secured a doctorate before moving with her husband to Western Australia, and who resumed archaeology after bringing up her family, the subject is now taught in the department of anthropology in the university, where she is currently an Associate Professor.[58] Prehistory is also a major component in the anthropology course at Brisbane and is taught in combination with other subjects at the James Cook University, Townsville, Queensland, Flinders

University, South Australia and La Trobe University, Victoria.[59]

Although the Cambridge department had no teaching post in New World archaeology it managed to make contributions ranging from the Dorset phase of Eskimo prehistory[60] to the high cultures of Mesoamerica and the Andes. The museum was for long dominated by Maya casts, and New World antiquities were richly displayed in its cases. Louis Clarke and later Geoffrey Bushnell were devoted to the subject and attracted many friends from the Americas. Even so there was more than a stroke of chance that determined two Cambridge men to make careers in Latin-American prehistory. Warwick Bray who took the tripos in 1958 had already taken a research doctorate in Mediterranean prehistory when presented with the opportunity of joining an

48   Norman Hammond at Cuello, 1980

undergraduate expedition to Colombia, and it was this that captured his interest in the local archaeology. In 1966 he was appointed Lecturer in Latin American Archaeology at London University jointly with the Institute of Archaeology and the Centre for Latin-American Studies. Although the amount of field work he has been able to carry out has been limited for logistical reasons, he soon began survey and excavation in Colombia. His command of Colombian archaeology became apparent when he acted as Academic Adviser to the Royal Academy Exhibition of gold-work at Burlington House in 1978–9, of which he wrote the Catalogue.[61]

Norman Hammond, who graduated in 1966, got his opportunity by responding to an entirely unexpected telephone call from Gordon Willey for a British volunteer for one of his Maya excavations. Like Bray, Hammond gained an abiding interest from an unexpected opportunity. Experience on the ground led him to adopt Maya civilization as a field for postgraduate research. From the outset he set his face against merely uncovering structures and their associated artefacts and aimed to account for the genesis and development of Maya civilization. In 1970 he undertook extensive survey in Belize (formerly British Honduras), concentrating his excavations at Lubaantun in the south of the country, and in 1971 located additional sites in the adjacent area. In this way he was able to present a study of a Maya realm instead of merely reporting on the excavation of a single monument.[62] After taking his doctorate, he continued to work on the major problems of Maya

49   Joan and David Oates at Tell Brak, 1985

archaeology as a Research Fellow of Fitzwilliam and Senior Lecturer at Bradford, becoming director of the Rutgers Archaeological Program and subsequently Professor of Archaeology at Boston University. His most exciting results to date stem from his excavations at Cuello in northern Belize, where he has revealed house platforms with associated agriculture and pottery dating back to around the end of the second millennium B.C.[63] In addition to active field reconnaissance and excavation Norman Hammond has kept a close eye on results obtained by other workers and has recently published what is widely accepted as the best synthesis of Maya civilisation presently available.[64]

Cambridge prehistorians made their first entry into south-west Asia in the person of Dorothy Garrod. As a Research Fellow of Newnham she pioneered and laid the basis of knowledge about the stone age in Palestine, having previously made a brief incursion into Iraqui Kurdistan. She supervised John Waechter's postgraduate research into the Natufian culture which she had herself been the first to recognize and some years later an Iraqui research student, Ghanim Wahida, completed the excavation of the Zarzi cave where she had revealed the first microlithic assemblage in Kurdistan.[65] Both these men made careers in academic archaeology, Waechter at the London Institute and Wahida at the university of Riyadh in Saudi Arabia. Further, the Cambridge Centre for Research on the Early History of Agriculture chose Palestine as one of its major fields of research[66] largely because of the animal bones recovered by Miss Garrod from the Mount Carmel caves. Another part of south-west Asia covered by the Early History of Agriculture project was south Anatolia which was penetrated by Sebastian Payne, who had taken the tripos in 1957 and was serving at the time as a fellow of the Project. He worked in close conjunction with David French, from whose excavations at the aceramic settlement of Can Hasan III the critical biological material came.[67]

Closer involvement with Mesopotamian archaeology came through David Oates who took a first in the Cambridge tripos of 1948 and went on to hold a fellowship at Trinity between 1951 and 1965. While still a fellow of Trinity he followed in the footsteps of Sir Aurel Stein by pursuing survey and excavation in northern Iraq in quest of Achaemenian and Parthian history.[68] On becoming resident director of the British School of Archaeology in Iraq (1966–9) he embarked on the excavation of Babylonian and Assyrian structures at Tell al-Rimah where between 1963 and 1971 he explored structures and recovered inscriptions. From the Directorship of the British School he moved to London where he succeeded Max Mallowan as professor of West Asiatic Archaeology at the Institute of Archaeology. Since 1976 he has conducted several seasons of excavation at the prehistoric site of Tell Brak in Syria. Meanwhile his wife Joan, who came to Cambridge as a graduate of Syracuse, New York, to undertake research on Al Ubaid pottery, carried on with her interest in early village life. Perhaps her most important excavation has been the one she undertook at Choga Mami, near Mandali close to the Iranian frontier. Many will appreciate her synthesis of the data recovered by several excavators bearing on the genesis and development of early village communities in Mesopotamia and the Zagros, since this is based on close personal study of the actual data.[69] Joan Oates attracted three notable Arab scholars to undertake postgraduate research at Cambridge and supervised their doctoral studies. All three are now professional archaeologists. They include Ghanim Wahida, who worked on the Palaeolithic and Epipalaeolithic of Zarzi in Iraqi Kurdistan discovered by Dorothy Garrod, and now teaches in the University of Bahrain; Walid Yasin al-Tikriti, archaeological adviser to the United Arab Emirates; and Behnam Abo Al Soof, Director of Antiquities for Northern Iraq. Another Cambridge prehistorian to excavate in Iraq was David Stronach who investigated a small prehistoric village at Ras al 'Amiya[70] with Al' Ubaid pottery.

Stronach was appointed first Director of the British Institute of Persian Studies established at Teheran in 1961, and in 1963 he instituted the periodical *Iran*. In the first volume he included the first of three reports on the excavation of two Achemenian capitals. Another important excavation during his time as Director was carried out at the port of Siraf[71] on the north

50   Aborigines transporting specimens by canoe from the excavation site to headquarters, Gua Cha, Malaysia, 1954

coast of the Gulf by David and Ruth Whitehouse, both trained at Cambridge. Meanwhile Charles McBurney had led an expedition from Cambridge to explore the Epipalaeolithic occupation of the cave of Ali Tappeh on the coastal plain of the Caspian.[72]

East of Iran Cambridge prehistorians contributed little to the archaeology of Asia except in the extreme south-east. Although John (later Sir John) Marshall was educated at Cambridge he came up well before prehistoric archaeology began to be taught there. The only important contribution made to the prehistory of India from Cambridge during the time covered in this book came from T. T. Paterson while holding a research fellowship at Trinity. As a young man he joined Helmut de Terra on the Carnegie Expedition sent out in 1935 to establish the glacial succession and fix the context of palaeolithic industries in India. One finding of importance for world prehistory was the definition of the pebble and flake industries of the Soan basin and their dating to the Middle Pleistocene.[73] The failure to establish a British Institute in India after independence, and the level of Indian salaries, meant that there was small opportunity for prehistorians from Britain to establish careers there. In any case Wheeler had trained a substantial number of Indians in field archaeology and Indian universities soon began to produce their own graduates. The academic treatment of Indian archaeology was badly neglected in British universities. Such work as there was was centred on the School of Oriental and African Studies and on the Institute of Archaeology of London University. It is only since Raymond and Bridget Allchin migrated to Cambridge in 1959 that teaching and research in Indian prehistory have come to be focussed on the Department of Oriental Studies at Cambridge.[74]

Although Cambridge undergraduates were free to attend courses on Chinese archaeology at Cambridge, the Far East offered little to Cambridge prehistorians in the way of opportunities for research or careers. In parts of south-east Asia on the other hand there were chances for both. H. D. Collings, one of the small band who took the Archaeological and Anthropological Tripos in 1930, made use of his appointment to the Raffles Museum at Singapore to make at least one discovery of importance to world prehistory. Although his interests centred on ethnology he had learned enough prehistory at Cambridge to recognize a primitive stone industry at the Kota Tampan rubber plantation on the upper reaches of the Perak river. The significance of his discovery, which he published promptly,[75] was recognized soon after by the Harvard prehistorian Hallam J. Movius. In his study of the early prehistory of southern and eastern Asia, ranging from the Soan basin of north-west India to north China and southward to Java, Movius gave a separate status to the Tampanian.[76]

When Mrs Ann Sieveking, who as Ann Paul had taken the Tripos in 1952, joined her husband Gale on his appointment as Curator of Museums in

Malaya, she decided to submit the Kota Tampan material to closer examination. In undertaking this in 1954 she had the collaboration of Donald Walker, who found himself seconded while on National Service from the Army Operational Unit (Far East) to the Geological Survey of the Federation. Their joint report, which for reasons beyond their control did not appear until 1962,[77] took full account of Collings' work and established that the Tampanian was of Middle Pleistocene age. It could there stand alongside not only the Soan of India and the Choukoutien assemblage from China, but also, as Ann Sieveking rightly insisted, with the Oldowayan of Africa.

Meanwhile Gale Sieveking, who with his wife and Donald Walker had not long previously shared in the excavations at Star Carr, was excavating the limestone shelter of Gua Cha, Kelantan, with the aim of exploring the later

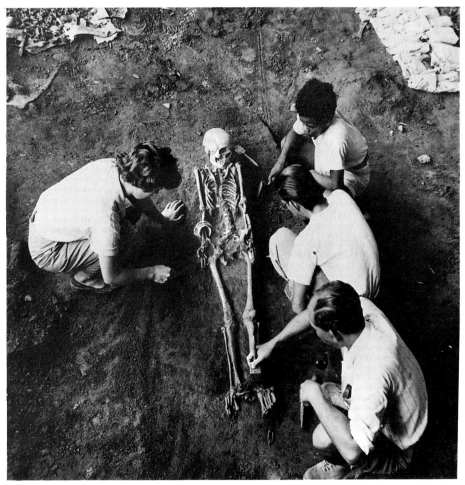

51   Ann Sieveking, with Ence Ibraham (pipe), Christian Oswald Theserra and Negrito, Gua Cha, 1954

prehistoric sequence in Malaya.[78] He succeeded in establishing two main levels. The lower layers produced a characteristic assemblage of Hoabhinian stone tools. Above them was a Neolithic cemetery of extended inhumations accompanied by polished stone axes, adzes and chisels and burials with groups of pots, many of them with comb decoration, grouped at their feet. In several instances the skeletons were wearing polished stone bracelets on their left arms. Before leaving Malaya to take up a post in the British Museum, Sieveking had time to salvage another Neolithic cemetery thrown out by guano diggers from the rock-shelter of Buki Tengku, Perlis.[79]

52   Charles Higham and Amphan Kijngam excavating a burial of c. 1000 B.C. at Ban Na Di,
     Thailand, 1981

The next attack on south-east Asian prehistory from Cambridge was aimed at Thailand and directed from New Zealand. Charles Higham's interest was kindled by W. G. Solheim's claim that bronze metallurgy had been developed earlier in Thailand than it had been in China. Following the five-year campaign launched from the University of Hawaii, Higham decided to test the radiocarbon chronology on which Solheim's case depended and at the same time to work more generally on the economic prehistory that lay behind the appearance of Thai civilization. He began his programme in 1969 and from the outset made a point of working with Thai colleagues. At the same time he went to great trouble to avoid unnecessary friction with American scholars in the same field. In particular he dug for two seasons with Chester Gorman of Philadelphia and since the latter's death has been at pains to accommodate his finds into the emerging picture of Thai prehistory. In the Mortimer Wheeler Archaeological Lecture for 1983 he gave an invaluable insight into the main problems opened up by the excavations at Non Nok Tha and Ban Chiang and since then has published a three-volume monograph making available a mass of evidence from Thailand.[80] Meanwhile he and his team at Otago are working on the analysis of the extremely important material excavated at Khok Phanom preparatory to publication.

The thrust from Australia and New Zealand into south-east Asia ought not to obscure the importance of research carried out from these countries in the Pacific region. The appointment of Wilfrid Shawcross and Peter Bellwood to the Auckland department gave a useful thrust to prehistoric research not merely in New Zealand itself[81] but also in the Cook Islands, the Marquesas and the Society Islands. Since moving to Australia, where he holds a Readership at the Australian National University, Bellwood has developed his grasp of the entire field and written what is widely regarded as the clearest and most comprehensive account of Polynesian prehistory in the light of modern archaeological research.[82]

CHAPTER 7

PREHISTORIANS BEYOND CAMBRIDGE: CONTINENTAL EUROPE AND BRITAIN

In the eastern and central parts of the Mediterranean basin the opportunities open to Cambridge prehistorians stemmed from the overlap between the fields covered by the Faculties of Archaeology and Anthropology and Classics. This applied particularly to Greece. There the main thrust from the Classical side appeared in Mycenaean and later studies, whereas that from Archaeology and Anthropology impinged mainly on the Stone Age. At Cambridge the later prehistory of Greece was largely created and taught by scholars who were nominally Classical. It is true that in some respects the most important advance made in Cambridge in Mycenaean studies was the demonstration by John Chadwick, following the initiative of Michael Ventris, that, as Ridgeway had long ago opined, the bearers of that culture spoke Greek.[1] Yet this in no way alters the fact that the methods used to explore their way of life and their prehistory differ in no important way from those applied to societies which were still preliterate. When Alan Wace gave his inaugural lecture as Laurence Professor of Classical Archaeology he was careful to address an impeccably Classical theme. This did not alter the fact that he occupied his chair by virtue of his achievements as a prehistoric archaeologist. When the time came for him to retire it was natural to resume work at Mycenae, where he found a further series of inscribed tablets. Among those who joined him at Mycenae was Lord William Taylour, who had taken the Archaeological and Anthropological Tripos in 1950 and took as a theme for his doctoral research the Mycenaean pottery from south Italy.[2] To enlarge his experience Lord William joined Carl Blegen at Pylos in the west Peloponnese, a site where the largest haul of inscribed Mycenaean tablets had been recovered in 1939. With this apprenticeship he embarked on his own campaign at Mycenae which culminated with the discovery in 1968 in the Citadel House of a richly furnished shrine with painted wall frescoes, idols and coiled serpents of fired clay.[3] In the meantime he had founded the Mediterranean Archaeological Trust to ensure the future of research in that field, and is currently applying its resources among other things to promote prehistoric excavation and research in Laconia. Although dedicated to the advance of knowledge about Greek prehistory Lord William Taylour has not overlooked the widespread public interest in the Mycenaeans.[4]

The first move on the part of Cambridge prehistorians based at the Department of Archaeology and Anthropology to explore the pre-Mycenaean prehistory of Greece also profited from Wace's example. It was the book he wrote with M. S. Thompson describing the exploration of the Neolithic settlement mounds of Thessaly[5] that pointed the way to Macedonia. Cambridge prehistorians had long been familiarized with the existence of settlement mounds in the Balkans largely through the writings of Gordon Childe, and had latterly been excited by the discoveries of James Mellaart in Anatolia. Not unnaturally they looked to Macedonia as a territory intermediate between the three. They therefore jumped at the opportunity afforded by Nea Nikomedeia on the western margin of the Macedonian Plain. The discovery, in the course of quarrying soil for an embankment, of a settlement mound with pottery that pointed to an early stage of Neolithic culture led to archaeological excavations in 1961 and 1963 directed by Robert Rodden, a Harvard graduate then working for a Cambridge research doctorate on the genesis of the Balkan Neolithic. The determination of a high radiocarbon date by the Cambridge Sub-department of Quaternary Research gave added stimulus to the work. Excavation revealed quantities of painted as well as of rusticated pottery, clay figurines, including some with coffee-bean eyes and stone studs, possibly nose-plugs, all of which were consistent with an Early Neolithic attribution.[6] The archaeological finds pointed to close

53 Mycenae, 1953: left to right, Helen Wace, Alan Wace, an American student, George Huxley, Lisa Wace, Linda Witherill, Lord William Taylour and a second student

analogies with material from southern Yugoslavia. Although a full report is still awaited, the importance of the discoveries at Nea Nikomedeia is brought out in a brief illustrated summary covering both seasons written by Robert Rodden and his wife,[7] who as Judith Wilkins had taken the Cambridge Tripos in 1958. Among the Cambridge students to share in the dig were two, Colin Renfrew and John Nandris, who in due course contributed notably to the prehistory of south-east Europe, Renfrew to the Cyclades in particular and Nandris to the Balkans. A notable and extremely helpful member of the party was R. W. Hutchinson a former Curator of Knossos, who had only recently retired from a lectureship in Classical Archaeology at Cambridge. Another was Eric Higgs, in charge of the animal remains recovered from the site. Already Higgs was dreaming of much earlier occupation by prehistoric man in Greece, while camping in his Land-Rover on the mountains overlooking the plain.

In the summer of 1962, between the two campaigns at Nea Nikomedeia, he had led the first Cambridge expedition to northern Greece in quest of Palaeolithic man. Although Macedonia itself proved disappointing, despite finding what could be claimed as the oldest artefact yet unearthed in Greece, a hand-axe of Acheulian type from Palaiokastron the expedition recovered abundant traces of Middle Palaeolithic flints in Epirus, notably in the Red Beds at Kokkinopilos.[8] During the ensuing years Eric Higgs and his fellow workers were able to show that this part of Greece was among the richest fields of palaeolithic archaeology between western Europe and the Ukraine. Excavations in the cave of Asprokhaliko revealed a well-defined Upper Palaeolithic stratified in several levels above an industry of Kokkinopilos type. In the third season a rich Upper Palaeolithic succession was found in the cave of Kastritsa overlooking the south shore of the lake of Ioannina. The need to establish the relationships between the successive phases of human settlement and the evolution of the physical environment was well recognized, and to this end Higgs was careful to introduce a team of experts in different branches of Quaternary research, drawing on London and the Netherlands as well as Cambridge.[9] The prospects opened up by Higgs and his colleagues in Epirus have since been more fully realized by a younger generation. The lead has been taken by Geoff Bailey who secured a first in the Cambridge Tripos in 1970 and currently holds a University Lectureship in the Cambridge Department. Revision of the Kastritsa material[10] and the systematic excavation of Klithi, an entirely new site in a adjacent gorge,[11] give every promise of making Greece one of the key territories of Pleistocene Europe.

As well as working on mainland Greece, Cambridge prehistorians have also operated in the islands, notably in Crete and the Cyclades. Until John Evans started to excavate in the Neolithic deposits, which Arthur Evans had recognized under the successive Minoan levels at Knossos, little was known about the predecessors of the Minoans. John Evans, who had taken a first in the Cambridge Tripos of 1949, and been appointed to the chair of Prehistoric Archaeology at the London Institute in 1956, carried out excavations between 1957 and 1960 and again in 1969 which gave a much more complete picture of the pre-Minoan culture. In terms of radiocarbon, Neolithic people had begun to settle at Knossos around 6000 B.C. and as far as we know they were among the first to occupy Crete. Excavation revealed signs of primitive dwellings as well as evidence of potting, weaving, tree-felling and farming. It also showed that the Neolithic Cretans were using obsidian obtained from Melos and made human figurines of fired clay and stone. In the midst of the Neolithic campaign at Knossos another Cambridge prehistorian, this time trained in the Department of Classics, Peter Warren, discovered and excavated for the first time a settlement dating from Arthur Evans' Early Minoan II as recognized at Knossos. While holding a Research Fellowship at Corpus Christi College, Warren excavated the site of Myrtos on the south coast of Crete and published the results fully and promptly.[13]

John Evans' next excavation in Greece was carried out in partnership with Colin Renfrew at Saliagos in the Cyclades.[14] Although now a small island between Paros and Antiparos, Saliagos was still attached to the latter as a peninsula at the time of the prehistoric settlement. The potential of the site was recognized by Colin Renfrew, who took a first in the Tripos of 1962, in the course of a routine survey undertaken for his doctoral research on the Neolithic and Early Bronze Age cultures of the Cyclades. A feature of the Saliagos excavations of 1964–5 is that they followed the usual Cambridge practice of including undergraduates who later made careers in prehistoric archaeology. These included in this case John Clegg, who later became a lecturer at Sydney, Ian Kinnes now an Assistant Keeper in the British Museum, and Andrew Fleming, who lectures at Sheffield University.

One reason why Renfrew was attracted to the site was the presence among the archaeological debris exposed on the surface of obsidian, a substance which had already engaged his interest as a clue to contacts within the Aegean world. By working with J. R. Cann, a Cambridge petrologist, he had shown that the sources of obsidian could often be inferred by noting their trace elements. In particular he felt confident that Melos was a frequent source of supply in the Aegean.[15] In the course of his doctoral research Renfrew identified a number of features likely to prove significant, among them Cycladic figurines.[16] As he showed in his book of 1972,[17] Renfrew regarded such things less for themselves than as clues to the development of Cycladic cultures. Between 1974 and 1977, while holding the chair of Archaeology at Southampton, Renfrew undertook excavations at Phylakopi on Melos which resulted in the discovery of a Mycenaean sanctuary.[18] In some respects this new sanctuary and its contents rivalled that previously discovered at Mycenae by Lord William Taylour.

Meanwhile John Ward-Perkins, an Oxford graduate who was appointed Director of the British School at Rome after the war and enjoyed a long tenure (1946–74), was well apprised of the need to study the prehistoric antecedents of the Roman state. Under Mortimer Wheeler's guidance at the London Museum he had made his reputation on the prehistoric Iron Age as well as on Roman Britain. During his last twenty years or so at Rome one of his main interests was to study the intensification of settlement of the territories of Veii, a city north of Rome, as far back as the Bronze Age. It was his conviction that prehistoric research was crucial to an understanding of the Roman world. He was succeeded as Director by David Whitehouse, who had taken the Cambridge Tripos in 1963, after holding a Rome Scholarship and a Wainwright Fellowship at Oxford. His wife, Ruth, who had taken a first in the Cambridge Tripos of 1964, made the earliest agricultural communities of southern Italy her subject for postgraduate research. Although mainly confined to the distribution in time and space of the pottery made by the Neolithic farmers,[19] her work still helped to draw attention to the prehistoric antecedents of Rome. Another Cambridge prehistorian to cultivate Italian

54   Colin Renfrew at Stonehenge

archaeology was David Trump, who had held a Rome Scholarship in Classical Studies after obtaining a first in the Cambridge Tripos of 1954. Working at the time he did it is perhaps less surprising that he directed attention almost entirely to the assemblages of artefacts which he assigned to the Middle and Late Apennine Cultures.[20]

The recent secondment of Graeme Barker from the Department of Archaeology and Prehistory at Sheffield to serve as Director of the British School at Rome points to a further advance by directing attention to territories and economies. Graeme Barker had taken the Cambridge Tripos in 1969. As an Associate of the British Academy project on the Early History of Agriculture, he shared the view that the advance of prehistory at that time involved paying greater attention to economies than to artefacts and attending to territories rather than to particular archaeological sites,[21] interests reflected both in his early papers and in his recent book.[22] While engaged in postgraduate research for his doctorate he had already pursued research on the economic prehistory of central Italy and in the course of this he had won the full support of John Ward-Perkins.

Apart from Gibraltar, the scene of Dorothy Garrod's first independent excavation, the only chance for Cambridge prehistorians to dig in Europe on British soil was offered by the Maltese islands. The foundations of Maltese archaeology had of course been laid by Themistocles Zammitt, who was Director of the Royal Museum in Malta from 1904 to 1935. The need for taking another look was signalled by the appointment of John Ward-Perkins as Professor of Archaeology in Malta, but this did not occur until the eve of the war, which claimed his active services. The turning point in Maltese prehistory came in 1952, when John Evans, then a Research Fellow of Pembroke College, was invited to catalogue the prehistoric antiquities of the islands.[23] Although this project was not fully realized until the publication of his book by the Athlone Press of London University in 1971, Evans was able to propose a five-fold division of Maltese prehistory as early as 1953.[24] One result was the appointment of another Cambridge graduate, David Trump, whose activities in Italy have already been noted, to the Curatorship of the Royal Museum in Malta for a five-year period (1958–63). During this time David Trump took the opportunity to make a number of key excavations, notably at Borġ im-Nadur and Bahrija in 1959 and at Skorba in 1960–4. As a result he was able to modify Evans' classification by adding two phases and transposing the chronological succession of another two.[25]

The situation for British prehistorians was very different in the rest of Europe. There were no colonial outposts and no British Institutes or Schools to prepare the ground. Field-work and excavation were very much in the hands of the various national authorities and Britons could take part only in close conjunction with colleagues in the several nations. The desire to undertake research on the Continent was certainly strong at Cambridge. At a time when Cambridge teaching in archaeology took shape the insular phase of British archaeology was already fading though still prevalent in the country at large. The concentration on Palaeolithic studies by Miles Burkitt and Dorothy Garrod was enough to dispel this for Cambridge, since for much of the Pleistocene Britain was geographically part of Europe. It never occurred to Burkitt or for that matter Reginald Smith of the British Museum to doubt that culturally speaking Britain was any other than a province of Europe. The first full-time Disney Professor was learned in the archaeology of imperial Russia, and for their later prehistory his students depended to a large extent on books written by Gordon Childe, an Australian whose reputation was founded on his understanding of European and above all of central European archaeology. Professor Chadwick's pupils who read Section B of the Cambridge Tripos were taught to think of the Celtic, Norse and Anglo-Saxon peoples in their European setting. Toty de Navarro, who retained his American citizenship, taught the Bronze Age very largely in terms of France, Germany and northern Europe. British archaeologists in general remained astonishingly provincial in outlook until after the Second World War, even though many of them were only too ready to attribute changes in British prehistory to invasion from the continent. Cambridge teaching from the outset emphasized the need to view British prehistory in relation to Europe prehistory as a whole, just as, as we saw in the previous chapter, it stressed the need to study prehistory as the unwritten history of the human race and not merely of Europeans and their closest neighbours. McBurney had a wide grasp of the Palaeolithic settlement of Europe, Clark specialized in the Scandinavian stone age, Daniel covered the megalithic phenomenon from the Mediterranean to the West Baltic and de Navarro specialized in the Early Iron Age of the Alpine zone of Europe.

Many of those who entered on postgraduate research in prehistoric archaeology at Cambridge not unnaturally followed their example and chose topics that involved travel, museum study and occasionally excavation on the European mainland. As examples one may cite the last three research students to come under my own supervision on retiring from the Disney chair. All three addressed themselves to the economies prevailing in different parts of Scandinavia in the course of the Stone Age. Each needed and received local assistance to pursue their research. Peter Rowley-Conwy, who took the tripos in 1973, and is now a research fellow of Clare Hall, worked under the supervision of Poul Kjaerum of Aarhus University while in Denmark and was given access to data recovered by Søren Andersen from his excavations. Marek Zvelebil and Priscilla Renouf came to Cambridge as graduate students, the former from Sheffield, the latter from Memorial University, Newfoundland. Marek Zvelebil was helped by his Finnish supervisor, Torsten Edgren, to gain access to the local evidence and as he acknowledged in his public dissertation he was aided by many other Finns.[27] Priscilla Renouf depended for her part on her Norwegian supervisor, Povl Simonsen of Tromsø, through whose good offices she was able to excavate the Nyelv Nedre Vest site on the south shore of Varanger Fjord in northern Norway.[28] Under a different supervisor, Iain Davidson, who graduated in 1970 and came under the strong influence of Eric Higgs' territorial approach to the study of prehistoric economies, concentrated on the analysis of biological data assembled by Spanish excavators and dated by radiocarbon from palaeolithic sites in eastern Spain. This he interpreted in the light of his own analysis of the potential of the territory from which it had been recovered by Spanish prehistorians.[29]

Effective studies of continental material from temperate Europe other than that available in public museums inevitably called for collaboration with European colleagues. When Dorothy Garrod herself took early retirement to engage in research she joined forces with Mlle de St Mathurin in order to explore the Upper Palaeolithic reliefs of Angles sur l'Anglin. Again, Lawrence Barfield, who graduated from Cambridge in 1958, began his postgraduate career by working at Bonn as assistant to the Professor of Prehistory and later as excavator for the Landesmuseum. Since joining the Department of Archaeology and Ancient History at Birmingham he has concentrated on the Neolithic cultures of northern Italy, where he has conducted excavations with Italian colleagues.[30] John Nandris, who took the Cambridge Tripos in 1962, followed by a Ph.D, has continued to develop his interest in Balkan prehistory, notably with the First Neolithic, since joining the London Institute of Archaeology as a lecturer.[31] As a final instance, Robin Dennell was able to secure the plant samples he needed only by establishing effective collaboration with Bulgarian colleagues.[32]

This is not to say that British archaeology was neglected. Far from being overlooked it was seen to be one of the main avenues for the employment of Cambridge graduates in archaeology. Since the war social change and technical advances have combined to enhance the need for professionals. Modern archaeology is not only expensive. It also calls for the long-term commitment of special knowledge and skills. Amateurs may still make important contributions. They may even play a vital role in observing and reporting clues brought to light in the course of day-to-day activities. Furthermore, amateurs of archaeology may be able to contribute special knowledge from fields in which they may be expert and this may help in the interpretation of archaeological traces. The fact remains that major advances in archaeology can no longer be sustained without the help of professionals and of the organizations that deploy them. For the most part these comprise the public services charged with the investigation, preservation and recording of ancient monuments, museums, and universities equipped to train professionals and advance research and understanding. On the other hand some projects are so demanding that they generate and sustain organizations of their own for conducting research and preparing for publication.

The attempts to recover the archaeology of Winchester and York are cases in point. At first sight it might seem odd that the directors of such enterprises concerned with two of the most important historic centres of England should have been products of the Cambridge Archaeological and Anthropological Tripos, both as it happens in the same year, 1961. Yet in view of what other graduates who passed through the same department have done in other parts of the world this should not be surprising. If David Oates could address himself to Babylonian and Assyrian structures in Mesopotamia, David Stronach Median and Parthian ones in Iran, and David Whitehouse and Neville Chittick Islamic ports on the coasts of the Persian Gulf or East Africa, this only confirms the value of prehistoric archaeology as it was presented at Cambridge. It was not so much that the Cambridge course offered a variety of options so much as that it was concerned first and foremost with the nature of archaeology as a means of recovering the unwritten past. The methods used to further this were and are equally valid regardless of the degree of literacy of the societies concerned. On the other hand archaeology faces its sternest test and evokes its most effective responses when confronted with traces of communities totally lacking written sources. Anyone trained in prehistoric archaeology is or ought to be all the better equipped to deal with material illuminated by ampler evidence. Again, the relatively smaller scale of most prehistoric communities accustoms archaeologists to view them in functional and structural terms. Moreover in the absence of written records the prehistorian is driven to resort to the natural sciences and develop ways of applying these to the fuller understanding of his data. Many of the methods developed by natural scientists for dating and interpreting archaeological finds can often be applied with even greater effect to the material traces of more complex societies.

Martin Biddle, who led the Winchester campaign, gave signal indications of his practical ability as an archaeologist by directing the excavations at Nonsuch Palace, Ewell, during his first long vacation as an undergraduate in the summer of 1959.[33] The project, in which more than five hundred persons took part, revealed plans of both courts of the structure built by Henry VIII, no surface trace of which remained, as well as recovering traces of the rich plasterwork that once covered the inner face of one of them. He was still an undergraduate when the Society of Antiquaries invited him to direct the new phase in the exploration of Winchester on behalf of the revived Winchester Exploration Committee. Although excavation only uncovered some 2% of the area within the city walls between 1961 and 1967, it brought an immense accession of knowledge about the antecedents and development of one of the country's most important medieval cities. A leading feature of the work described in the Albert Reckitt Lecture for 1983 is the way in which its progress has been documented.[34] The total information recovered has been systematically stored in the Historic Resources Centre of the Winchester

City Museum. The obligation to publish was recognized from an early stage and in 1968 the Winchester Research Unit was set up to produce a series of Winchester Studies. Of the eleven volumes planned three had already been published at the time of the Reckitt Lecture, a fourth was in print, and several others were at an advanced stage of preparation. Between them they will cover the pre-Roman and Roman phases of settlement, the Anglo-Saxon minster and the medieval city, ranging from its domestic life, including the health and diet of its citizens, to the functioning of the Castle and of Wolvesey Palace.

Peter Addyman was a University Lecturer at Southampton when persuaded by Maurice Barley, chairman of the joint working party of the Council for British Archaeology and the Yorkshire Philosophical Society, to move to York and take on the Directorship of the York Archaeological Trust.[35] By deploying the techniques of modern archaeology and using a

55   Martin Biddle

wide range of scientific aids the Trust has succeeded in throwing an exceptionally full light on the Viking settlement at Coppergate. By making the discoveries, including the wooden houses preserved in the water-logged deposits, available for public display, and devising original methods for giving visitors access to the archaeological finds in such a way as to enhance their understanding of the Viking community, Peter Addyman and his colleagues have not only heightened appreciation of Viking Jorvik but have ensured its future by putting it on a secure financial basis.

Valuable contributions have also been made to British archaeology by graduates of the Cambridge department who joined one or other of the Royal Commissions responsible for making inventories of ancient monuments, or the Inspectorates concerned with their protection. In some cases their energies were fully absorbed in contributing to the collective advance of archaeology. Others found occasion to make individual contributions as well. Among those to join the English Commission were R. M. Butler, A. P. Baggs, who later transferred to the Victoria County History, and R. D. Gem, who later divided his time between the National Council for the Care of Churches and other archaeological work, men who graduated respectively in 1951, 1956 and 1966. Two joined the Welsh Commission, G. M. White, who took the Diploma in 1932, after the Classical Tripos, and Christopher Houlder who graduated in 1950. Mollie White (later Mrs Clark) assisted at

56   Peter Addyman (right) amid the clutter of a construction site in York

Giant's Hills and Arminghall and later excavated on her own account in West Sussex.[36] Christopher Houlder made a noteworthy contribution by excavating the Neolithic stone implement factory at Mynydd Rhiw in Caernarvonshire.[37]

The first Cambridge prehistorian to join the Inspectorate of Ancient Monuments was J. R. C. Hamilton, who completed the Cambridge Tripos in 1939. During his early phase while based in Edinburgh Hamilton published the results of excavating two major sites in the Shetlands,[38] but the latter part of his career was spent in London supervising rescue archaeology and ensuring publication. Mike Thompson, who graduated in 1950 and ended up as Chief Inspector for Wales and Monmouth, made several contributions of note to prehistoric archaeology during his spare time. He learned Russian, like a good Pembroke man, so as to make the work of Russian archaeologists available to English readers. This allowed him to translate three of the principle archaeological works published in Russia[39] since Ellis Minns wrote his *Scythians and Greeks*. Thompson also wrote a useful book dealing with the contribution of General Pitt Rivers.[40] John Hurst, a year junior at Cambridge, had already begun his card index of deserted medieval villages as an undergraduate. The Deserted Medieval Village Research Group which he founded did much to promote interest in what proved to be a useful clue to economic and demographic change in medieval history. At the same time he has made himself an authority on medieval pottery.[41] Above all he and his group have persevered relentlessly since 1948 with excavation and field survey at Wharram Percy on the Yorkshire Wolds in order to establish its prehistoric and Roman antecedents and trace its development during historic times up to its abandonment around 1500.[42]

Museums have always offered careers to prehistoric archaeologists, and the most prestigious of these is the British Museum. Since the Second World War the Museum has been obliged to expand its staff to cope with the increased specialization of knowledge and the vastly heavier burden of satisfying lay interest. During the period covered by this book Cambridge was a main source of supply. The first to join what is now the Department of Prehistoric and Romano-British Antiquities since the war was John Brailsford, who had taken Sections A and B of the Cambridge Tripos culminating in 1939 with a first. Before taking early retirement for reasons of health Brailsford made some notable contributions to the Early Iron Age in Britain. His publication of the pottery and small finds from the farming settlement at Little Woodbury[43] rounded off an initiative of the Prehistoric Society that has in some ways revolutionized our approach to the Iron Age in southern Britain. Probably his greatest interest has been in the metal objects symbolizing Celtic chieftainship.[44] The illustrated book displaying masterpieces of British Iron Age smiths in the British Museum[45] reveals a depth of feeling and understanding that remind us of the loss sustained by his premature retirement.

Another early recruit was Gale Sieveking, who took the Cambridge Tripos in 1949 and joined the British Museum in 1962 after serving as Curator of Museums, Federation of Malaya. Throughout his time in the British Museum Sieveking, who ended up as a Deputy Keeper, concentrated on the Stone Age. One of the projects in which he was involved was to establish the context of the Lower Palaeolithic implements in the Pleistocene deposits at High Lodge, Mildenhall,[46] of which the museum housed extensive collections. Excavation established the stratigraphy but no agreement has yet been reached with geological opinion about the precise context of the sequence.

57   John Hurst (left) and his long-time collaborator, Maurice Beresford of Leeds University, during excavations at Wharram Percy

Another topic was the possibility of defining the sources of flint by determining trace elements, as had previously been done for axes stemming from stone quarries. This research was closely linked with the British Museum's new survey and excavations at Grimes Graves, Norfolk.[47]

Ian Longworth, who took a first in 1957 and obtained his doctorate in 1960, joined the Department after a brief spell in the National Museum of Antiquities at Edinburgh. In 1973 he succeeded John Brailsford as Keeper of the Department of Prehistoric and Romano-British Antiquities. As head of a rapidly expanding department reinforced by research assistants but faced with the need to devise new displays for the public and meet diverse problems of conservation and dating, Ian Longworth still found time and energy enough to make distinguished contributions to learning. In doing so he was sustained by the conviction held since he was a research student that prehistoric hand-made pottery was a notable embodiment of continuity, while at the same time being a sensitive indicator of regional tastes. His early commitment to Neolithic and Bronze Age pottery was reflected in his detailed and comprehensive treatment of the Neolithic wares from the henge monument at Durrington Walls[48] and above all in his great corpus of some 2,255 collared urns of the British Bronze Age.[49]

Three men, each of whom had taken the Cambridge Tripos followed by research doctorates, joined Ian Longworth's department. Of these the senior, Ian Stead, graduated in 1958 and later that year made trial excavations with local support in an Early Iron Age hill-fort at Grimthorpe, Yorkshire. More extensive excavations at the site were organized in 1961–2 by the Inspectorate of Ancient Monuments, of which he had by then become a member. He later transferred to the Department of Prehistoric and Romano-British Antiquities, of which he is now Deputy Keeper. His interest still centres on the Early Iron Age. His Early Iron Age excavations in east Yorkshire[50] and in the Ardennes and Champagne[51] have done much to enhance the value of the Museum's existing collections as well as to advance knowledge in general. As far as Britain is concerned his most important work has probably been the recovery of La Tène burials under square-ditched barrows of a type made visible in their thousands in eastern Yorkshire air photography. More recently Ian Stead has been prominent in bringing out the importance of the prehistoric bog corpse from Lindow Moss.[52]

The other two, Ian Kinnes and Timothy Potter, both took the Cambridge Tripos in 1966. Kinnes has specialized so far on megaliths, having made a total excavation of the tomb of Les Fouillages, Guernsey,[53] whereas Potter, who made important excavations in Etruria while attached to the British School at Rome,[54] is responsible for the Romano-British aspect of the Department's work.

The British Museum has also recruited products of the Cambridge Tripos for other Departments. These include the new Keeper of the Department of

Western Asiatic Antiquities, T. C. Mitchell, who graduated in 1954, and D. S. W. Kidd, who took a first in 1970 and joined the Department of Medieval and Later Antiquities. Finally, the present Director, Sir David Wilson, took the Cambridge Tripos in 1953 and came to the Museum after a distinguished career in Anglo-Saxon and Medieval Archaeology at University College, London. Sir David has wisely continued his scholarly interests[55] while meeting the heavy demands imposed by his official duties in the Museum.

Other graduates from the Cambridge department to join museums in London included H. G. Wakefield, who took a first in 1937 and entered the Victoria and Albert Museum where he became Head of Circulation, and Keith Muckleroy who joined the Institute of Maritime Archaeology in St Andrews and later the staff of the National Maritime Museum after gaining a first in 1974. In St Andrews he wrote a book which, in the words of the doyen of the subject in Britain, 'for the first time established the place of maritime archaeology as an important part of archaeological research'. His early death has been a serious loss to this branch of archaeology.[56] Oxford museums also proved attractive. Andrew Sherratt, who took the Tripos in 1968 followed by a research doctorate, entered the Department of Antiquities in the Ashmolean where he has maintained the tradition of combining scholarly production with the discharge of curatorial duties.[57] Others joined

58   Ian Stead with one of the Iron Age chariot burials at Driffield, Yorkshire

the Pitt Rivers Museum after holding archaeological posts in Africa. Bernard Fagg became Curator in 1964 after a long spell in Nigeria and held the post until ill-health led to his early retirement. Ray Inskeep, whose previous post was at the University of Cape Town, is still an Assistant Curator as well as holding a University Lectureship in Prehistory and Archaeology. Notable contributions have also been made to other museums in Britain by Cambridge graduates. These include Euan Mackie[58] at the Hunterian in Glasgow and Rainbird Clarke who obtained a first at Cambridge in 1936 and presided over Norwich Castle Museum as Curator until his premature death. While he was in charge he made the Museum a veritable magnet for new discoveries, which he was careful to make widely available by prompt publication.[59]

Yet the most important service rendered by Cambridge to prehistory was not to staff the various services concerned with the preservation and display of monuments and antiquities, important though these were. It was to bring prehistory to the point at which it became acceptable as a subject for teaching and research in university institutions and to provide the necessary staff. The contributions made by Cambridge in this respect overseas have already been

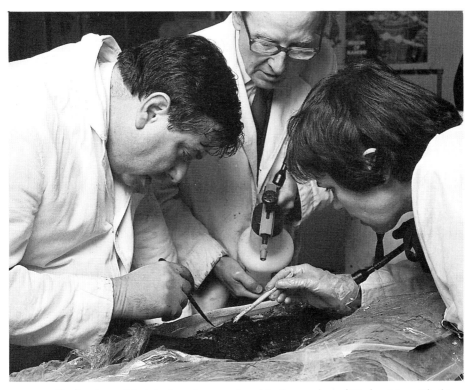

59   Stead examining the Iron Age man found in the peat bog of Lindow Moss, Cheshire, 1984. Conducting the autopsy is the surgeon James Bourke

noted. In respect of Britain it should be stressed that in the case of staffing the influence from Cambridge was almost confined to England. Edinburgh, Cardiff and Belfast established their own departments of archaeology in 1926, 1958 and 1963. Furthermore it did not greatly affect those English universities where archaeology grew up as a component of classics or history and in which prehistoric archaeology has generally played a comparatively minor role. Within the triangle of Yorkshire, the Isle of Wight and North Foreland, which includes the universities of Oxford, London, Sheffield and Southampton as well as Cambridge itself it was strong and cumulatively overwhelming.

One may begin with London where the Institute of Archaeology was already established before the Second World War.[60] The process of re-staffing began with Gordon Childe's retirement in 1956. In order to ensure the smooth running of the Institute in its new premises it was plainly necessary to appoint as director a senior archaeologist who could be relied upon to act as a sound administrator, and the university was fortunate to acquire just such a man in W. P. Grimes. In the short term on the other hand it was hardly possible to replace Childe as a prehistorian of European, indeed of world renown. The University took the obvious course and appointed the most brilliant young man it could find to fill the chair of European Prehistory. It chose John D. Evans, who had taken a first in the Cambridge Tripos of 1949 and been elected a Research Fellow of Pembroke, the college of Minns and Wace. Before Grimes retired he presided over the widening of the Institute's intake in 1968 to include undergraduates. When Evans took over as Director in 1973 he was soon faced with the prospect of increasing financial stringency. The Institute was only able to survive until the recent amalgamation with University College by virtue of attracting students from all over the world. A main reason why they came was the excellence of the teaching and here a conspicuous part was played by academics who like the new Director himself emanated from Cambridge. When Evans became Director his place as Professor of European Prehistory was filled by Roy Hodson who had joined the Institute as a lecturer after taking the Cambridge Diploma in Prehistoric Archaeology.[61] Hodson brought a keen sense of the value of mathematics, something which had been enhanced through his continued contact with Professor D. G. Kendall, Director of the Statistical Laboratory at Cambridge. One of his lecturers, John Nandris, who had taken the Cambridge Tripos in 1962, has specialized as we have already noted in the prehistory of eastern Europe and notably of the Balkans. For some years the Old Stone Age was covered by John Waechter, one of Dorothy Garrod's former research students. New World archaeology was taught by Warwick Bray, who held a joint lectureship with the Centre for Latin-American Studies. The chair of West Asiatic archaeology was filled by another Cambridge product, David Oates, who succeeded Seton Lloyd on the latter's retirement. Now that the Institute is part of University College it may be noted that the former Reader of Anglo-Saxon Archaeology and later Professor of Medieval Archaeology, at present Director of the British Museum, and the present Reader, James Graham-Campbell,[62] who took the Tripos in 1968, were both products of the Cambridge department.

The Rankin Lectureship in Prehistoric Archaeology in the School of Archaeological and Oriental Studies at Liverpool was held from 1948 until his death in 1976 by Terence Powell who took the Cambridge Tripos in 1937. Powell served during his first five years as Honorary Secretary of the Prehistoric Society and was President from 1970 to 1974. His main scholarly interests were British megalithic tombs and the graphic arts of the prehistoric Britons and Europeans.[63] This was reflected in his fierce opposition to the materialist trend of much modern European prehistory. Although never strong he went to some trouble to provide field experience for his pupils. His successor, Joan Taylor, was also a product of Cambridge to which she came as a postgraduate student from the United States. The subject of her research was gold-working during the Bronze Age in Britain and continental Europe. Since working at Liverpool she has published a corpus of Bronze Age gold-work from Britain.[64]

The first English universities outside Cambridge and Liverpool to mount courses in prehistoric archaeology for undergraduates were Sheffield and Southampton. Sheffield began to recruit in 1965 and was lucky to attract Colin Renfrew, who had taken his research doctorate on the prehistoric cultures of the Cyclades and been elected to a Research Fellowship at St John's that same year. His lively teaching and prowess in research ensured his early promotion to a Senior Lectureship and in 1972 to a Readership. Renfrew was accompanied when he came to Sheffield by his newly married wife, the former Jane Ewbank who had taken the Cambridge Tripos in 1964 and had since embarked on postgraduate research. Her subject, the palaeo-ethnobotany of Neolithic Greece and Bulgaria,[65] was happily compatible with her husband's field-work in the East Mediterranean. In 1972 Colin Renfrew left to take up the chair at Southampton vacated by Barry Cunliffe on his election to the Oxford chair of European Archaeology. Meanwhile the department at Sheffield was strengthened by half a dozen lecturers from Cambridge. Paul Mellars had joined the Sheffield department as a lecturer after obtaining a first in the Cambridge Tripos in the same year as Cunliffe and Renfrew. Mellars, who has since been retrieved by Cambridge, earned promotion at Sheffield to a Senior Lectureship on account of his exemplary research on the economy relating to the Stone Age shell-mounds of Oronsay in the Inner Hebrides, work on which he focussed the special knowledge of experts in several branches of Quaternary research.[66] Andrew Fleming, who graduated at Cambridge in 1965, brought a special interest in land utilization and was particularly concerned to see what inferences could be drawn from surface features, notably those exposed in the existing moorland regions of England.[67] John Collis, who took the Cambridge Tripos a year later, had a particularly close concern with the Early Iron Age societies of Britain and continental Europe.[68] Robin Dennell and Graeme Barker both took the Cambridge Tripos in 1969 and spent some time with Eric Higgs working as associates of the Early History of Agriculture Project. Robin Dennell specialized in the plant resources of prehistoric communities, but since becoming established at Sheffield has developed a more comprehensive interest in the economies of prehistoric Europe.[69] Graeme Barker's study of land use in central Italy since prehistoric times noted earlier in this chapter led to his secondment from Sheffield to direct the British School at Rome and pursue a subject pioneered by a former Director.[70] Finally one of Sheffield's own graduates, Marek Zvelebil, returned as a lecturer after gaining his doctorate at Cambridge for research on the interface between hunters and farmers during prehistoric times in northern Europe.[71]

When Southampton decided to start a chair of Archaeology in 1966 it chose Barry Cunliffe who had taken a first at Cambridge in 1962 along with Colin Renfrew and others. While still an undergraduate he had begun the excavation at Fishbourne, just outside Chichester,[72] that revealed the Roman palace, and he completed this while holding his first post, a lectureship in the Department of Classics at Bristol. While at Bristol he had also explored the Roman baths at Bath[73] and began to excavate the Saxon Shore Fort at Portchester. While holding the chair at Southampton he excavated the Roman and Anglo-Saxon phases at this crucial site[74] as well as publishing reports on Roman Bath and the first-century palace at Fishbourne. For most of his time at Southampton he had the assistance as a lecturer of Peter Addyman, who had taken the Cambridge Tripos in 1961 along with Martin Biddle. After a five-year stint at Southampton Addyman moved to York to take on the direction of the Archaeological Trust.

The vacancy at Southampton caused by Cunliffe's move to Oxford brought Colin Renfrew from Sheffield to fill his place. During his tenure of the Southampton chair, which lasted until he returned to Cambridge as Disney Professor in 1981, Renfrew continued to be extremely active both as author and excavator. He carried out important excavations on Orkney[75] between 1972 and 1974 before returning to the Aegean to undertake what proved to be an exciting excavation at Phylakopi on Melos.[76] As a writer he concentrated on the dynamics of change, on which he edited and contributed extensively.[77] Among those appointed to lectureships in his time at Southampton was Stephen Shennan who took the Cambridge Tripos in 1971. His wife is Susan Lathbury, who graduated at Southampton and took a Cambridge Ph.D on a topic of social archaeology,[78] the theme of Renfrew's Southampton inaugural. It is significant that Stephen Shennan has recently co-edited a volume of contributions on social structure in prehistoric Europe with Colin Renfrew,[79] who had already published a collected series of his own essays on social archaeology.[80] A later recruit to Southampton was Clive Gamble, who had taken the Cambridge Tripos the year after Shennan and undertook research there on the relationship between animal communities and prehistoric economies in western Europe. At Southampton he has so far concentrated on the economic strategies employed by the prehistoric inhabitants of Europe during the Old Stone Age.[81]

When Barry Cunliffe moved to the chair of European Archaeology at Oxford he found himself in a university where prehistoric archaeology was very differently situated. It was not an undergraduate subject. Instead it was a

60   Barry Cunliffe guiding visitors around the excavations at Hengistbury Head, Dorset

resource drawn upon to serve scholars in fields ranging from anthropology, history, classics, oriental studies and a number of natural sciences as well as providing teaching to a limited number of postgraduates. Since he was not troubled with having to teach undergraduates he was free to complete the publication of Portchester and to undertake the excavation of two major sites of the British Iron Age, Danebury and Hengistbury Head.[82] The Ashmolean Museum close by, which ministered to a wide range of interests, was a separate institution. Another centre of great importance more particularly for early prehistory was the Research Laboratory for Archaeology and the History of Art, which brings to bear the resources of physics and chemistry. One of its prime tasks is to advance scientific dating methods including radiocarbon analysis. The staff member responsible for ensuring the correct source of archaeological samples was until recently John Gowlett, a specialist in early prehistory who had taken a first at Cambridge in 1972.

Relations between prehistory, the human sciences and biology are cultivated by the Faculty of Anthropology and Geography and in particular by the Department of Ethnology and Prehistory situated in the Pitt Rivers Museum. Teaching in prehistory for the Postgraduate Diploma in Prehistory, one of three stemming from the Diploma of Anthropology devised in 1907 by E. B. Tylor, a contemporary of Haddon and virtual founder of ethnology at Oxford, is given by a staff of University Lecturers in Prehistoric Archaeology. All three were trained at Cambridge – Ray Inskeep whose work in Africa has already been noticed, and who combines his lectureship with the Assistant Curatorship of the Pitt Rivers Museum, Denis Britton, and Derek Roe who took a first in the Tripos of 1961. The last mentioned combines his lectureship with the Honorary Directorship of the Donald Baden-Powell Quaternary Research Centre, which although forming part of the Pitt Rivers Museum occupies its own building and serves as a focus of palaeolithic prehistory at Oxford.[85] When the Board of Anthropology and Geography appoints a supervisor for a candidate in prehistory, it chooses as a rule one of the three lecturers but it might also call upon the Professor of European Archaeology or Andrew Sherratt of the Ashmolean. All five are products of the Cambridge Faculty of Archaeology and Anthropology.

Prehistorians from Cambridge have taught the subject at several other English universities. Durham, where the present chair was founded only in 1972, acquired Anthony Harding, who graduated at Cambridge in 1969 and wrote his doctoral dissertation in 1972–3. Harding's standing in the field of Bronze Age Europe has already been established by two books, one a general text written with his former supervisor John Coles, the other addressed more specifically to the subject of his own research on the relations between the Mycenaeans and the rest of Europe.[86] Ruth Whitehouse, whose contributions to Italian prehistory have received notice earlier in this chapter, now directs archaeology courses for the Department of Classics and Archaeology

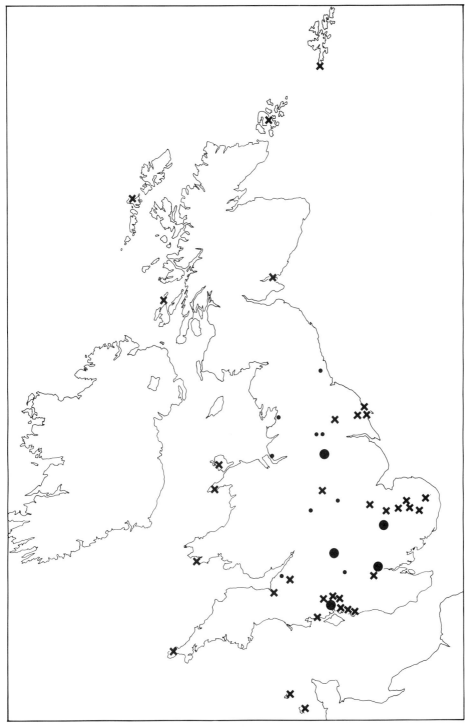

61   Map : Activities of Cambridge prehistorians in Britain
X Main excavations   ● ● Posts in universities

at Lancaster University which include field archaeology and laboratory work. A more pronounced emphasis on laboratory work is made by the School of Archaeological Sciences established at Bradford University, where Norman Hammond was foundation Senior Lecturer from 1975 to 1977 before moving to America and which has recruited two other Cambridge products, John Bintliff[87] and James Lewthwaite,[88] who graduated in 1971 and 1974 respectively. Both men have laid special emphasis on the links between environment, economy and settlement during prehistoric times. In the Midlands, Cambridge has provided two lecturers for the Department of Archaeology and Ancient History at Birmingham, J. J. Orchard who had previously been Assistant Director of the British School in Iraq and came as lecturer in Near Eastern Archaeology, and Lawrence Barfield, whose work in North Italy has already been noted. Stanley Thomas, who took the Cambridge Tripos in 1948 and spent some time in Sweden, where he assisted at Carl-Axel Althin's Ageröd excavations,[89] joined the Department of Archaeology at Leicester where he remained until his death. R. M. Jacobi took a lectureship at Lancaster and has recently transferred to Nottingham University. Finally, Bob Chapman, who took the Cambridge Tripos in 1971, joined the Department of Archaeology at Reading. While pursuing his own work[90] he has found time to act for a period (1980–4) as Honorary Secretary of the Prehistoric Society.

EPILOGUE

When Cambridge first began to offer courses in prehistoric archaeology to undergraduates there was virtually no call for professional prehistorians. The university established anthropology, which then included prehistory, as it still does in many parts of the world, not in order to meet a pressing vocational demand, but in response to a powerful idea. In the course of the nineteenth century thought had been transformed in many fields by the idea of evolution, the conviction that existing forms both in nature and society could best be understood as marking stages in a temporal process. It is significant that before there was any call for professional prehistorians support for the teaching of prehistoric archaeology in the context of anthropology came from humane scholars as well as from natural scientists in a wide range of disciplines.

The need for professional prehistorians first became perceptible in the aftermath of the First World War when public concern for the archaeological heritage began to be taken seriously in Britain and overseas. For much of the period covered in the present book Cambridge was one of the few universities equipped to produce the graduates needed to take up prehistoric archaeology as a career or provide the teaching required to produce a cadre of professionals. The number of candidates sitting for the archaeological option of the Cambridge Tripos in Archaeology and Anthropology, even when this was reshaped and widened by the new regulations adopted after the Second World War, remained small. For the first decade the number taking the new Part II and choosing the archaeology option averaged only half a dozen. In the second decade the numbers doubled and in the final years of the period up till 1974 there were around fifteen. Of this modest intake an exceptionally large proportion aimed at and attained professional careers in prehistoric archaeology. Not surprisingly academic standards were high. They reached a peak in the early 1960s. Of the eighteen who graduated in 1961 six obtained upper seconds and another a first. All seven of these became professional prehistorians. In 1962 no less than five of the dozen graduates were awarded firsts. These included the present Professors at Oxford, Cambridge and Otago as well as a University Lecturer at Cambridge.

The last twenty years have witnessed a marked increase in the academic provision for prehistoric archaeology. Archaeology, including in nearly every case prehistoric archaeology, is now taught in some twenty British universities for single honours degrees, as well as in two others in joint courses with other subjects. At the same time the subject has been widely adopted by universities in the English-speaking world beyond, notably in Australia, New Zealand, the United States, Canada, several African states and India. Between them these have sponsored research on an unprecedented scale and have made possible for the first time the development of a truly world prehistory based on archaeological findings. The success of Cambridge and other universities, many of them staffed by Cambridge graduates, means that the intake of students to archaeological courses far exceeds the likely opportunities to pursue prehistoric archaeology as a career. This is true despite the increase in opportunities becoming available as more countries enter upon a post-industrial phase in which leisure activities, many of them geared to further education, provide increasingly varied avenues of employment. The growth of a wider appreciation for prehistoric archaeology has created the opportunity for its own range of professional employment. This stems from a greater concern for the archaeological heritage of different regions and the deployment of larger numbers of trained archaeologists in rescuing, recording and displaying the archaeological evidence, as well as the diffusion of knowledge about the prehistoric past in a variety of media. In many ways archaeology is exceptionally well placed to profit from modern conditions. It is labour-intensive without competing with established industries and it enriches the cherished environment by increasing its historical interest. Its use in youth training schemes, at present tentative, already points to one way in which it can help to solve the problem which besets modern societies able to satisfy material needs with a diminishing proportion of the population. At the same time the universities have taken a lead in calling for greater technical advances in the recovery of archaeological data and the refining of the concepts needed for throwing light on social development in the prehistoric past.

Despite the increased call for professional archaeologists it has long ceased to be realistic for university teachers of archaeology to pretend that their subject is any longer primarily vocational. The emergence of prehistoric archaeology at Cambridge in the context of anthropology described in this book occurred at what proved to be precisely the right moment in the history of the subject. Yet the very success of the pioneering phase at Cambridge has ensured that it can now be viewed in the context of another age. So long as the need to produce professionals exists – and as we have seen this is more likely to intensify than diminish – the subject will retain a vocational appeal, but increasingly archaeology is likely to be valued by universities primarily for its educational importance. History has traditionally been thought a suitable subject for the education of princes. It is a sign of the times that when the present Prince of Wales came up to Trinity he chose to take Part I of the

Archaeological and Anthropological Tripos in 1968 before going on to History to complete his Tripos. The fact that his younger brother Prince Edward took the same avenue at Jesus, taking Part I of the Archaeological and Anthropological Tripos in 1984, suggests that the initiative was found rewarding. On the face of it one might think that anyone programmed for the twenty-first century might well profit by approaching history from the wider background offered by archaeology and anthropology.

Prehistoric archaeology of the kind offered in greater detail in Part II of the Cambridge Tripos and now taught in different ways in so many universities offers a unique opportunity to view the world in a modern perspective. It not only emphasizes the degree to which human behaviour has been shaped by culture rather than merely by genetic endowment. It also displays the astonishing variety of patterns devised by people living at different times and places, at varying levels of social evolution and adapted to a wide range of ecological circumstances. The fruitful study of prehistory calls upon a great variety of interests, abilities and knowledge. One sign of the catholicity of its appeal is to be seen in the wide range of subjects with which it is paired in joint honour courses in British universities, notably ancient history, history, geography and English studies. In addition a few universities combine archaeology with natural science and one at least offers a single honours degree in archaeological science.

From the student's point of view one of the main attractions of prehistoric archaeology is the way it brings them even at an undergraduate level to the very brink of the unknown. Even by applying existing concepts and techniques great areas remain to be explored. By developing and applying new ones there are exciting prospects of enlarging and deepening knowledge about the prehistoric past and the ways in which human societies took shape and changed before they began to leave written records behind them in the comparatively recent past. At the same time the actual practice of archaeology provides scope for a wide range of skills and attributes. If the reconstruction of prehistory calls for high qualities of the imagination controlled by intellectual grasp and aesthetic awareness, the acquisition of the primary data involves practical aptitudes and a wide range of experience. Aerial reconnaissance, a wide range of ground survey methods and the ability acquired only by experience to interpret the sometimes evanescent indications of human activity in the more or less remote past are only a few of the skills and qualities likely to be involved in field archaeology. Again, excavation calls for an ability to work with a variety of natural scientists in the collection and analysis of finds and samples. A sensitivity to stylistic nuances is only one of many requirements when it comes to interpreting discoveries in terms of prehistory. Few subjects address a more searching appeal to the interests and abilities of students. Few can be more richly educational.

NOTES

Abbreviations

Ant. J.	*Antiquaries Journal*
BAR	British Archaeological Reports
BSA	*Annual of the British School at Athens*
CAH	*Cambridge Ancient History*
CBA	Council for British Archaeology
Geog. J.	*Geographical Journal*
J. Arch. Science	*Journal of Archaeological Science*
JHS	*Journal of Hellenic Studies*
JRAI	*Journal of the Royal Anthropological Institute*
PBA	*Proceedings of the British Academy*
Phil. Trans. Royal Soc.	*Philosophical Transactions of the Royal Society*
PPS	*Proceedings of the Prehistoric Society*
PPSEA	*Proceedings of the Prehistoric Society of East Anglia*
Proc. R.I.A.	*Proceedings of the Royal Irish Academy*
PSAS	*Proceedings of the Society of Antiquaries of Scotland*
UJA	*Ulster Journal of Archaeology*

1: Introductory

(1) This has recently been treated by P. Levine, *The Amateur and the Professional: Antiquarians, Historians and Archaeologists in Victorian England, 1838–1886*, Cambridge, 1986.

(2) O. G. S. Crawford, *The Long Barrows of the Cotswolds*, Gloucester, 1925, passim.

(3) Lt-Gen. A. H. L. F. Pitt-Rivers, *Excavations in Cranborne Chase*, vols. I–IV, privately printed, 1887–98.

(4) J. G. D. Clark, *Sir Mortimer and Indian Archaeology*, New Delhi, 1979.

(5) Sir A. Keith, *The Life-work of Lord Avebury (Sir John Lubbock), 1834–1913*, edited by the Hon. Mrs A. Grant Duff (daughter), London, 1924.

(6) Dr Thurnam presented his conclusions in seven lectures to the Society of Antiquaries between 1867 and 1870: *Archaeologia*, XLII, 1869, 161–244; XLIII, 1870, 285–552.

(7) Sir J. Evans, *The Ancient Stone Implements, Weapons and Ornaments of Great Britain*, London, 1872; *The Ancient Bronze Implements, Weapons, and Ornaments, of Great Britain and Ireland*, London, 1881.

(8) J. Evans, *Time and Chance: The Story of Arthur Evans and his Forebears*, London, 1943.

(9) C. J. Thomsen, *Ledetraad til Nordisk Oldkyndighed*, Copenhagen, 1836. Translated in Lord Ellesmere's *A Guide to Northern Antiquities*, London, 1948. See G. E. Daniel, *The Three Ages: An Essay on Archaeological Method*, Cambridge, 1943.

(10) S. Nilsson, *Skandinaviska Nordens Ur-invånare*, 2 vols, Lund, 1838–65.

(11) O. Klindt-Jensen, *A History of Scandinavian Archaeology*, London, 1975. Translated by G. R. Poole.

(12) *Danmarks Oldtid*, I–III, Copenhagen, 1938–40.
(13) J. M. Crook, *The British Museum*, London, 1972.
(14) T. D. Kendrick and C. F. C. Hawkes, *Archaeology in England and Wales, 1914–31*, London, 1932.
(15) O. Impey and A. Macgregor (eds.), *The Origins of Museums: The Cabinet of Curiosities in Sixteenth- and Seventeenth-century Europe*, Oxford, 1985.
(16) T. K. Penniman, *A Hundred Years of Anthropology*, London, 1935, 90.
(17) E. B. Tylor, *Primitive Culture*, London, 1871.
(18) *Archaeologia*, XIII, 1800, 204–5.
(19) D. A. E. Garrod, *The Upper Palaeolithic Age in Britain*, Oxford, 1926, 19.
(20) H. Breuil, 'Les Subdivisions du paléolithique supérieur et leur signification', *Congrès international d'Anthropologie et d'Archéologie préhistoriques Compte Rendu*, Sess. XIV, Geneva, 1912, 165–238.
(21) W. J. Sollas, *Ancient Hunters and Their Modern Representatives*, London, 1911, 1915 and 1924.
(22) T. D. Kendrick, *The Axe Age: A Study in British Prehistory*, London, 1925, 2–5.
(23) W. M. Flinders Petrie, *Stonehenge: Plans, Descriptions and Theories*, London, 1880. R. J. C. Atkinson stated in his *Stonehenge* (Harmondsworth, 1960, 193), that Petrie's book contained 'the most accurate plan of Stonehenge ever likely to be made'.
(24) J. Evans, *Time and Chance*, London, 1943, 359.
(25) Inaugural Lecture, 19 October 1887, Oxford.
(26) F. J. Haverfield, *The Romanization of Roman Britain*, London, 1905; R. G. Collingwood, *The Archaeology of Roman Britain*, London, 1930.
(27) C. H. Read, 'Anthropology at the Universities', *Man*, VI, 1906, 56–9.
(28) H. J. Rose, 'Robert Ranulph Marett, 1866–1943', *PBA*, XXIX, 1943, 357–70.
(29) C. F. C. Hawkes, *Archaeology and the History of Europe: An Inaugural Lecture*, Oxford, 1948, 13.
(30) *Ibid.*, 4.
(31) A. Sherratt, 'Archaeology in Oxford', *Oxford Magazine*, 1986, No. 11, 11–13.
(32) F. Roe and J. May, *Guide to Undergraduate University Courses in Archaeology*, London, 2nd edn, 1983, 35.
(33) A valedictory volume of *Liverpool Annals* appeared with a cumulative index in 1948.
(34) V. G. Childe, *Man Makes Himself*, London, 1936; *What Happened in History*, Harmondsworth, 1942.
(35) *Conference on the Future of Archaeology, Aug. 6–8, 1943; Conference on the Problems and Prospects of European Archaeology, Sept. 16–17, 1944*, University of London Institute of Archaeology, Occasional Papers nos. 5 & 6.
(36) A. F. E. Zeuner published the first edition of his *Dating the Past* in 1946 (London).
(37) W. F. Grimes, 'Archaeology and the University', *13th Annual Report and Bulletin of the London University Institute of Archaeology for 1955–6*, 37–48.

2: Anthropology at Cambridge, 1904–20

(1) S. J. Hickson, *A Naturalist in North Celebes*, London, 1889.
(2) W. B. Spencer and F. J. Gillen, *The Native Tribes of Central Australia*, London, 1899; and *The Northern Tribes of Central Australia*, London, 1904.
(3) D. J. Mulvaney and J. H. Calaby, *'So Much That is New': Baldwin Spencer 1860–1929*, Melbourne, 1985, 70.
(4) A. C. Haddon, 'Baron Anatole von Hügel', *Man*, XXVIII, 1928, 169–71; 'Baron Anatole von Hügel', *Nature*, CXXII, 1928, 322–3.
(5) A. H. Quiggin, *Haddon the Head-Hunter*, Cambridge, 1942; H. J. Fleure, 'Alfred Cort Haddon 1855–1940', *Obituary Notices of the Royal Society*, III, 1941, 449–65.
(6) A. C. Haddon, 'Sir William Ridgeway', *Man*, XXVI, 1926, 175–6; 'Sir William Ridgeway', *Nature*, CXVIII, 1926, 275–6; R. S. Conway, 'Sir William Ridgeway 1853–1926', *PBA*, XII, 1926, 326–36.

(7) A. R. Radcliffe-Brown, *The Andaman Islanders: A Study in Social Anthropology*, Cambridge, 1922.

(8) B. Malinowski, *Argonauts of the Western Pacific*, London, 1922.

(9) M. Fortes, *Social Anthropology at Cambridge since 1900: An Inaugural Lecture*, Cambridge, 1953, passim.

(10) W. J. Perry, *The Children of the Sun: A Study in the Early History of Civilization*, London, 1923.

(11) W. J. Perry, *The Megalithic Culture of Indonesia*, Manchester, 1918.

(12) J. D. Freeman, 'Henry Devenish Skinner: a Memoir', in *Anthropology in the South Seas. Essays presented to H. D. Skinner* (J.D. Freeman and W. R. Geddes, eds.), New Plymouth, N.Z., 1959, 9–27.

(13) N. Hammond, *Ancient Maya Civilization*, Cambridge, 1982, 46–8.

(14) *JRAI*, xxxix, 1908, 10–25.

(15) Classical Library, Cambridge: pamphlet OL, Box C.9.

(16) E. C. Quiggin (ed.), *Essays and Studies presented to William Ridgeway on his Sixtieth Birthday, 6 August 1913*, Cambridge, 1913.

(17) W. Ridgeway, *The Early Age of Greece*, vol. I, Cambridge, 1901.

(18) W. Ridgeway, 'What People produced the Objects called Mycenaean', *JHS*, xvi, 1896, 77–119.

(19) D. S. Robertson, 'Sir William Ridgeway', *The Cambridge Review*, xlviii, 1926, 12–13. A good idea of Ridgeway's appearance as a lecturer may be had from the drawing by Frances Darwin (Mrs F. M. Cornford) (fig. 2) reproduced in J. G. Stewart's *Jane Ellen Harrison: A Portrait From Letters*, London, 1959, 16.

(20) J. G. D. Clark, *The Study of Prehistory: An Inaugural Lecture*, Cambridge, 1954, 1–3.

3: Prehistoric archaeology at Cambridge, 1920–39

(1) M. C. Burkitt, *Prehistory: A Study of Early Cultures in Europe and the Mediterranean Basin*, Cambridge, 1921; 2nd edn, 1925.

(2) E. H. Minns, *Scythians & Greeks*, Cambridge, 1913.

(3) E. D. Phillips, 'In Memoriam Ellis Hovell Minns', *Artibus Asiae*, xvii, 1954, 168–73; J. G. D. Clark, 'Ellis Hovell Minns 1874–1953', *PBA*, lxxi, 1985, 597–602.

(4) *PBA*, xxviii, 1942, 47–99 and pls. i–xxviii.

(5) J. G. D. Clark, 'The Prehistoric Society: From East Anglia to the World', *PPS*, li, 1985, 1–13.

(6) Sir R. Lankester, 'On the Discovery of a Novel Type of Flint Implements Below the Base of the Red Crag in Suffolk, Proving the Existence of Skilled Workers of Flint during the Pliocene Age', *Phil.Trans.Royal Soc.*, Ser. B, ccii, 1912, 283–336.

(7) J. M. de Navarro, 'Hector Munro Chadwick 1870–1947', *PBA*, xxxiii, 1947, 307–330.

(8) *Studies on Anglo-Saxon Institutions*, Cambridge, 1905; *The Origin of the English Nation*, Cambridge, 1907.

(9) 'Prehistoric Routes between Northern Europe and Italy defined by the Amber Trade', *Geog.J.*, lxvi, 1925, 481–507.

(10) J. M. de Navarro, *The Finds from the Site of La Tène*, vol. I, *Scabbards and the Swords found in them*, London, 1972.

(11) J. D. Clark, 'Louis Seymour Bazett Leakey 1903–1972', *PBA*, lix, 1973, 447–71.

(12) L. S. B. Leakey, *The Stone Age Cultures of Kenya Colony*, Cambridge, 1931.

(13) M. C. Burkitt, *The Old Stone Age: A Study of Palaeolithic Times*, Cambridge, 1933.

(14) L. S. B. Leakey, *Adam's Ancestors: An Up-To-Date Outline of What is Known About the Origin of Man*, London, 1934.

(15) L. S. B. Leakey, *The Stone Age Races of Kenya*, London, 1935.

(16) L. S. B. Leakey, *Stone Age Africa: an Outline of Prehistory in Africa*, London, 1936.

(17) M. C. Burkitt, *South Africa's Past in Stone and Paint*, Cambridge, 1928.

(18) J. G. D. Clark, 'Gertrude Caton Thompson 1888–1985', *PBA*, lxxi, 1985, 523–31.

(19) E.g. (with Guy Brunton), *The Badarian Civilization and Pre-Dynastic Remains Near Badari*, London, 1928; (with E. W. Gardner), *The Desert Fayum*, London, 1934.

(20) G. Caton Thompson, 'Dorothy Annie Elizabeth Garrod 1892–1968', *PBA*, LV, 1969, 339–61.

(21) D. A. E. Garrod, 'Nova et Vetera: A Plea for a New Method in Palaeolithic Archaeology', *PPSEA*, V, 1928, 260–72; *Bulletin of the American School of Prehistoric Research*, VI, 1930.

(22) J. J. Hawkes, *The Bailiwick of Jersey*, Jersey, 1939; *A Guide to the Prehistoric and Roman Monuments of England and Wales*, London, 1951; *The Atlas of Early Man*, London, 1976.

(23) D. A. E. Garrod and D. M. A. Bate, *The Stone Age of Mount Carmel: Excavations at the Wady el-Mughara*, vol. I, Oxford, 1937; T. D. McCown and Sir A. Keith, *The Stone Age of Mount Carmel: The Fossil Human Remains from the Levalloiso-Mousterian*, vol. II, Oxford, 1939.

(24) D. A. E. Garrod, 'Nova et Vetera: A Plea for a New Method in Palaeolithic Archaeology', *PPSEA*, V, 1928, 260–72; 'The Upper Palaeolithic in the Light of Recent Discovery', *PPS*, IV, 1938, 1–26.

(25) Cambridge, 1923. Reissued in 1948 with an extra Appendix giving the author's reflections.

(26) *The Archaeology of Cornwall and Scilly*, London, 1932.

(27) H. O'Neill Hencken, 'Ballinderry Crannog No. 1', *Proc.R.I.A.*, XLIII, 1936, Sect.C, 103–239; 'Ballinderry Crannog No. 2', *Proc.R.I.A.*, XLVII, 1942, Sect. C, 1–76; 'Lagore Crannog: an Irish Royal Residence of the 7th to 10th centuries A.D.', *Proc.R.I.A.*, LIII, 1950, Sect.C, 1–247.

(28) E. C. Curwen, *The Archaeology of Sussex*, 2nd rev. edn, London, 1954, pl. VI.

(29) T. D. Kendrick and C. F. C. Hawkes, *Archaeology in England and Wales 1914–1931*, London, 1932.

(30) Apart from Burkitt's own books those recommended for the Cambridge course on early prehistory comprised: M. Boule, *Les Hommes Fossiles: Eléments du Paléontologie Humaine*, Paris, 1921, H. Breuil, 'Les Subdivisions du paléolithique supérieur et leur signification', *Congrès international d'Anthropologie et d'Archéologie préhistoriques Compte Rendu*, Sess. XIV, Geneva, 1912, 161–238; and H. Obermaier, *Fossil Man in Spain*, New Haven, 1925, Translated by C. D. Matthew.

(31) M. C. Burkitt, *Our Early Ancestors: An Introductory Study of Mesolithic, Neolithic and Copper Age Cultures in Europe and Adjacent Regions*, Cambridge, 1926.

(32) V. Gordon Childe, *The Dawn of European Civilization*, London, 1925.

(33) *The Aryans: A Study of Indo-European Origins*, London, 1926; *The Most Ancient East: the Oriental Prelude to European Prehistory*, London, 1928; *The Danube in Prehistory*, Oxford, 1929.

(34) Oxford, 1926, 181–90.

(35) *The Mesolithic Age in Britain*, Cambridge, 1932, Appendix VII.

(36) *The Mesolithic Settlement of Northern Europe*, Cambridge, 1936.

(37) Sir H. Godwin, *Fenland: Its Ancient Past and Uncertain Future*, Cambridge, 1978, ch. 3; 'Professor Sir Harry Godwin, F.R.S., 1901–1985 – a tribute', *J. Arch. Science*, XIII, 1986, 299–306.

(38) H. and M. E. Godwin, 'British Maglemose Harpoon Sites', *Antiquity*, VII, 1933, 36–48.

(39) S. B. J. Skertchley, *The Geology of the Fenland*, Memoirs of the Geological Survey, England and Wales, London, 1877; S. H. Miller and S. B. J. Skertchley, *The Fenland Past and Present*, Wisbech, 1878.

(40) G. Fowler, 'The Extinct Waterway of the Fens', *Geog.J.*, LXXXIII, 1934, 30–9. A brief note had appeared in 'Old River-Beds in the Fenlands', *Geog.J.*, LXXIX, 1932, 210–2.

(41) Pollen analysis was first demonstrated to be an effective method for zoning deposits and recovering the history of ecological change in 1916 by Lennart van Post and it was to him that Knut Faegri and Johs. Iversen dedicated their *Text-book of Modern Pollen-analysis* published by Munksgaard, Copenhagen in 1950. The method was first applied to samples from British sites by the Swede G. Erdtman during the 1920s. The Godwins were the first British scientists to apply it systematically in this country.

(42) C. W. Phillips, 'The Fenland Research Committee, its Past Achievements and Future Prospects', In *Aspects of Archaeology in Britain and Beyond: Essays presented to O. G. S. Crawford* (ed. W. F. Grimes), London, 1951, 258–73; H. Godwin, *Fenland*, ch. 5; *Cambridge & Clare*, Cambridge, 1985, 174–6.
(43) H. Godwin, *The History of the British Flora: A Factual Basis for Phytogeography*, Cambridge, 1956.
(44) H. Godwin and M. H. Clifford, 'Studies of the Post-Glacial History of British Vegetation. I. Origin and Stratigraphy of Fenland Deposits near Woodwalton, Hunts.; II. Origin and Stratigraphy of Deposits in Southern Fenland', *Phil.Trans.Royal Soc.*, Ser.B, CCXXIX, 1938, 323–406.
(45) H. Godwin, 'III. Fenland Pollen Diagrams; IV. Post-glacial Changes of Relative Land- and Sea-level in the English Fenland', *ibid.*, CCXXX, 1940, 239–303.
(46) J. G. D. Clark (in collaboration with H. and M. E. Godwin and W. A. Macfadyen of the Fenland Research Committee), 'Report on an Early Bronze Age Site in the South-eastern Fens', *Ant. J.*, XIII, 1933, 266–96; H. and M. E. Godwin, J. G. D. Clark and M. H. Clifford, 'A Bronze Age Spearhead found in Methwold Fen, Norfolk', *PPSEA*, VII, 1934, 395–8; J. G. D. Clark, H. and M. E. Godwin and M. H. Clifford, 'Report on Recent Excavations at Peacock's Farm, Shippea Hill, Cambridgeshire', *Ant. J.*, XV, 1935, 284–319; J. G. D. Clark, 'Report on a Late Bronze Age Site in Mildenhall Fen, West Suffolk', *Ant. J.*, XVI, 1936, 29–50; J. G. D. Clark and H. Godwin, 'A Late Bronze Age Find near Stuntney, Isle of Ely', *Ant. J.*, XX, 1940, 52–71.
(47) C. W. Phillips, *My Life in Archaeology*, Gloucester, 1987.
(48) C. W. Phillips, 'The Excavation of the Giants' Hills Long Barrow, Skendleby, Lincolnshire', *Archaeologia*, LXXXV, 1935, 37–106.
(49) J. G. D. Clark, 'The Timber Monument at Arminghall and its Affinities', *PPS*, II, 1936, 1–51.
(50) J. G. D. Clark, 'The Prehistoric Society: from East Anglia to the World', *PPS*, LI, 1985, 1–13.
(51) A. M. Tallgren, 'The Method of Prehistoric Archaeology', *Antiquity*, XI, 1937, 152–61.
(52) London, 1939. A much revised third edition appeared in 1957.

4: Prehistoric archaeology at Cambridge, 1946–74: expansion of the syllabus and provision for excavation

(1) J. G. D. Clark, 'Geoffrey Hext Sutherland Bushnell 1903–1978', *PBA*, LXV, 1979, 587–93; G. H. S. Bushnell, *The Archaeology of the Santa Elena Peninsula in South-west Ecuador*, Cambridge, 1951.
(2) G. H. S. Bushnell, *Peru*, London, 1956, 1963; *The First Americans: The Pre-Columbian Civilizations*, London, 1968; (with A. Digby), *Ancient American Pottery*, London, 1955.
(3) J. G. D. Clark, *Archaeology and Society*, London, 1939; 3rd edn, 1957.
(4) Fellow of Emmanuel College and University Lecturer in Classics, Cambridge. Editor (with A. J. B. Wace) of *A Companion to Homer*, London, 1962.
(5) Jocelyn Toynbee held the Lawrence Chair of Classical Archaeology at Cambridge from 1951 to 1962. She published *Art in Roman Britain*, London and *Art in Britain under the Romans*, Oxford in 1962 and 1964, as well as works of wider scope.
(6) F. H. Stubbings, 'Alan John Bayard Wace 1879–1957', *PBA*, XLIV, 1958, 263–80.
(7) I. E. S. Edwards, 'Stephen Ranulph Kingdon Glanville 1900–1956', *PBA*, XLIV, 1958, 231–40.
(8) Martin Plumley held the chair from 1957 to 1977 during which time he directed many seasons of excavation for the Egypt Exploration Society in Nubia.
(9) B. and R. Allchin, *The Birth of Indian Civilization: India and Pakistan before 500 B.C.*, Harmondsworth, 1968.
(10) T. Cheng, *Archaeology in China*, Cambridge, 1959.
(11) G. E. Daniel, *The Prehistoric Chamber Tombs of England and Wales*, Cambridge, 1950; (with T. G. E. Powell), *Barclodiad y Gawres: the Excavation of a Megalithic Chamber Tomb in Anglesey, 1952–3*, Liverpool, 1956; *The Megalith Builders of Western Europe*,

London, 1958; *The Prehistoric Chamber Tombs of France: A Geographical, Morphological and Chronological Survey*, London, 1960.

(12) J. M. Coles, 'Scottish Late Bronze Age Metalwork: Typology, Distributions and Chronology', *PSAS*, xciii, 1959–60, 16–134.

(13) (with E. S. Higgs) *The Archaeology of Early Man*, London, 1969; *Field Archaeology in Britain*, London, 1972; *Archaeology by Experiment*, London, 1973; *The Archaeology of Wetlands*, Edinburgh, 1984.

(14) B. Hope-Taylor contributed through his skills as excavator and draughtsman, both displayed in *Yeavering: an Anglo-British Centre of Early Northumbria*, London, 1977.

(15) G. E. Daniel, *A Hundred Years of Archaeology*, London, 1950; *A Hundred and Fifty Years of Archaeology*, London, 1975.

(16) O. G. S. Crawford and A. Keiller, *Wessex from the Air*, Oxford, 1928; J. K. S. St Joseph (with D. Knowles), *Monastic Sites from the Air*, Cambridge, 1952; (with M. W. Beresford), *Medieval England: an Aerial Survey*, Cambridge, 1958; (with E. R. Norman), *The Early Development of Irish Society: the Evidence of Aerial Photography*, Cambridge, 1969.

(17) J. G. D. Clark, 'Report on Excavations on the Cambridgeshire Car Dyke, 1947', *Ant. J.*, xxix, 1949, 145–63.

(18) Preliminary reports on the 1949 and 1950 seasons appeared respectively in J. G. D. Clark, 'A Preliminary Report on Excavations at Star Carr, Seamer, Scarborough, Yorkshire 1949', *PPS*, xv, 1949, 52–69, and 'Second Season 1950', *PPS*, xvi, 1950, 109–29.

(19) J. G. D. Clark, *Excavations at Star Carr: An Early Mesolithic Site at Seamer near Scarborough, Yorkshire*, Cambridge, 1954.

(20) J. G. D. Clark and C. I. Fell, 'An Early Iron Age Site at Micklemoor Hill, West Harling, Norfolk and its Pottery', *PPS*, xix, 1953, 1–40.

(21) J. G. D. Clark with E. S. Higgs and I. Longworth, 'Excavations at the Neolithic Site at Hurst Fen, Mildenhall, Suffolk (1954, 1957 and 1958)', *PPS*, xxvi, 1960, 202–45.

(22) E. S. Higgs, 'Excavations at a Mesolithic Site at Downton, near Salisbury, Wiltshire', *PPS*, xxv, 1959, 209–32.

(23) J. G. D. Clark and H. Godwin, 'The Neolithic in the Cambridgeshire Fens', *Antiquity*, xxxvi, 1962, 10–23.

(24) R. G. West and C. B. M. McBurney, 'Quaternary Deposits at Hoxne, Suffolk, and their Archaeology', *PPS*, xx, 1954, 131–54.

(25) C. B. M. McBurney, 'Report on the First Season's Fieldwork on British Upper Palaeolithic cave deposits', *PPS*, xxv, 1959, 260–9.

(26) C. B. M. McBurney and P. Callow, 'The Cambridge Excavations at La Cotte de St Brelade, Jersey: A Preliminary Report', *PPS*, xxxvii, Part II, 1971, 167–207.

(27) *La Cotte de St Brelade 1961–1978: Excavations by C. B. M. McBurney*, edited by P. Callow and J. M. Cornford, Norwich, 1986.

(28) C. B. M. McBurney, 'The Stone Age of the Libyan Littoral: The Results of a War-time Reconnaissance', *PPS*, xiii, 1947, 56–84.

(29) C. B. M. McBurney and R. W. Hey, *Prehistory and Pleistocene Geology in Cyrenaican Libya: A Record of Two Seasons' Geological and Archaeological Fieldwork in the Gabel Akhdar Hills*, Cambridge, 1955.

(30) C. B. M. McBurney, *The Haua Fteah, Cyrenaica and the Stone Age of the South-east Mediterranean*, Cambridge, 1967.

(31) C. B. M. McBurney, 'The Cave of Ali Tappeh and the Epi-palaeolithic in N. E. Iran', *PPS*, xxxiv, 1968, 385–413.

(32) C. B. M. McBurney, 'Early Man in the Soviet Union: The Implications of Some Recent Discoveries', *PBA*, lxi, 1975, 171–221.

(33) R. J. Rodden, 'Excavations at the Early Neolithic Site at Nea Nikomedeia, Greek Macedonia (1961 Season)', *PPS*, xxviii, 1962, 267–88.

(34) S. I. Dakaris, E. S. Higgs and R. W. Hey, 'The Climate, Environment and Industries of Stone Age Greece: Part I', *PPS*, xxx, 1964, 199–244.

(35) E. S. Higgs and C. Vita-Finzi, 'The Climate, Environment and Industries of Stone Age Greece: Part II', *PPS*, xxxii, 1966, 1–29.

(36) E. S. Higgs, C. Vita-Finzi, D. R. Harris and A. E. Fagg, 'The Climate, Environment and Industries of Stone Age Greece: Part III', *PPS*, XXXIII, 1967, 1–29.

(37) G. N. Bailey and P. Callow (eds.), *Stone Age Prehistory: Studies in Memory of Charles McBurney*, Cambridge, 1986.

(38) H. J. Movius, *Excavations of the Abri Pataud, Les Eyzies (Dordogne)*, Vol. 2. H. M. Bricker and N. David, *The Périgordian VI (Level 3) Assemblage*, Harvard, 1984.

(39) C. B. M. McBurney, 'Evidence for the Distribution in Space and Time of Neanderthaloids and Allied Strains in Northern Africa', In *Hundert Jahre Neanderthaler: Neanderthal Centenary, 1856–1956* (ed. G. H. R. von Koenigswald), Köln, 1958, 253–64.

(40) R. Foley, *Off-site Archaeology and Human Adaptation in Eastern Africa: an Analysis of Regional Artefacts Density in the Amboseli, Southern Kenya*, Oxford, 1981; *Hominid Evolution and Community Ecology: Prehistoric Human Adaptation in Biological Perspective*, London, 1984.

5: Prehistoric archaeology at Cambridge, 1946–74: Quaternary Research and economic history

(1) J. E. Marr, 'Man and the Ice Age', *PPSEA*, III, 1920, 177–91.

(2) M. C. Burkitt, *Prehistory: A Study of Early Cultures in Europe and the Mediterranean Basin*, Cambridge, 1921, 54.

(3) W. B. R. King and K. P. Oakley, 'The Pleistocene Succession in the Lower Parts of the Thames Valley', *PPS*, II, 1936, 52–76.

(4) H. Hamshaw Thomas, 'Albert Charles Seward 1863–1941', *Obituary Notices of the Royal Society*, III, 1941, 867–80.

(5) Sir H. Godwin, *Cambridge & Clare*, Cambridge, 1985.

(6) R. G. West, *Pleistocene Geology and Biology with especial reference to the British Isles*, London, 1968, 1977.

(7) R. G. West, 'Pleistocene History of the British Flora', In *Studies in the Vegetational History of the British Isles* (D. Walker and R. G. West, eds.), Cambridge, 1970, 1–11.

(8) H. Godwin, 'Studies of the Post-glacial History of British Vegetation, VI, Correlations in the Somerset Levels', *The New Phytologist*, XL, 1941, 108–32.

(9) A. R. Clapham and H. Godwin, 'Studies of the Post-glacial History of British Vegetation, IX, Prehistoric Trackways in the Somerset Levels', *Phil.Trans.Royal Soc.*, Ser.B, CCXXXIII, 1948, 249–73; H. Godwin, 'Prehistoric wooden trackways of the Somerset Levels: their construction, age and relation to climatic change', *PPS*, XXVI, 1960, 1–36.

(10) H. S. L. Dewar and H. Godwin, 'Archaeological Discoveries in the Raised Bogs of the Somerset Levels, England', *PPS*, XXIX, 1963, 17–49.

(11) J. G. D. Clark, 'Neolithic Bows from Somerset, England, and the Prehistory of Archery in North-western Europe', *PPS*, XXIX, 1963, 50–98.

(12) J. M. Coles, 'Later Bronze Age activity in the Somerset Levels', *Ant. J.*, LII, 1972, 269–75.

(13) *Somerset Levels Papers*, no. 1, 1975; J. Coles, *The Archaeology of Wetlands*, Edinburgh, 1984.

(14) W. F. Libby, 'Atmospheric Helium Three and Radiocarbon from Cosmic Radiation', *Physical Review*, LXIX, 1946, 671–2.

(15) W. F. Libby, E. C. Anderson and J. R. Arnold, 'Age Determination by Radiocarbon Content: World-Wide Assay of Natural Radiocarbon', *Science*, CIX, 1949, 227–8.

(16) A. G. Engelkemeir, W. H. Hamill, M. C. Inghram and W. F. Libby, 'The Half-Life of Radiocarbon (C 14)', *Physical Review*, LXXV, 1949, 1825–33.

(17) J. R. Arnold and W. F. Libby, 'Age Determinations by Radiocarbon Content: Checks with Samples of Known Age', *Science*, CX, 1949, 678–80.

(18) Details about the work of the Sub-Department are available in the *Reporter* under the heading: Reports, Botany Dept.

(19) H. Godwin, 'Carbon-14 Dating: Symposium in Copenhagen, September 1–4', *Nature*, CLXXIV, 1954, 868; H. Levi, 'Radiocarbon Dating: Conference in Cambridge', *Nature*, CLXXVI, 1955, 727–8; F. Johnson, J. R. Arnold and R. F. Flint, 'Radiocarbon Dating', *Science*, CXXV, 1957, 240–2; H. Godwin, 'Carbon-dating Conference at Groningen,

September 14–19, 1959', *Nature*, CLXXXIV, 1959, 1365–6 and H.T. Waterbolk, 'The 1959 Carbon-14 Symposium at Groningen', *Antiquity*, XXXIV, 1960, 14–8; H. Goodwin, 'Radiocarbon Dating: Fifth International Conference', *Nature*, XCCV, 1962, 943–5.

(20) F. C. Fraser and J. E. King, 'Second Interim Report on the Animal Remains from Star Carr, Seamer', *PPS*, XVI, 1950, 124–9.

(21) J. G. D. Clark and H. Godwin, 'The Neolithic in the Cambridgeshire Fens', *Antiquity*, XXXVI, 1962, 10–23.

(22) Clark, 'Neolithic Bows', 55.

(23) E. V. Wright and D. M. Churchill, 'The Boats from North Ferriby, Yorkshire, England, with a Review of the Origins of the Sewn Boats of the Bronze Age', *PPS*, XXXI, 1965, 1–24.

(24) Q 655.

(25) E. S. Higgs et al., 'Stone Age Greece: Part III', passim.

(26) C. B. M. McBurney, *Haua Fteah*, 49 and 71.

(27) J. G. D. Clark, 'Radiocarbon Dating and the Spread of Farming Economy', *Antiquity*, XXXIX, 1965, 45–8; 'Radiocarbon Dating and the Expansion of Farming Culture from the Near East over Europe', *PPS*, XXXI, 1965, 58–73.

(28) J. G. D. Clark, *World Prehistory*, Cambridge, 1961, 243.

(29) J. G. D. Clark, *World Prehistory: A New Outline*, Cambridge, 2nd edn, 1969.

(30) J. G. D. Clark, *World Prehistory in New Perspective*, Cambridge, 3rd edn, 1977, 461.

(31) J. Iversen, *Land Occupation in Denmark's Stone Age: A Pollen Analytical Study of the Influence of Farmer Culture on the Vegetational Development*, Copenhagen, 1941.

(32) Godwin reacted to Iversen's pioneer study in his 'Age and Origin of the "Breckland" Heaths of East Anglia', *Nature*, CLIV, 1944, 6–7, and in his recognition of the impact of prehistoric agriculture in the Somerset Levels, 'Correlation Between Climate, Forest Composition, Prehistoric Agriculture and Peat Stratigraphy in Sub-Boreal and Sub-Atlantic Peats of the Somerset Levels', *Phil. Trans. Royal Soc.*, Ser.B, CCXXXIII, 1948, 275–86.

(33) V. G. Childe, *What Happened in History*, Harmondsworth. This book, originally published in 1942, remains a classic.

(34) J. G. D. Clark, 'The Economic Approach to Prehistory', *PBA*, XXXIX, 1953, 215–38.

(35) J. G. D. Clark, 'Seal-hunting in the Stone Age of North-western Europe: A Study in Economic Prehistory', *PPS*, XII, 1946, 12–48; 'Whales as an Economic Factor in Prehistoric Europe', *Antiquity*, XXI, 1947, 84–104; 'The Development of Fishing in Prehistoric Europe', *Ant. J.*, XXVIII, 1948, 45–85; 'Fowling in Prehistoric Europe', *Antiquity*, XXII, 1948, 116–30.

(36) J. G. D. Clark, 'Farmers and Forests in Neolithic Europe', *Antiquity*, XI, 1945, 57–71; 'Forest Clearance and Prehistoric Farming', *Economic History Review*, XVII, 1947, 45–51; 'Sheep and Swine in the Husbandry of Prehistoric Europe', *Antiquity*, XXI, 1947, 122–36.

(37) J. G. D. Clark, 'Folk-culture and the Study of European Prehistory', In *Aspects of Archaeology in Britain and Beyond: Essays Presented to O. G. S. Crawford* (W. F. Grimes, ed.), London, 1951, 49–65.

(38) London, 1952.

(39) J. M. Coles and B. J. Orme, *Prehistory of the Somerset Levels*, Cambridge, 1980.

(40) J. G. D. Clark, 'The Economic Approach to Prehistory'.

(41) H. de Terra and T. T. Paterson, *Studies on the Ice Age in India and Associated Human Cultures*, Washington, 1939.

(42) Whereas the first edition (1961) ran to 283 pp., the third and current edition (1977) needed 554 pp.

(43) Namely Harry Godwin, Grahame Clark, Christopher Hawkes and Stuart Piggott, E. M. Jope and Sir Joseph Hutchinson.

(44) E. S. Higgs (ed.), *Papers in Economic Prehistory: Studies by Members and Associates of the British Academy Major Research Project in the Early History of Agriculture*, Cambridge, 1972; *Palaeoeconomy: Being the Second Volume of Papers in Economic Prehistory by Members and Associates of the British Academy Major Research Project in the Early History of Agriculture*, Cambridge, 1975; and M. R. Jarman, G. N. Bailey and

H. N. Jarman (eds.), *Early European Agriculture: Its Foundations and Development*, Cambridge, 1982.

(45) J. G. D. Clark, 'Domestication and Social Evolution', In *The Early History of Agriculture: A Joint Symposium of the Royal Society and the British Academy*, organised by J. Hutchinson, J. G. D. Clark, E. M. Jope and R. Riley, Oxford, 1976, 5–11.

(46) J. G. D. Clark, *Star Carr: a Case Study in Bioarchaeology*, Reading, Mass., 1972.

(47) J. G. D. Clark, 'Neothermal Orientations', In *The Early Postglacial Settlement of Northern Europe: An Ecological Perspective* (Paul Mellars, ed.), London, 1978, 1–10; *Mesolithic Prelude: the Palaeolithic-Neolithic Transition in Old World Prehistory*, Edinburgh, 1980.

(48) D. L. Clarke, *Analytical Archaeology*, London, 1968; *Analytical Archaeologist: Collected Papers of David L. Clarke*, London, 1979.

(49) D. L. Clarke, *Beaker Pottery of Great Britain and Ireland*, 2 vols, Cambridge, 1970.

(50) I. H. Longworth, *Collared Urns of the Bronze Age in Great Britain and Ireland*, Cambridge, 1984.

(51) J. J. Taylor, *Bronze Age Goldwork of the British Isles*, Cambridge, 1980.

6: Prehistorians beyond Cambridge: Africa, Australasia, America and Asia

(1) M. C. Burkitt, *South Africa's Past in Stone and Paint*, Cambridge, 1928.

(2) A. J. H. Goodwin and C. van Riet Lowe, 'The Stone Age Cultures of South Africa', *Annals of the South African Museum*, XXVII, 1929, 1–289.

(3) R. R. Inskeep, *The Peopling of Southern Africa*, Cape Town, 1978.

(4) J. E. Parkington, 'Stone-tool Assemblages, Raw Material Distributions and Prehistoric Subsistence Activities: The Late Stone Age of South Africa', In *Stone Age Prehistory: Studies in Memory of Charles McBurney* (G. N. Bailey and P. Callow, eds.), Cambridge, 1986, 181–94.

(5) G. and M. Sampson, *Riversmead Shelter: Excavations and Analysis*, Bloemfontein, 1967; C. G. Sampson, *The Stone Age Archaeology of Southern Africa*, New York, 1974.

(6) For a memoir with a good bibliography see J. D. Clark, 'Louis Seymour Bazett Leakey 1903–1972', *PBA*, LIX, 1973, 447–71.

(7) L. S. B. Leakey (ed.) assisted by S. Cole, *Proceedings of the Pan-African Congress on Prehistory, 1947*, Oxford, 1952.

(8) G. Ll. Isaac, *Olorgesailie: Archaeological Studies of a Middle Pleistocene Lake Basin in Kenya*, Chicago, 1977.

(9) J. D. Clark, *Stone Age Sites in Northern Rhodesia and the Possibilities of Future Research*, Livingstone, 1939; *The Stone Age Cultures of Northern Rhodesia*, Claremont, 1950.

(10) J. D. Clark (ed.) assisted by S. Cole, *Third Pan-African Congress on Prehistory, Livingstone, 1955*, London, 1957.

(11) J. D. Clark, *Kalambo Falls Prehistoric Site*, 2 vols., Cambridge, 1969–74.

(12) J. D. Clark, *Atlas of African Prehistory*, Chicago, 1967; *The Prehistory of Africa*, London, 1970; (as editor) *Cambridge History of Africa*, vol. I, *From the Earliest Times to c.500 B.C.*, Cambridge, 1982.

(13) J. D. Clark, *Cambridge History of Africa*, I, 14.

(14) T. Shaw, *Excavation at Dawu: Report on an Excavation in a Mound at Dawu, Akuapim, Ghana*, London, 1961.

(15) C. T. Shaw, 'Report on Excavations Carried Out in the Cave known as 'Bosumpra' at Abetifi, Kwahu, Gold Coast Colony', *PPS*, X, 1944, 1–67.

(16) A. W. Lawrence, *Trade Castles & Forts of West Africa*, London, 1963.

(17) O. Davies, *West Africa before the Europeans: Archaeology and Prehistory*, London, 1967.

(18) M. Posnansky, *Myth and Methodology – The Archaeological Contribution to African History: an Inaugural Lecture Delivered on 12th February, 1969, at the University of Ghana, Legon*, Accra, 1969.

(19) B. Fagg, 'Preliminary Report on a Microlithic Industry at Rop Rock shelter, Northern Nigeria', *PPS*, X, 1944, 68–9.

(20) B. E. B. Fagg, 'The Nok Culture in Prehistory', *Journal of the Historical Society of Nigeria*, I, 1959, 288–93; 'Recent Work in West Africa: New Light on the Nok Culture', *World Archaeology*, I, 1969, 41–50.

(21) T. Shaw, *Archaeology and Nigeria: An Expanded Version of an Inaugural Lecture Delivered at the University of Ibadan on 29 Nov. 1963*, Ibadan, 1963.

(22) T. Shaw, *Igbo-Ukwu: an account of Archaeological Discoveries in Eastern Nigeria*, 2 vols., London, 1970; *Unearthing Igbo-Ukwu: Archaeological Discoveries in Eastern Nigeria*, Ibadan, 1977.

(23) T. Shaw, 'Archaeology in Nigeria', *Antiquity*, XLIII, 1969, 187–99; *Nigeria: Its Archaeology and Early History*, London, 1978.

(24) R. C. Soper, 'The Stone Age in Northern Nigeria', *Journal of the Historical Society of Nigeria*, III, 1965, 175–94.

(25) P. Allsworth-Jones, 'Middle Stone Age and Middle Palaeolithic: the Evidence from Nigeria and Cameroun', In *Stone Age Prehistory: Studies in Memory of Charles McBurney* (G. N. Bailey and P. Callow, eds.), Cambridge, 1986, 153–68.

(26) G. Connah, 'Archaeological Research in Benin City, 1961–64', *Journal of the Historical Society of Nigeria*, II, 1963, 465–77; *Three Thousand Years in Africa: Man and his Environment in the Lake Chad Region of Nigeria*, Cambridge, 1981.

(27) G. Connah, 'Settlement Mounds of the Firki – The Reconstruction of a Lost Society', *Ibadan*, XXVI, 1969, 48–62; *The Archaeology of Benin: Excavations and Other Researches in and around Benin City, Nigeria*, Oxford, 1975; *African Civilizations: Precolonial Cities and States in Tropical Africa: An Archaeological Perspective*, Cambridge, 1987.

(28) D. W. Phillipson, *African Archaeology*, Cambridge, 1985.

(29) H. N. Chittick, *Kilwa: an Islamic Trading Centre on the East African Coast*, 2 vols., Nairobi, 1974; *Manda: Excavations at an Island Port on the Kenya Coast*, Nairobi, 1984.

(30) H. N. Chittick and R. I. Rotberg (eds.), *East Africa and the Orient: Cultural Syntheses in Precolonial Times*, New York, 1975.

(31) B. M. Fagan, *Iron Age Cultures in Zambia*, vol. I, London, 1967; B. Fagan with D. W. Phillipson and S. G. H. Daniels, *ibid.*, vol. II, 1969.

(32) R. C. Soper published most of his results in *Azania*, VI, 1971, 'The Banku Studies Project', 1–4; 'A General Review of the Early Iron Age of the Southern Half of Africa', 5–37; 'Early Iron Age Pottery Types from East Africa: Comparative Analysis', 39–52; 'Iron Age Sites in Chobi Sector, Murchison Falls National Park, Uganda', 53–87; 'Resemblances Between East African Early Iron Age Pottery and Recent Vessels from the North-eastern Congo', 233–41.

(33) For a preliminary report see *Azania*, IX, 1974, N. Chittick, 'Excavations at Aksum, 1973–4: A Preliminary Report', 159–205.

(34) A. E. Close, *The Identification of Style in Lithic Artefacts from North East Africa*, Cairo, 1977; A. Close, F. Wendorf and R. Schild, *The Afian: A Study of Stylistic Variation in a Nilotic Industry*, Dallas, 1979.

(35) D. J. Mulvaney and J. H. Calaby, *'So Much That is New': Baldwin Spencer 1860–1929*, Melbourne, 1985, 69.

(36) J. D. Freeman, 'Henry Devenish Skinner: a Memoir', In *Anthropology in the South Seas: Essays Presented to H. D. Skinner* (J. D. Freeman and W. R. Geddes, eds.), New Plymouth, N.Z., 1959, 9–27.

(37) D. F. Thompson, 'The Seasonal Factor in Human Culture Illustrated from the Life of a Contemporary Nomadic Group', *PPS*, V, 1939, 209–21; 'Some Wood and Stone Implements of the Bindibu Tribe of Central Western Australia', *PPS*, XXX, 1964, 400–22.

(38) D. J. Mulvaney, 'The Stone Age of Australia', *PPS*, XXVII, 1961, 56–107.

(39) D. J. Mulvaney, *The Prehistory of Australia*, London, 1969.

(40) R. A. Binns and I. McBryde, 'Preliminary Report on a Petrological Study of Ground-edge Artefacts from North-eastern New South Wales, Australia', *PPS*, XXXV, 1969, 229–35; *A Petrological Analysis of Ground-edge Artefacts from Northern New South Wales*, Canberra, 1972; I. McBryde, 'Artefacts, Language and Social Interaction: A Case Study from South-eastern Australia', In *Stone Age Prehistory: Studies in Memory of Charles McBurney* (G. N. Bailey and P. Callow, eds.), Cambridge, 1986, 77–93.

(41) J. Golson, 'Culture change in Prehistoric New Zealand', In *Anthropology in the South Seas: Essays Presented to H. D. Skinner* (D. J. Freeman and W. R. Geddes, eds.) New Plymouth, N.Z., 1959, 29–74.

(42) F. W. Shawcross, 'Archaeological Investigations at Ongari Point, Kati-kati, Bay of Plenty', *N.Z. Archaeological Society Newsletter*, June 1964, 79–98; 'An Investigation of Prehistoric Diet and Economy on a Coastal Site at Galatea Bay, New Zealand', *PPS*, XXXIII, 1967, 107–31; 'Ethnographic Economics and the Study of Population in Prehistoric New Zealand: Viewed Through Archaeology', *Mankind*, VII, 1970, 279–91.

(43) P. Bellwood, 'Fortifications and Economy in Prehistoric New Zealand', *PPS*, XXXVII, 1971, 56–95; 'Varieties of Ecological Adaptation in Southern Cook Islands', *Archaeology and Physical Anthropology in Oceania*, VI, 1971, 146–69; *Man's Conquest of the Pacific: The Prehistory of Southeast Asia and Oceania*, London, 1978; *The Polynesians: Prehistory of an Island People*, London, 1978.

(44) J. Golson and P. W. Gathercole, 'The Last Decade in New Zealand Archaeology', *Antiquity*, XXXVI, 1962, 168–74 and 271–8.

(45) C. F. W. Higham and R. H. Parker (with an appendix by Nai Pote Keakoon), *Prehistoric Research in North-East Thailand 1969–70: A Preliminary Report*, Dunedin, N.Z., 1970.

(46) J. Golson, 'Old Guards and New Waves: Reflections on Antipodean Archaeology, 1954–75', In Papers presented to John Mulvaney (C. C. Macknight and J. Peter White, eds.), *Archaeology in Oceania*, XXI, no. 1, 1986, 2–12.

(47) R. Jones, 'Archaeological Reconnaissance in Tasmania, Summer 1963/1964', *Oceania*, XXXV, 1965, 191–201; 'The Demography of Hunters and Farmers in Tasmania', In *Aboriginal Man and Environment in Australia* (D. J. Mulvaney and J. Golson, eds.), Canberra, 1971, 271–87; (with K. Kierman and D. Ranson), 'New Evidence from Fraser Cave for Glacial Age Man in South-West Tasmania', *Nature*, CCCI, 1983, 28–32.

(48) J. Golson, 'The Making of the New Guinea Highlands', In *The Melanesian Environment: Change and Development* (J. H. Winslow, ed.), Canberra, 1977, 45–56.

(49) S. Bulmer, 'Prehistoric Stone Implements from the New Guinea Highlands', *Oceania*, XXXIV, 1964, 246–68.

(50) J. Chappell, 'Stone Axe Factories in the Highlands of East New Guinea', *PPS*, XXXII, 1966, 96–121.

(51) M. Strathern, 'Stone Axes and Flake Tools: Evaluations from Two New Guinea Highlands Societies', *PPS*, XXXV, 1969, 311–29.

(52) S. and R. Bulmer, 'The Prehistory of the Australian New Guinea Highlands', *American Anthropologist*, LXVI, No.4 Part 2, 1964, 39–76 and 309–22.

(53) J. P. White, 'New Guinea and Australian Prehistory: The Neolithic Problem', *Aboriginal Man and Environment in Australia* (D. J. Mulvaney and J. Golson, eds.), Canberra, 1971, 182–95; (with J. F. O'Donnell), *A Prehistory of Australasia, New Guinea and Sahul*, Sydney, 1982.

(54) A. Steensberg, *New Guinea Gardens: A Study of Husbandry with Parallels in Prehistoric Europe*, London, 1980.

(55) R. V. S. Wright, 'Prehistory in Cape York Peninsula', In *Aboriginal Man and Environment in Australia* (D. J. Mulvaney and J. Golson, eds.), Canberra, 1971, 133–40.

(56) R. V. S. Wright (ed.), *Archaeology of the Gallus Site, Koonalda Cave*, Canberra, 1971.

(57) J. Clegg, 'The Archaeological Approach to Prehistoric Pictures in Australia', In *Stone Age Prehistory: Studies in Memory of Charles McBurney* (G. N. Bailey and P. Callow, eds.), Cambridge, 1986, 55–65.

(58) Much of her research on the Romans in the Fens was later made available in P. Salway, S. J. Hallam and J. I. Bromwich, *The Fenland in Roman Times: Studies of a Major Area of Peasant Colonization with a Gazetteer Covering all Known Sites and Finds*, edited by C. W. Phillips, London, 1970. Professor Sylvia Hallam's many contributions to the archaeology and anthropology of Western Australia include the monograph *Fire and Hearth: a Study of Aboriginal Usage and European Usurpation in South-western Australia*, Canberra, 1975.

(59) I. McBryde, 'Educational Goals of University Schools of Prehistory and Archaeology: Mechanik Trades in the Ivory Tower?', *Australian Archaeology*, XI, 1980, 72–80.

(60) G. Rowley, 'The Dorset Culture of the Eastern Arctic', *American Anthropologist*, XLII, 1940, 490–9.

(61) W. Bray and M. E. Mosley, 'An Archaeological Sequence from the Vicinity of Buga, Colombia', *Nawpa Pacha*, VII–VIII, 1969–70, 85–104; W. Bray, *The Gold of El Dorado: Catalogue for the Royal Academy Exhibition (1978–9)*, London, 1978.

(62) N. Hammond, *Lubaantun: A Classic Maya Realm*, Cambridge, Mass., 1975.

(63) N. Hammond, 'Early Maya Ceremonial at Cuello, Belize', *Antiquity*, LIV, 1980, 176–90; personal communication, 1987.

(64) N. Hammond, *Ancient Maya Civilization*, Cambridge, 1982.

(65) G. Wahida, 'The Re-excavation of Zarzi, 1971', *PPS*, XLVII, 1981, 19–40.

(66) E. S. Higgs (ed.), *Papers in Economic Prehistory: Studies by Members and Associates of the British Academy Major Research Project in the Early History of Agriculture*, Cambridge, 1972.

(67) *Ibid.*, chs. 7 and 8.

(68) D. Oates, *Studies in the Ancient History of Northern Iraq*, London, 1968; 'Excavations at Tell Brak, 1978–81', *Iraq*, XLIV, 1982, 187–204; 'Excavations at Tell Brak, 1983–84', *Iraq*, XLVII, 1985, 159–73.

(69) J. Oates, 'The Background and Development of Early Farming Communities in Mesopotamia and the Zagros', *PPS*, XXXIX, 1973, 147–81.

(70) D. Stronach, 'Excavations at Ras al 'Amiya', *Iraq*, XXIII, 1961, 95–137.

(71) A full report is still awaited. Interim reports began to appear in D. Whitehouse, 'Excavations at Sīrāf: First Interim Report', *Iran*, VI, 1968, 1–22.

(72) C. B. M. McBurney, 'Preliminary report on stone age reconnaissance in N.E. Iran', *PPS*, XXX, 1964, 382–99; 'The Cave of Ali Tappeh and the Epi-Palaeolithic in N.E. Iran', *PPS*, XXXIV, 1968, 385–413.

(73) H. de Terra and T. T. Paterson, *Studies on the Ice Age in India and Associated Human Cultures*, Washington, 1939.

(74) B. and R. Allchin, *The Rise of Civilization in India and Pakistan*, Cambridge, 1982.

(75) H. D. Collings, 'Pleistocene Site in the Malay Peninsula', *Nature*, CXLI, 1938, 575–6.

(76) H. J. Movius, Jr, 'The Lower Palaeolithic Cultures of Southern and Eastern Asia', *Trans. Am. Phil. Soc.*, XXXVIII, 1948, 329–420.

(77) D. Walker and A. de G. Sieveking, 'The Palaeolithic Industry of Kota Tampan, Perak, Malaya', *PPS*, XXVIII, 1962, 103–39. Since Dr Ann Sieveking returned to Britain she has focussed her attention on palaeolithic art. Her most recent contribution has been her definitive *Catalogue of Palaeolithic Art in the British Museum*, London, 1987.

(78) G. de G. Sieveking, 'Excavations at Gua Cha, Kelantan, 1954', *Federation Museums Journal*, I and II, 1954–5, 75–138.

(79) G. de G. Sieveking, 'The Prehistoric Cemetery at Bukit Tengku Lembu, Perlis', *Federation Museums Journal*, VII, 1962, 25–54.

(80) C. F. Higham, 'The Ban Chiang Culture in Wider Perspective: Mortimer Wheeler Lecture, 1983', *PBA*, LXIX, 229–61; C. Higham, *Prehistoric Investigations in Northeast Thailand*, Oxford, 1984.

(81) P. Bellwood, 'Fortifications and economy in prehistoric New Zealand', *PPS*, XXXVII, 1971, 56–95; W. Shawcross, 'An archaeological assemblage of Maori combs', *J. Polynesian Soc.*, LXXIII, 382–98; and 'Kauri Point Swamp: the ethnographic interpretation of a prehistoric site', *Problems in Economic and Social Archaeology* (ed. G. de G. Sieveking *et al.*), 277–305. London, 1976.

(82) P. Bellwood, *The Polynesians: Prehistory of an Island People*. London, 1977, rev. ed. 1987.

7: Prehistorians beyond Cambridge: continental Europe and Britain

(1) M. Ventris and J. Chadwick, 'Evidence for Greek Dialect in the Mycenaean Archives', *JHS*, LXXIII, 1953 84–103; J. Chadwick, *The Decipherment of Linear B*, Cambridge, 1958. Cambridge, 1958.

(2) Lord W. D. Taylour, *Mycenaean Pottery in Italy and Adjacent Areas*, Cambridge, 1958.

(3) Lord W. D. Taylour, 'Mycenae, 1968', *Antiquity*, XLIII, 1969, 91–7.

(4) Lord W. D. Taylour, *The Mycenaeans*, London, 1964, 19.

(5) A. J. B. Wace and M. S. Thompson, *Prehistoric Thessaly: Being some Account of Recent Excavations and Explorations in North-eastern Greece from Lake Kopais to the Borders of Macedonia, Cambridge, 1912.*

(6) R. J. Rodden, 'Excavations at the Early Neolithic Site at Nea Nikomedeia, Greek Macedonia (1961 Season)', *PPS*, xxviii, 1962, 267–88.

7 R. J. Rodden, 'An Early Neolithic Village in Greece', *Scientific American*, ccxii, April, 1965, 82–92.

(8) E. S. Higgs, 'A Middle Palaeolithic Industry in Greece. Preliminary Report', *Man*, lxiii, 1963, 2–3.

(9) S. I. Dakaris, E. S. Higgs and R. W. Hey, 'The Climate, Environment and Industries of Stone Age Greece. Part i', *PPS*, xxx, 1964, 199–244; E. S. Higgs and C. Vita-Finzi, 'The Climate, Environment and Industries of Stone Age Greece. Part ii', *PPS*, xxxii, 1966, 1–29; E. S. Higgs, C. Vita-Finzi, D. R. Harris and A. E. Fagg, 'The Climate, Environment and Industries of Stone Age Greece. Part iii', *PPS*, xxxiii, 1967, 1–29.

(10) G. N. Bailey, P. L. Carter, C. S. Gamble and H. P. Higgs, 'Asprochalicho and Kastritsa: Further Investigations of Palaeolithic Settlement and Economy in Epirus (North-West Greece)', *PPS*, xlix, 1983, 15–42.

(11) G. N. Bailey, P. L. Carter, C. S. Gamble, H. P. Higgs and C. Roubet, 'Palaeolithic Investigations in Epirus: the Results of the First Season's Excavations in Klithi, 1983', *BSA*, lxxix, 1984, 7–22.

(12) J. D. Evans, 'Excavations in the Neolithic Settlement of Knossos, 1957–60. Part i', *BSA*, lix, 1964, 132–240; 'Knossos Neolithic. Part ii', *BSA*, lxiii, 1968, 239–276; 'Neolithic Knossos: the Growth of a Settlement', *PPS*, xxxvii, Part 2, 1971, 95–117.

(13) P. Warren, *Myrtos: An Early Bronze Age Settlement in Crete*, London, 1972.

(14) J. D. Evans and C. Renfrew, *Excavations at Saliagos near Antiparos*, London, 1968.

(15) J. R. Cann and C. Renfrew, 'The Characterisation of Obsidian and its Application to the Mediterranean Region', *PPS*, xxx, 1964, 111–33.

(16) C. Renfrew, 'Cycladic Metallurgy and the Aegean Early Bronze Age', *American Journal of Archaeology*, lxxi, 1967, 1–20; J. A. Charles, 'Early Arsenical Bronzes – A Metallurgical View', *American Journal of Archaeology*, lxxi, 1967, 21–6; C. Renfrew, 'The Development and Chronology of the Early Cycladic Figurines', *American Journal of Archaeology*, lxxiii, 1969, 1–32.

(17) C. Renfrew, *The Emergence of Civilization: The Cyclades and the Aegean in the Third Millennium B.C.*, London, 1972.

(18) C. Renfrew, *The Archaeology of Cult: The Sanctuary of Phylakopi*, London, 1985.

(19) R. D. Whitehouse, 'Settlement and Economy in Southern Italy in the Neothermal Period', *PPS*, xxxiv, 1968, 332–367; 'The Neolithic Pottery Sequence in Southern Italy', *PPS*, xxxv, 1969, 267–310.

(20) D. H. Trump, 'The Apennine culture of Italy', *PPS*, xxiv, 1958, 165–200; *Central and Southern Italy before Rome*, London, 1966.

(21) G. W. W. Barker, 'The Conditions of Cultural and Economic Growth in the Bronze Age of Central Italy', *PPS*, xxxviii, 1972, 170–208; 'Prehistoric Territories and Economies in Central Italy', In *Palaeoeconomy: being the Second Volume of Papers in Economic Prehistory by Members and Associates of the British Academy Major Research Project in the Early History of Agriculture* (E. S. Higgs, ed.), Cambridge, 1975, 111–75.

(22) G. W. W. Barker, *Prehistoric Farming in Europe*, Cambridge, 1985.

(23) J. D. Evans, *The Prehistoric Antiquities of the Maltese Islands: A Survey*, London, 1971.

(24) J. D. Evans, 'The Prehistoric Culture-sequence in the Maltese Archipelago', *PPS*, xix, 1953, 41–94.

(25) D. H. Trump, 'The Later Prehistory of Malta', *PPS*, xxvii, 1961, 253–62; *Skorba: Excavations carried out on behalf of the National Museum of Malta, 1961–3*, Oxford, 1966.

(26) P. A. Rowley-Conwy, 'Continuity and Change in the Prehistoric Economies of Denmark 3700 B.C. to 2300 B.C.', unpublished Ph.D. dissertation, Cambridge, 1980.

(27) M. Zvelebil, *From Forager to Farmer in the Boreal Zone: Reconstructing Economic*

Patterns Through Catchment Analysis in Prehistoric Finland, Oxford, 1981.
(28) M. A. P. Renouf, 'Prehistoric Coastal Economy in Varangerfjord, North Norway: the Analysis of Faunal Material and the Study of Subsistence Patterns in the Inner Area of Varangerfjord During the Younger Stone Age, from 5800 to 2500 B.P.', unpublished Ph.D. dissertation, Cambridge, 1982.
(29) I. Davidson, 'The Late Palaeolithic Economy in Eastern Spain', unpublished Ph.D dissertation, Cambridge, 1981; 'The Geographical Study of Late Palaeolithic Stages in Eastern Spain', In *Stone Age Prehistory: Studies in Memory of Charles McBurney* (G. N. Bailey and P. Callow, eds.), Cambridge, 1986, 95–118.
(30) L. H. Barfield, *Northern Italy before Rome*, London, 1971.
(31) J. Nandris, 'Lepenski Vir', *Science J.* iv, January, 1968, 64–70; 'The development and relationships of the earlier Greek Neolithic', *Man*, v, 1970, 192–213; 'Some Features of Neolithic Climax societies', *Studia Praehistorica*, i–ii, 1978, 198–211.
(32) R. W. Dennell, 'The Interpretation of Plant Remains: Bulgaria', In *Papers in Economic Prehistory: Studies by Members and Associates of the British Academy Major Research Projects in the Early History of Agriculture* (E. S. Higgs, ed.), Cambridge, 1972, 149–159; R. W. Dennell and D. Webley, 'Prehistoric Settlement and Land Use in Southern Bulgaria', In *Palaeoeconomy* (E. S. Higgs, ed.), Cambridge, 1975, 97–109.
(33) J. Dent and M. Biddle, *Nonsuch 1960: the Banqueting House, with an Account of Last Year's Excavation of the Palace Site*, Ewell, 1960.
(34) M. Biddle, 'A Study of Winchester: Archaeology and History in a British Town, 1961–1983', *PBA*, lxix, 1983, 93–135.
(35) P. V. Addyman, 'York in its Archaeological Setting', In *Archaeological Papers from York presented to M. W. Barley* (P. V. Addyman and V. E. Black, eds.), York, 1984, 7–21.
(36) G. M. White, 'Prehistoric Remains from Selsey Bill', *Ant. J.*, xiv, 1934, 40–52; 'A Settlement of the South Saxons', *Ant. J.*, xiv, 1934, 393–400; 'A New Roman Inscription from Chichester', *Ant. J.*, xv, 1935, 461–4; 'The Chichester Amphitheatre: Preliminary Excavations', *Ant. J.*, xvi, 1936, 149–59.
(37) C. H. Houlder, 'The Excavation of a Neolithic Stone Implement Factory at Mynydd Rhiw in Caernarvonshire', *PPS*, xxvii, 1961, 108–43.
(38) J. R. C. Hamilton, *Excavations at Jarlshof, Shetland*, Edinburgh, 1956; *Excavations at Clickhimin, Shetland*, Edinburgh, 1968.
(39) A. L. Mongait, *Archaeology in the USSR*, Harmondsworth, 1961; S. A. Semenov, *Prehistoric Technology: An Experimental Study of the Oldest Tools and Artefacts from Traces of Manufacture and Wear*, London, 1964; S. I. Rudenko, *Frozen Tombs of Siberia: The Pazyryk Burials of Iron Age Horsemen*, London, 1970.
(40) M. W. Thompson, *General Pitt-Rivers: Evolution and Archaeology in the Nineteenth Century*, Bradford-on-Avon, 1977.
(41) J. G. Hurst, D. S. Neal and H. J. Van Beuningen, *Pottery Produced and Traded in North-west Europe, 1350–1650*, Rotterdam, 1986.
(42) J. G. Hurst, 'The Wharram Research Project: Results to 1983', *Medieval Archaeology*, xxviii, 1984, 77–111.
(43) J. W. Brailsford, 'Excavations at Little Woodbury', *PPS*, xv, 1949, 156–68.
(44) J. W. Brailsford and J. E. Stapley, 'The Ipswich Torcs', *PPS*, xxxviii, 1972, 219–34; R. J. Taylor and J. W. Brailsford, 'British Iron Age Strap-unions', *PPS*, li, 1985, 247–72.
(45) J. W. Brailsford, *Early Celtic Masterpieces from Britain in the British Museum*, London, 1975.
(46) G. de G. Sieveking, 'High Lodge Palaeolithic Industry', *Nature*, ccxx, 1968, 1065–6.
(47) G. de G. Sieveking *et al.*, 'Prehistoric Flint Mines and their Identification as Sources of Raw Material', *Archaeometry*, xiv, 1972, 151–76; G. de G. Sieveking *et al.*, 'A New Survey of Grimes Graves: First Report', *PPS*, xxxix, 1973, 182–218; G. de G. Sieveking and M. B. Hart (eds.), *The Scientific Study of Flint and Chert: Proceedings of the Fourth International Flint Symposium Held at Brighton Polytechnic, 10–15 April 1983*, Cambridge, 1986.
(48) G. J. Wainwright with I. H. Longworth, *Durrington Walls: Excavations, 1966–8*, London, 1971.

(49) I. H. Longworth, *Collared Urns of the Bronze Age in Great Britain and Ireland*, Cambridge, 1984.

(50) I. M. Stead, *The La Tène Cultures of Eastern Yorkshire*, York, 1965; 'An Iron Age Hill-fort at Grimthorpe, Yorkshire, England', *PPS*, xxxiv, 1968, 148–90; 'La Tène burials between Burton Fleming and Rudston, North Humberside', *Ant. J.*, lvi, 1976, 217–26.

(51) J. L. Flouest and I. M. Stead, *Iron Age Cemeteries in Champagne: the Third Interim Report on the Excavations carried out between 1971 and 1978*, London, 1979.

(52) I. M. Stead, J. B. Bourke and D. Brothwell, *Lindow Man: the Body in the Bog*, London, 1986.

(53) I. Kinnes, 'Les Fouaillages and Megalithic Origins', *Antiquity*, lvi, 1982, 24–30.

(54) T. W. Potter, *A Faliscan Town in South Etruria: Excavations at Narce, 1966–71*, London, 1976.

(55) D. M. Wilson, *Anglo-Saxon Art from the Seventh Century to the Norman Conquest*, London, 1984; *The Bayeux Tapestry: the Complete Tapestry in Colour*, London, 1985.

(56) K. Muckleroy, *Maritime Archaeology*, Cambridge, 1978.

(57) A. Sherratt (ed.), *The Cambridge Encyclopedia of Archaeology*, Cambridge, 1980.

(58) E. W. Mackie, 'The Origin and Development of the Broch and Wheelhouse Building Cultures of the Scottish Iron Age', *PPS*, xxi, 1965, 93–146.

(59) R. R. Clarke, 'A Hoard of Metalwork of the Early Iron Age from Ringstead, Norfolk', *PPS*, xvii, 1951, 214–25; 'The Early Iron Age Treasure from Snettisham, Norfolk', *PPS*, xx, 1954, 27–86; *East Anglia*, London, 1960.

(60) J. D. Evans, 'The First Half-Century – and After', *Institute of Archaeology Golden Jubilee Lecture Series*, no. 1, 1987.

(61) F. R. Hodson, 'The La Tène cemetery at Münsingen-Rain', *Acta Bernensia*, v, 1968; F. R. Hodson, D. G. Kendall and P. Tautu (eds.), *Mathematics in the Archaeological and Historical Sciences: Proceedings of the Anglo-Romanian Conference, Mamaia, 1970, Organised by the Royal Society of London, and the Academy of the Socialist Republic of Romania*, Edinburgh, 1971; F. R. Hodson (ed.), *The Place of Astronomy in the Ancient World: A Joint Symposium of the Royal Society and the British Academy organised by D. G. Kendall*, London 1974; J. E. Doran and F. R. Hodson, *Mathematics and Computers in Archaeology*, Edinburgh, 1975; F. E. Barth and F. R. Hodson, 'The Hallstatt Cemetery and its Documentation: Some New Evidence', *Ant. J.*, lvi, 1976, 159–76.

(62) J. Graham-Campbell, 'The 9th-century Anglo-Saxon Horn-Mount from Burghead, Morayshire, Scotland', *Medieval Archaeology*, xvii, 1973, 43–51; (with J. Close-Brooks), 'The Mote of Mark and Celtic Interlace', *Antiquity*, l, 1976, 48–53.

(63) G. E. Daniel and T. G. E. Powell, 'The Distribution and Date of the Passage-Graves of the British Isles', *PPS*, xiv, 1949, 169–87; T. G. E. Powell and G. E. Daniel, *Barclodiad y Gawres: The Excavation of a Megalithic Chamber Tomb in Anglesey 1952–3*, Liverpool 1956; *The Celts*, London, 1958; *Prehistoric Art*, London, 1966; 'From Urartu to Gundestrup: The Agency of Thracian metal-work', In *The European Community in Later Prehistory: Studies in Honour of C. F. C. Hawkes* (J. Boardman, M. A. Brown and T. G. E. Powell, eds.), London, 1971, 183–210; 'Presidential Address: A Midterm Review', *PPS*, xxxix, 1973, 1–5; 'The Inception of the Iron Age in Temperate Europe', *PPS*, xlii, 1976, 1–14.

(64) J. J. Taylor, 'Early Bronze Age Gold Neck-rings in Western Europe', *PPS*, xxxiv, 1968, 259–65; *Bronze Age Goldwork of the British Isles*, Cambridge, 1980.

(65) J. Renfrew, *Palaeoethnobotany: The Prehistoric Food-Plants of the Near East and Europe*, London, 1973.

(66) P. Mellars, 'Fire Ecology, Animal Populations and Man: A Study of Some Ecological Relationships in Prehistory', *PPS*, xlii, 1976, 15–45; 'Excavation and Economic Analysis of Mesolithic Shell Middens on the Island of Oronsay (Inner Hebrides), In *The Early Postglacial Settlement of Northern Europe* (P. Mellars, ed.), London, 1978, 371–96; *Excavations on Oronsay: Prehistoric Human Ecology on a Small Island*, Edinburgh, 1987.

(67) A. Fleming, 'Territorial Patterns in Bronze Age Wessex', *PPS*, xxxvii, 1971, 138–66; 'Early Settlement and the Landscape in West Yorkshire', In *Problems in Economic and*

Social Archaeology (G. de G. Sieveking, I. H. Longworth and K. E. Wilson, eds.), London, 1976, 359–73; 'The Prehistoric Landscape of Dartmoor. Part I. South Dartmoor', *PPS*, XLIV, 1978, 97–123; 'The Prehistoric Landscape of Dartmoor. Part II. North and East Dartmoor', *PPS*, XLIX, 1983, 195–241.

(68) J. R. Collis (ed.), *The Iron Age in Britain: a Review*, Sheffield, 1977; J. R. Collis, *Oppida: Earliest Towns North of the Alps*, Sheffield, 1984; *The European Iron Age*, London, 1984.

(69) R. W. Dennell, 'The Economic Importance of Plant Resources Represented on Archaeological Sites', *J. Arch. Science*, III, 1976, 229–47; *European Economic Prehistory: A New Approach*, London, 1983.

(70) G. Barker, 'Early Neolithic Land Use in Yugoslavia', *PPS*, XLI, 1975, 85–104; *Prehistoric Farming in Europe*, Cambridge, 1985.

(71) M. Zvelebil (ed.), *Hunters in Transition: Mesolithic Societies of Temperate Eurasia and their Transition to Farming*, Cambridge, 1986.

(72) B. Cunliffe, *Excavations at Fishbourne 1961–69*, 2 vols., London, 1971.

(73) B. Cunliffe, *Roman Bath*, London, 1969.

(74) B. Cunliffe, *Excavations at Porchester Castle*, vol. I, *Roman*, London, 1975; vol. II, *Saxon*, London, 1975.

(75) C. Renfrew, *Investigations in Orkney*, London, 1979.

(76) C. Renfrew, *The Archaeology of Cult: The Sanctuary at Phylakopi*, London, 1985.

(77) C. Renfrew (ed.), *The Explanation of Culture Change: Models in Prehistory*, London, 1973.

(78) S. Shennan, 'The Social Organisation at Branc', *Antiquity*, LIX, 1975, 279–88.

(79) C. Renfrew and S. Shennan (eds.), *Ranking, Resource and Exchange: Aspects of the Archaeology of Early European Society*, Cambridge, 1982.

(80) C. Renfrew, *Approaches to Social Archaeology*, Edinburgh, 1984.

(81) C. Gamble, 'Hunting Strategies in the Central European Palaeolithic', *PPS*, XLV, 1979, 35–52; 'Culture and Society in the Upper Palaeolithic of Europe', In *Hunter-Gatherer Economy in Prehistory: A European Perspective* (G. Bailey, ed.), Cambridge, 1983, 201–11; *The Palaeolithic Settlement of Europe*, Cambridge, 1986; J. A. J. Gowlett and R. E. M. Hedges (eds.), *Archaeological Results from Accelerator Dating*, Oxford, 1987.

(82) B. Cunliffe, *Hengistbury Head*, London, 1978; *Danebury: An Iron Age Hillfort in Hampshire*, vols. 1–2, *The Excavations, 1969–1978*, London, 1984.

(83) J. A. J. Gowlett, 'Culture and Conceptualisation: the Oldowan-Acheulian Gradient', in *Stone Age Prehistory: Studies in Memory of Charles McBurney* (G. N. Bailey and P. Callow, eds.), Cambridge, 1986, 243–60.

(84) D. Britton, 'Traditions of Metal-Working in the Later Neolithic and Early Bronze Age of Britain: Part I', *PPS*, XXIX, 1963, 258–325.

(85) D. A. Roe, 'British Lower and Middle Palaeolithic Handaxe Groups', *PPS*, XXXIV, 1968, 1–82; *A Gazetteer of British Lower and Middle Palaeolithic Sites*, London, 1968; *Adlun in the Stone Age: the Excavations of D. A. E. Garrod in the Lebanon, 1958–63*, Oxford, 1983; *The Lower and Middle Palaeolithic Periods in Britain*, London, 1981.

(86) J. M. Coles and A. F. Harding, *The Bronze Age in Europe: An Introduction to the Prehistory of Europe c.2000–700 B.C.*, London, 1979; A. Harding, *The Mycenaeans and Europe*, London, 1984.

(87) J. L. Bintliff, 'Mediterranean Alluviation: New Evidence from Archaeology', *PPS*, XLI, 1975, 78–84; *Natural Environment and Human Settlement in Prehistoric Greece, Based on Original Fieldwork*, Oxford, 1977; 'An Archaeological Survey of the Lower Catchment of the Ayiofarango Valley', *BSA*, LXXII, 1977, 13–84.

(88) J. Lewthwaite, 'The Transition to Food Production: A Mediterranean perspective', In *Hunters in Transition: Mesolithic Societies of Temperate Eurasia and their Transition to Farming* (M. Zvelebil, ed.), Cambridge, 1986, 53–66.

(89) S. E. Thomas, 'Appendix I: Sjöholmen. Site 179: A Re-examination', In C. A. Althin, *The Chronology of the Stone Age Settlements of Scania, Sweden*, Lund, 1954, 169–87.

(90) R. Chapman, I. Kinnes and K. Randsborg (eds.), *The Archaeology of Death*, Cambridge, 1981.

INDEX

Abetifi, Ghana 105
Abri Pataud, Dordogne 78
Achimota Museum, Ghana 104
Addyman, Peter 137f., 146
Afghanistan 75
Africa 29, 43, 52, 72, 101-11
agriculture, early history 93
air photography 50, 56, 64f., 76
Aksum, Ethiopia 108, 110
Ali Tappeh, Iran 73, 124
Allchin, Bridget & Raymond 62, 124
Allsworth-Jones, Philip 107
Al Soof, Benham Abo 123
Al-Tikriti, Walid Yasin 123
American School of Prehistoric Research 46
Americanist studies 5, 40, 61, 87, 120ff.
Anatomy Department, Cambridge 15, 17
Andaman Islands 21
Anglo-Saxon studies, Cambridge 20f., 29, 37f., 64, 67
animal bone identification 68, 72ff., 95
Anthropology at Cambridge 1, 6, 11, 15-29, 59, 61, 89ff., 99
Antiquaries, Society of, London 3, 7, 13, 52, 57, 83, 93, 136
Antiquity 98
Archaeology, history 1-14, 64
Arminghall, Norfolk 56
Ashmolean Museum, Oxford 6, 12, 142, 148
Asprochaliko, Epirus 76f., 130
Auckland University, N.Z. 114f.
Australia 2, 15f., 68, 72, 76, 88, 108, 111-20
Australian National University 69, 113-16, 118
Azania 110

Babington, C. 29
Baden-Powell Quaternary Research Centre, Oxford 6, 148
Bahrain University 123
Bailey, Geoff 62, 77f., 130
Ballinderry Crannog, Ireland 50
Ban Chiang, Thailand 127

Ban Na Di, Thailand 126
Bantu migrations 110
Barfield, Lawrence 135, 150
Barker, Graeme 133, 146
Bath, Roman 146
Bégouën, Comte Henri 31
Bellwood, Peter 115f., 127
Benin, Nigeria 101, 106f.
Berkeley, University of California 102ff., 111
Biddle, Martin 136f.
Bilsborough, Alan 78
Bintliff, J.C. 150
bioarchaeology 96
Birmingham University 106, 150
Boston University, USA 122
Boule, Marcellin 8, 35
bows, neolithic 81, 87
Bradford University 150
Brailsford, John 37, 52, 139
Bray, Warwick 61, 120f., 144
Breuil, Abbé Henri 8, 11, 35f., 45f., 78f.
Bristol University 146
British Academy 91, 93ff., 108
British archaeology 135-49
British Institute in East Africa 108ff.
British Institute of Persian Studies 70
British Museum 4f., 11, 16, 52, 69, 79, 84, 96, 139-42
British Museum of Natural History 16, 47, 68, 79
British School of Archaeology, Athens 9, 75
British School of Archaeology, Iraq 122f.
British School of Archaeology, Jerusalem 46
British School at Rome 132, 141, 146
Britton, Denis 148
Brown, G.F. 29
Burdo, Father 72
Burkitt, M.C. ix, 8, 30f., 34-7, 43, 52f., 59, 79, 91, 101f., 104, 134
Bushnell, Geoffrey 60f., 120
Butler, R.M. 138

Calgary University, Canada 78
Callow, Paul 78